FROM DENMARK TO THE CARIBOO

"An intriguing and very readable true story of three adventurous Danish sisters caught up in the British Columbia gold rush."

JEAN BARMAN
award-winning author of *British Columbia in the Balance: 1846–1871*

"The absence of women from our history has been a huge loss to scholarship. We need this book. *From Denmark to the Cariboo* tells the story of three sisters who moved to the Cariboo in the late 1800s. In telling their stories, the author includes the stories of other women of the Cariboo. Meticulously researched, it shows the opportunities and constraints in the society of those days, giving us a detailed look at how women dealt with them."

MARION McKINNON CROOK
bestselling, award-winning author of *Always Pack a Candle:
A Nurse in the Cariboo-Chilcotin*

"It was a joy to delve into this captivating book about three level-headed sisters from Denmark who ventured to Van Winkle and Barkerville during the Cariboo gold rush, each of them experiencing remarkable adventures, finding a husband, and overcoming hardships."

ROLF BUSCHARDT CHRISTENSEN
President, Federation of Danish Associations in Canada

"A remarkably well-researched history book. The biographies of three sisters who came from cultured Denmark to the Cariboo gold camps in 1870 reveal a new version of the emerging role of women in the developing societies of early BC. The book reads like a novel that you can't put down."

LIZ BRYAN

author of *Adventure Roads of BC's Northwest Heartland*
and *Pioneer Churches along the Gold Rush Trail*

"*From Denmark to the Cariboo* gives intriguing insight into the lives of three Danish sisters who arrived in Van Winkle, a rustic gold rush town near Barkerville, in the 1870s and became part of the fabric of the community. Family values and the role of women in society are strong undercurrents in this delightful narrative."

SAGE BIRCHWATER

bestselling author of *Talking to the Story Keepers:
Tales from the Chilcotin Plateau*

"The remarkable story of three sisters who immigrated to British Columbia during the gold rush era, woven together with a wealth of historical details."

MARIANNE VAN OSCH

author of *A Mill Behind Every Stump*

from
DENMARK
to the
CARIBOO

from
DENMARK
to the
CARIBOO

THE EPIC JOURNEY OF
THE LINDHARD SISTERS

LINDA PETERAT

Copyright © 2022 Linda Peterat

All rights reserved. No part of this publication may be reproduced, stored in a retrieval system, or transmitted in any form or by any means—electronic, mechanical, audio recording, or otherwise—without the written permission of the publisher or a licence from Access Copyright, Toronto, Canada.

Heritage House Publishing Company Ltd.
heritagehouse.ca

Cataloguing information available from Library and Archives Canada

978-1-77203-393-9 (paperback)
978-1-77203-394-6 (e-book)

Edited by Jesse Marchand
Cover design by Setareh Ashrafologhalai
Interior design by Jacqui Thomas
Front cover photograph: Image G-06712
courtesy of Royal BC Museum and Archives
Maps by Ken Mather

The interior of this book was produced on 100% post-consumer recycled paper, processed chlorine free, and printed with vegetable-based inks.

Heritage House gratefully acknowledges that the land on which we live and work is within the traditional territories of the Lkwungen (Esquimalt and Songhees), Malahat, Pacheedaht, Scia'new, T'Sou-ke, and W̱SÁNEĆ (Pauquachin, Tsartlip, Tsawout, Tseycum) Peoples.

We acknowledge the financial support of the Government of Canada through the Canada Book Fund (CBF) and the Canada Council for the Arts, and the Province of British Columbia through the British Columbia Arts Council and the Book Publishing Tax Credit.

26 25 24 23 22   1 2 3 4 5

Printed in Canada

TABLE *of* CONTENTS

Introduction 1

— PART ONE —
LAURA LINDHARD BEEDY DODD 11

Mid-Century Denmark 14

Opportunities Abound 17

To America 22

An Older Sister Dilemma 29

Van Winkle on Lightning Creek 37

Beedy and Lindhard 40

Mining Town Entrepreneurs 48

A Growing Family, a Growing Community 63

Return to Stanley 72

Merchant and Postmistress 79

Retiring to California 89

— PART TWO —

CAROLINE LINDHARD BATES HARRISON 93

To the New Country *97*

Far from Fashion *101*

A Secret Revealed *108*

A New Gamble *112*

Freighter, Farmer, Steamboat Captain *115*

Sisters Reunited *125*

Family Loss *132*

An Estate Unsettled *135*

Social Pacesetters of Sausalito *143*

A Stepson's Return *150*

The Family Branches *153*

Forward on Her Own *158*

— PART THREE —
CHRISTINE LINDHARD HAMILTON *165*

A Most Unpleasant Journey *169*

Sisters Together *174*

Soda Creek *178*

A Northern Partnership *184*

Losing Family, Finding Family *196*

Nieces of Caroline and Commodore Harrison *209*

Conclusions 218

Acknowledgements 227

Notes 231

Bibliography 251

Index 262

Lindhard Family Tree.
COURTESY D. STOUT

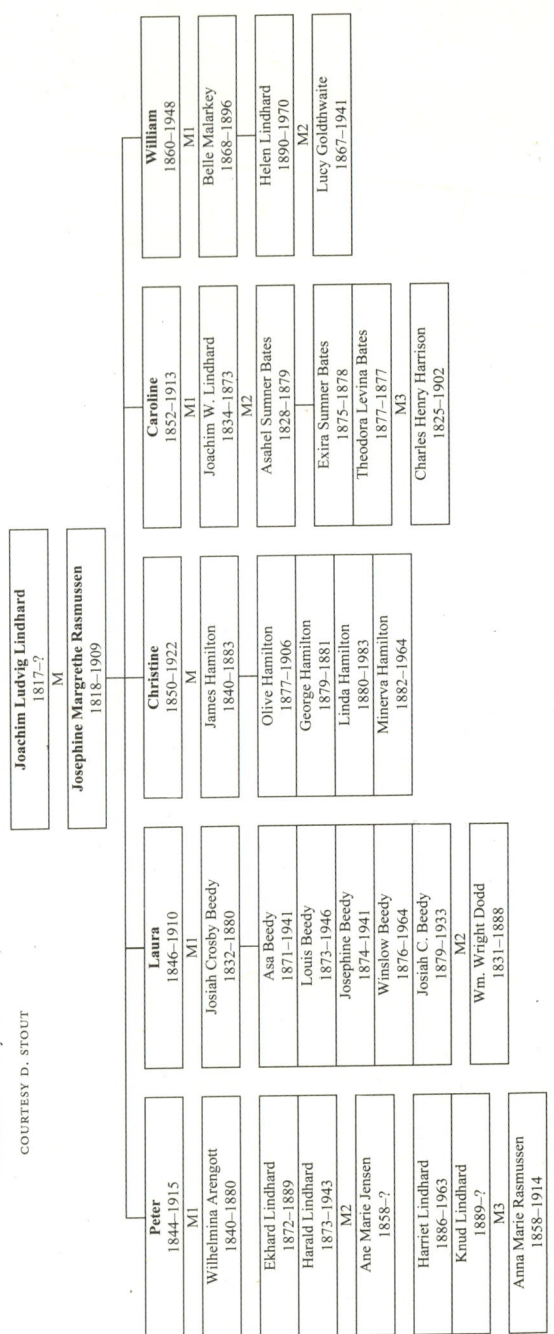

INTRODUCTION

I THINK OF HISTORY AS a large jigsaw puzzle. There are pieces missing, some pieces don't seem to fit, the colours aren't quite right, but once you start working on it you can't leave it. You are drawn into the puzzle. One thing leads to another. I began this puzzle wanting to know more about James Hamilton, partner in F.J. Barnard and Company in 1872. The information I had was contradictory. One source said he had no family. A second source said he left a wife and three daughters. Which was right? And who were they? What were their names? And who was Hamilton? These questions opened the door to the bigger project that I could not leave.

The project grew to encompass the stories of three sisters, Laura, Christine, and Caroline Lindhard, who left their home in Denmark in the 1870s for the opportunities and adventures that early British Columbia, specifically the Cariboo, had to offer. They arrived 150 years ago, before British Columbia had become a province in the Dominion of Canada. It was a new society that offered opportunities and a break from the constraints and traditions of their European homeland. Laura and Caroline arrived in the spring of 1870, accompanied by two male cousins, one who had already spent more than a decade in the gold-rush communities of California, the Fraser River, and the Cariboo. Christine joined her sisters four years later in 1874.

2

While some believe enough has been written about women in the nineteenth century and we should focus more on recent history, there are many stories yet to be told of newcomer women in early British Columbia that demand a place in the larger picture of that time. The stories we have of nineteenth-century women in British Columbia have often been gleaned from letters and journals held in archives.[1] Lesser known are stories of those who didn't keep journals or leave letters but were probably the majority of women—those who were middle class and entrepreneurial and had fewer moments to reflect on and document their daily activities. Busy trying to secure a comfortable existence and a better future for themselves and their children, they regarded their lives as common and unremarkable. The Lindhard sisters were part of this largely quiet group of women who accompanied or followed men to the frontier communities of the 1860s and later.

British Columbia's history of the late nineteenth century has frequently been told by men who have ignored the presence and influence of women and given attention to stereotypes perpetuated about women of the time. Our understanding of newcomer women is dominated by three tropes: the tragic, the entertaining, and the exceptional. There is the often-told story of Sophia Groves Cameron or Elizabeth Harper Tingley, women who followed their husbands into remote British Columbia and met with early, tragic deaths.[2] The entertaining women, such as Fanny Bendixen, Mary Sheldon, and Hattie Lucas ran saloons and entertainment houses in the Barkerville area. The hurdy-gurdy girls often figure in this category, although their presence in Barkerville was quite brief.[3] The exceptional women were those who sought gold, operated pack trains, and excelled at running saloons, boarding houses, and hotels. Entrepreneurial and independent, this third stereotype characterized women as exceptional because they chose a life of self-determination rather than follow the dominant nineteenth-century script for women of wife and mother.[4] Many women's stories have fit within these three stereotypes and have been reductionist portrayals that fail to enlarge our understanding of the activities and multiple roles women played in British Columbia's early years as a province. Furthermore, the stories we have of newcomer women of the time largely overlook the vast majority who were entrepreneurial, middle class, attached to families, *and* attempting to seize the same opportunities as men while securing better futures for themselves and the next generation. The stereotypes offer slim fragments of the lives they lived.

Entrepreneurial women, especially those who were self-employed or who employed others in the nineteenth century, have been rarely studied.[5] The general assumption was that women didn't pursue economic activities, and yet many did have to fend for themselves and the economic futures of their children when they were frequently widowed or abandoned. Life expectancy for men was around forty to fifty years in the 1880s, and many, especially in mining communities, died young. Even if women were not fending for themselves, they were active contributors in building their communities and family businesses in partnership with husbands. It's not surprising that women's entrepreneurial work of the nineteenth century is under-studied because women were themselves largely invisible in the public record. If married, their identities and activities were submerged by their husbands, whose activities dominated in the newspapers of the time.

Historians are challenged to tell stories from a variety of perspectives.[6] This account fits within the cluster of research that focuses on uncovering women's experiences.[7] This remains a needed focus when studying nineteenth-century women because their lives are obscured and their presence in the frontier societies of 150 years ago is usually absent in many documents that remain. In addition to being absent, what little that is known about women of the time often shows them as supporting rather than autonomous actors. Many more stories need to be told.

Laura and Caroline Lindhard arrived in pre-Confederation British Columbia in 1870, accompanied by two male cousins who had followed the gold-rush dream in earlier years to California and to the Fraser River in 1858. By the 1870s, Joachim (a.k.a. Henry) Lindhard had realized some financial success and security on British Columbia's frontier. The Cariboo Wagon Road had reached the mining regions of the interior by 1865. The transcontinental railway across the United States was completed by 1869 and provided more comfortable, faster, and safer travel from New York to San Francisco than the ocean routes through Panama or around Cape Horn. Transportation was easier and western settlement in Canada and the United States accelerated. But the Lindhard sisters' destination was the Cariboo of British Columbia, where life was more isolated and society less established. The last leg of their journey was by sternwheeler from Victoria to New Westminster and Yale, then by stagecoach from Yale to Van Winkle near Barkerville.

As I learned more about the Lindhard sisters, at least four features of their lives drew me further into their stories. First, they emigrated from Denmark and therefore their immigrant stories were different from many of the early British Columbia women who arrived from England or eastern Canada. Why would young women leave Denmark in the 1870s for frontier British Columbia? Since they were from neither the British colonial class nor the aspiring group of eastern Canadians, how did they find a place in this new society? What challenges did they face?

Second, the Lindhard sisters were young when they left their Denmark home, and within a few years they experienced many personal changes. Their ages when they arrived ranged between eighteen years for Caroline, in 1870, and twenty-four for both Laura, in 1870, and Christine, in 1874. Within a few years of reaching the Cariboo, they married, bore children, experienced deaths of husbands, became sole supporters of their young children, and re-married. Faced with various unexpected events, what options were open to them as women in this new society? What decisions did they make to secure their and their children's futures?

Third, the Lindhard sisters were part of a different economic segment of British Columbia best characterized as the entrepreneurial middle class. They and their husbands held shares in mining companies, and they operated farms, ranches, stores, post offices, roadhouses, saloons, freighting businesses, and a variety of other businesses serving miners and settlers in the society. While they "settled" for short periods in the Cariboo, they remained mobile, with strong attachments to Victoria and San Francisco. Ultimately, the family base in the San Francisco area drew most of the next generation, but the lure of the Cariboo and British Columbia never fully extinguished. What forces limited the extent to which the sisters settled in British Columbia? How did they negotiate the colonial politics of late nineteenth-century British Columbia?

Last, while the three sisters began their British Columbian stories as young immigrants to the new society, their lives as adult women took three distinctly different directions. In the 1870s, women were legally restricted in society; they were without the right to vote and were denied the same economic freedoms as men. While legal rights were slowly changing, women's choices were circumscribed by societal norms and legal technicalities. They had limited options for higher education and careers. As maturing women, the Lindhard sisters pursued different paths. Their lives became a series of responses to circumstances and choices made within the constraints on women's lives of the time. Historian Lenore Davidoff describes sibling relationships as "life's longest relationship" that often endures even when distance and time intervene.[8] What happened to the sisterly bonds as the three women matured, formed their own families, and seized the opportunities they found?

With so many questions about the lives of the Lindhard sisters, I set about to piece together as many fragments as I could find about their lives. In the absence of sufficient diaries, letters, and other written remnants, historians must assess what they can.[9] The Lindhard sisters didn't leave correspondence or diaries that could provide a

Introduction

window on their sisterly ties and confidences. Therefore, the insights I could draw are limited about the private emotional-social-psychological reactions and aspirations that they might have communicated to each other in letters. My interpretations are drawn from the women's actions that were publicly reported.

I made extensive use of digitized newspapers. The California Digital Newspaper Collection, the newspaper collection available through Open Library University of British Columbia, and the *Daily British Colonist* available through University of Victoria (now through archive.org) were invaluable to this work. Social columns and passenger lists were especially useful in providing a window into the sisters' actions and more general events of the time. I checked newspaper reports against birth, marriage, and death records and census records, wills, and probate records found in archives in Canada and the United States. I searched school records, land records, court records, and mining licences held in various archives. I also consulted city and provincial directories available online and in archives. Through this process, I was able to construct life accounts from a wide range of fragments gleaned online, in archives, and published texts.

Often the process required reading between the lines, then re-reading the lines, as information I may have first overlooked became significant in relation to a recently discovered fragment. For those unfamiliar with the way women's lives were obscured in nineteenth-century newspapers, birth announcements are one example:

SATURDAY, SEPTEMBER 12, 1874

BIRTHS: *At Van Winkle, on Sunday morning, 6th September, the wife of Mr. J. C. Beedy, of a daughter.*[10]

Traces of women's lives appeared in news columns, but again exact identities were obscure. In 1872, Barkerville celebrated both July 1 (Dominion Day in Canada) and July 4 (Independence Day in the

United States) and "Mr. and Mrs. Lindhard from Vanwinkle" were noted as visitors to the town on the "occasion of the sports and amusements."[11] Newspapers often recorded people arriving and leaving on the stagecoaches and steamers. On September 28, 1872, it was noted that Mrs. Lindhard left Barkerville on Sunday, September 22, on the stage for Yale.[12] In both cases, since first names were not used, the exact identity of Mrs. Lindhard is only recognizable when one knows her husband's identity and activities in Van Winkle. When Mr. J.W. Lindhard died on June 9, 1873, he received a lengthy three-paragraph tribute in the *Cariboo Sentinel* with reference made to "the bereaved family" but no family members were named.[13]

The Barkerville Archives were extremely useful in this project for the photographs and documents they hold. Books with dates and Laura's or her son Asa Beedy's name inside the cover gave clues as to what they read and studied and where Asa had studied. Account books from the various stores and partnerships provided a compelling glimpse into the daily activities and business practices of gold-rush-era merchants. The business records kept by John Boyd at Cottonwood and Cold Spring House were valuable for the detail they provided on business and social activities. I had access to letters written by the Lindhard sisters' children and grandchildren containing reminiscences that were possessions of family descendants who very generously shared these treasures.

Each of the chapters that follow is focused on one of the Lindhard sisters. Chapter 1 is about Laura, the oldest sister who journeyed to the Cariboo in 1870. In the mining town of Van Winkle she married and had children, then left the province for five years after the death of her first husband. She married again and returned to Stanley, where she remained as merchant and postmistress until retirement in 1899. Chapter 2 is focused on Caroline, who accompanied Laura to Van Winkle in 1870 at the young age of eighteen. She married twice, to men in the Cariboo, before moving to the San Francisco area where she created a family base that served her extended family for over twenty years. She pursued real estate investments and attained an affluent lifestyle that she generously shared. Chapter 3 is focused on Christine, who came to join her sisters in British Columbia in 1874. She married, had children, was widowed, and left the province after nine years. She was drawn to communal living, which she participated in for the rest of her life after leaving British Columbia. Each chapter traces the events and activities of their lives from 1870 to approximately 1900, through marriages, births, deaths, business decisions, good times, and bad. Their children play a large part in their lives and each account includes the children until they marry and start their own families. The sisters' lives entwined, and the sisterly bonds were stretched and sometimes frayed. They shared strong commitments to family and community although the paths to realizing those commitments diverged.

In constructing the accounts of the women's lives, I engaged in a process Jean Barman describes as bringing together "traces, from which meaning must be inferred."[14] The traces that I assembled about each sister's life took on meaning as they were arranged beside and in relationship to her other sisters and family members. In this way, meaning arose from within the family context and the larger societal and political unfoldings. The process that feminists have referred to as "reading between the lines" was also relevant. When identities were obscured or names were omitted or erroneously reported, reading newspaper accounts critically was important. I triangulated data sources, and when that wasn't possible or sources contained errors, I filled in details through speculation and probability assessments. Knowing the family and societal contexts made these procedures possible.

A crucial strategy in constructing the stories of the Lindhard sisters was to place them as much as possible within the context of their times. What were the social, political, and economic conditions? What impacts did these conditions have on their choices and decisions? What structures and discourses would have been at play in shaping their beliefs and life choices? There are limitations to the extent that we can understand nineteenth-century lives. The interpretive procedures I used of filling in the blanks and reading between the lines are prone to presentism. In other words, my interpretations risk a bias of interpreting past events and conditions through my own twenty-first-century perspective. My own perspective was formed by being born a white female about a century after the Lindhard women. My formative years were in a rural agriculture area of southern Manitoba where some elements of pioneer life persisted—no electricity, semi-isolation, a self-sufficient rural daily existence, one-room schools, cold snowy winters—some of the same elements the Lindhards may have experienced in northern British Columbia. I tried to offset the influence of presentism by broadly reading texts about and from the nineteenth century that could enrich my understanding of that era. In doing so, I pored through old newspapers, imagining I was reading the newspapers they may have read and trying to imagine how they could have been thinking and feeling. I read books that they may have read at the time. This helped to imagine various scenarios before deciding on the most likely. In the chapters that follow, I periodically describe the context of events and activities the Lindhard sisters were experiencing or observing in their travels and in Victoria, the Cariboo, and San Francisco. I invite the reader to imagine themselves in the time and place the Lindhards lived and enjoy the journey.

Laura Lindhard Beedy Dodd (1846–1910).
PHOTO COURTESY J. PASNAU

— *Part One* —

LAURA LINDHARD
BEEDY DODD

LAURA LINDHARD BEEDY DODD came to British Columbia when she was twenty-four years old. She travelled to the Cariboo in 1870, accompanied by her sister Caroline, who was six years younger, and their cousins Theodor and Joachim Lindhard.

Born Laurine (Laura) Martine Elise Lindhard on January 28, 1846, in Stege, Denmark, Laura was the eldest daughter and second child of Joachim Lindhard and Josephine Margrethe Rasmussen Lindhard. Stege is a small port city on the island of Moen in southeastern Denmark. As a centre of the lucrative herring fishery, it received city rights as early as 1268 and in the 1800s became a centre for merchant shipping. Stege's location gave it a feeling of isolation and separateness from the country's mainland and the more urban Copenhagen.

Laura's father, Joachim, was a master carpenter and with his wife, Josephine, raised three daughters and two sons, William and Peter (a.k.a. Harold). Peter was two years older than Laura and the oldest child in the family. The family lived close to Joachim's brother Jorgen Hansen Lindhard, married to Bolette Nielsen Lindhard. It was their children, eldest son Joachim and youngest son Theodor, who accompanied Laura and Caroline on their journey to North America. Cousin Joachim was twelve years older than Laura and had left Stege to see the world when he was fourteen. Laura was only three years old at the time he left, and she hardly knew him. She was closer to Theodor, who had been like a younger brother to her as they grew up together.

MID-CENTURY DENMARK

WHEN LAURA WAS BORN in the mid-nineteenth century, it was a time of change and turmoil in Denmark. The country was almost bankrupt by 1813 due to its sixteenth-century wars with Sweden and the war with England in 1801–14 that resulted in the loss of Norway to Sweden. The First and Second Schleswig Wars in 1848–51 and 1864 against Prussia resulted in Denmark's loss of the Schleswig-Holstein region. In 1849, the people of Denmark demanded an end to absolute rule by the monarchy, and Frederik VII, who ruled at the time, agreed to create the country's first constitution. Enlightenment thinking was sweeping through Europe, and some began to question whether Denmark could survive as a nation.[1]

These tumultuous times gave rise to Nikolai Frederik Severin Grundtvig, who has been described as a poly-historian. A Danish bishop and poet, he was influenced by German idealistic thought, French and American republicanism, British liberalism, and Slavonic nationalism.[2] He was critical of the revolutions and conditions he witnessed in these countries and argued for a reformist way to enlightenment. As a result, he turned to education and argued that vocational and cultural education could make individuals the equal of their fellow beings and facilitate the transition from absolute government to a people's government. The task was to educate citizens to understand themselves not only as self-governing and self-loving but also as morally obligated to the community—be that a people, a nation, or a state.

Since education was central to Grundtvig's philosophy, he has also been regarded as an education philosopher and his influence undoubtedly shaped the schooling that Laura and her sisters experienced in Denmark. By 1814, Denmark had introduced compulsory schooling for all children between the ages of seven and fourteen, the second country in the world after Prussia to do so. After 1844, Grundtvig's idea of a folk's school, or people's school, took hold. The goals of education in the people's school included helping children become useful citizens of the state, creating a sense of identity, an uplifting community life, and a passion for learning. He wrote of the importance of educating the mind and heart and of schooling in the Danish language. Grundtvig's thinking permeated Danish society and affected Laura's views of self, community, and nation that she carried into her life in North America.

Sadly, Grundtvig was of his time, and when he wrote of education, identity, and nation, he considered only male citizens. In his opinion, matters of state were not issues for women and children.[3] Grundtvig didn't fully grasp the changes that were afoot among the people, including women's desire for equal opportunities and freedoms, such as those possible in the frontiers and new societies.

A restlessness prevailed in Denmark by 1870. The recent wars with Germany ended badly for Denmark. It lost Crown lands, and the disillusionment and loss of faith in the future stirred some Danes toward emigration.[4] The economy was industrializing and shifting from a base in rural agriculture to urbanized manufacture. This made for a mobile population—especially of young men who were in excess numbers in rural areas and unlikely to secure land of their own. Their options were either moving to the city in search of industrial work or emigrating to countries where work and land ownership might be possible. The political and economic conditions contributed to

Mid-Century Denmark

"social buoyancy" among young rural Danes who sought better living conditions and greater independence.[5]

Laura followed the experiences of her cousin Joachim through the letters he wrote home from California, where he had arrived in 1849, and later from the Colony of British Columbia. When he arrived in California, he was an impressionable sixteen-year-old and wrote glowingly of the vastness and riches of the land. He found plenty of opportunities for employment in the gold mining towns and tried his hand in the search for gold. All the Lindhard family members read his letters, and his writing stirred conversation about what life was like in the "new world" he was experiencing. Laura began to wonder if the opportunities Joachim had found might also be for her.

The Lindhard families debated social theories, the future of the Danish nation, and the roles of women and men. They were witnessing changes around them as Denmark's economy transitioned from agriculture to manufacture. Stege became a centre for merchant shipping and warehouses soon lined the waterfront. Laura and her sisters felt the restlessness of the times and the social buoyancy that they might capture in their futures. But would it be possible in Stege?

OPPORTUNITIES ABOUND

LAURA'S EARLY YEARS FOLLOWED a common pattern for young people in Denmark. School was compulsory for children to age fourteen. The Danish Constitution of 1849 granted religious freedom, but the Lutheran Church remained the state church. Unless people formally opted out, everyone was born into the Lutheran Church and within months of birth, children were baptized. Laura was baptized on May 18, 1846, almost four months after her birth on January 28. In 1736, King Christian VI had passed a law requiring all young people to be confirmed at age fourteen, a practice that signified their passage into adulthood and entrance into social and religious life. After 1810, an additional requirement before confirmation was proof of vaccination against smallpox or of having had smallpox. Without proof of vaccination, one could not be confirmed and without being confirmed one could not marry, attend school, become an apprentice, serve in the military, be a godparent, or vote.[6] Laura was confirmed at age fourteen in 1860.

Laura's entrance to adulthood in 1860 coincided with her mother giving birth to the youngest family member, William Laurist Lindhard. With two younger sisters aged eight and ten, Laura's help was needed at home. Any immediate ambitions for further schooling or employment were delayed while she helped her mother with the daily tasks of childcare and homemaking. Opportunities for women to be employed were limited and most looked forward to marrying and forming their own families. The common employment was as farm helpers or domestics. Learning the domestic arts was important in Laura's family. She and her sisters learned needlework and how to sew their own clothes. Baking and cooking were also accomplishments that were a source of pride. With a baby in the family to care for, Laura and her younger sisters had an apprenticeship readily available within their own family!

Laura wasn't keen to rush into marriage. She listened to her cousin Joachim when he came home in 1867 fired with enthusiasm for his current life in Van Winkle in the Colony of British Columbia. He had exciting and funny stories to tell of the people he knew and the riches gained and lost on Lightning Creek in the Cariboo. Many young people that she knew, young men especially, were leaving Denmark to try their luck in the United States and British North America and she wondered what she might find there. When Joachim convinced his younger brother, Theodor, to join him the next year, Laura seriously began to think that joining them might be a possibility and not just a dream.

Laura left her family home sometime before 1870 to live with a farm family headed by Jorgen Andersen Wendelbo and Dorethe Katrine Frikke Wendelbo in Kattrup Sogn. She may have been a farm helper or domestic for the family. The 1870 Danish census described her as a visitor, a designation that suggests she was a long-term visitor.

In 1869, cousins Joachim and Theodor returned to Denmark for Christmas, joining many fellow countrymen who returned each year on the Christmas ship.[7] The transcontinental railway in the United States had opened months before and Joachim was eager to see how much shorter the journey would be for him now when he wanted to travel home from the Cariboo. He also believed that with train travel making the trip easier, this might be the right time to convince his cousins to accompany him back to Van Winkle.

PART ONE: LAURA LINDHARD BEEDY DODD

Joachim reminded Laura that she was approaching the age in Denmark when friends plot to give an unwed woman or man at age twenty-five or thirty a "pepper shower." This was a tradition that dated to the 1500s when merchants travelled a lot and as a result often remained unwed on their thirtieth birthday. Having escaped the pepper shower himself and now at age thirty-five, he promised Laura that in Van Winkle there would be no pepper showers and there would be many unmarried men, some of whom were quite wealthy.[8]

Joachim had been in the Colony of British Columbia for twelve years and was now settled in the village of Van Winkle, twenty-two kilometres (fourteen miles) west of Barkerville. In 1866 he bought the Van Winkle store from Mssrs. Schorling & Company, and it had been so busy that three years later he had taken Josiah Crosby Beedy (a.k.a. J.C. Beedy) as a partner. The autumn of 1869 had kept him in Van Winkle well past what was departure time for many residents of the Cariboo. First there was the visit of the new governor, Sir Anthony Musgrave, in late September. Then the court case when Aime Guilloteau accused him of stealing lumber from the roof of his barn.[9] Fortunately, the judge dismissed the case because the value of the lumber was inconsequential, and Joachim provided evidence that the lumber had been taken from a mining claim site he had purchased. It was the principle of the thing Joachim argued. Guilloteau had no right to the lumber, and he had therefore asked his employees to retrieve the lumber for him.[10] That was behind him now and he was able to leave Van Winkle in November and leave his partner, Josiah Beedy, in charge for the months they would be in Denmark. Ah Fung, his cook, and other employees would capably manage his businesses while he was away.

Joachim was convinced that mining on Lightning Creek would realize large profits. So far, his investments had paid off. He operated the saloon that had become a meeting place for the community, hosting lectures and election voting. He had rooms to rent, a saloon serving drinks and meals to travellers and miners, a store providing

Opportunities Abound

supplies and equipment for the miners, and a butcher shop he had operated for several years. He was a major shareholder in the Van Winkle Company that was mining on Lightning Creek and he held shares in the Union Jack Company. He was sure that one day the mining companies would make him rich because the Van Winkle claim was at the convergence of three streams—Lightning and Van Winkle creeks and Perkins Gulch. He believed these three creeks had been depositing gold onto Van Winkle Company's piece of bedrock for centuries.[11] Both he and Josiah were convinced that Lightning Creek would provide them bountiful returns.

When Laura was home in Stege over Christmas of 1869, she listened to Joachim's exciting tales of his business and mining experiences on Lightning Creek. He employed helpers and needed workers to assist with his businesses. Laura was impressed when he told them of recently meeting Sir Anthony Musgrave, the new governor of the Colony of British Columbia. Musgrave had visited Van Winkle at the end of September and Joachim had shared lunch with him and toured him through the Van Winkle Company's claim, explaining to him the difficulties the mining companies were having in reaching the gold deposits on Lightning Creek. Lightning Creek did not give up its gold easily and it was proving especially difficult to hold back the slum (silt and water combination) that kept flooding over the rich bedrock.[12] Joachim was pleased to point out to Musgrave that the mines held great promise of wealth and employment for the area and perhaps the government could lend some assistance in helping the miners overcome the challenges they faced. While Musgrave could promise no assistance, Joachim was satisfied that he was now aware of the challenges.[13] He might have to call on him again in the future.

British Columbia was on the verge of becoming a new province in the Dominion of Canada, joining the vision of a nation sea to sea. The Yale Convention had been held in 1868, a gathering of twenty-six elected delegates from throughout the colony that approved a resolution calling for immediate union with Canada. Governor Musgrave's main mission was to persuade all British Columbians to support joining the Dominion of Canada.[14] There was widespread enthusiasm for joining Canada among Barkerville residents, and Joachim and Josiah were fully wrapped up in the idea. They could see that the whole Cariboo area would benefit if transportation and communication were improved, as was being promised if British Columbia joined Canada.

Laura was intrigued by the newness of everything Joachim described: a soon-to-be new province; a new town in the Cariboo where they had to build everything they needed; a new road and railway and easier transportation. Her sister Caroline, who was a young eighteen years, romantically inclined and spontaneous, was totally enthralled. When Joachim suggested that Caroline and Laura accompany him and Theodor to the Cariboo, Caroline was ready to go! It was the sisters' parents who were adamant that Laura accompany Caroline, and they expected her to be a supportive and stabilizing companion for her young sister.

To AMERICA

LAURA AND CAROLINE WERE in the vanguard of women adventurers of the time. Prior to 1870, mostly single men emigrated from Denmark, seeking work in America. Some intended to stay, but others were temporary workers seeking to improve their economic conditions and return to their homeland. An 1868 article in *Putnam's Magazine* commented, "If the social history of the world is ever written, the era in which we live will be called the nomadic period. With the advent of ocean steam navigation and the railway system began a travelling mania which has gradually increased until half the earth's inhabitants . . . are on the move."[15]

The Lindhards were booked in two cabins on the *Saxonia* for the trip departing from Hamburg, Germany, to New York on March 9, 1870. The *Saxonia* was a large, 95 × 13 metre (311 × 42 foot), three-masted steamship operated by the Hamburg America Line. The *Saxonia* was no longer a new ship. It had launched in 1857 and made regular crossings between Hamburg and New York.

Two well-known American sisters—Louisa May Alcott and her sister May—with friend Alice Bartlett were travelling from New York to France on the *Lafayette* in the spring of 1870.[16] Their paths almost crossed with the Lindhards, who arrived in New York on March 26. The young women were seeking adventure in Europe at a time when Americans were fascinated by everything European—its news, books, clothes, letters, and fashion. The fascination with everything European may have eased the way for Laura and Caroline as they travelled across North America.

While the steamships were able to cross the Atlantic more quickly, travelling on the *Saxonia* for seventeen days was not luxurious. There was a usual pattern to the journey. The first day after departure was pleasurable, but once out to sea most people were seasick. For others, boredom set in. Louisa May Alcott wrote to her parents after seven days on the *Lafayette*, "This is a mean letter but absolutely nothing happens aboard a steamer."[17] The Alcotts practised French during their crossing in preparation for life in France, and it's likely that Laura and Caroline used the time to practice English. They needed to learn English quickly if they were to be helpful to Joachim in his businesses. Joachim would have been a good tutor since he had been away from Denmark for twenty-two years and had clearly mastered English grammar and the writing conventions of America.[18]

One adventurer, who wrote of his crossing the Atlantic in 1869, noted the strong headwinds that slowed progress: "Passengers who had been jubilant as to the prospects of the voyage now shook their heads and bemoaned their lot. The attendance at meals was agreeably select."[19] Others complained of the incessant noise of the ship groaning, creaking, and cracking; the eternal close contact with the crew and other passengers; the food; and the impossibility of any exercise in the cramped quarters. So, while the speed of crossing the Atlantic had improved considerably, it was not a comfortable cruise!

After seventeen days at sea, New York appeared in sight. This is when it dawned on Laura that there was now no turning back. She was uncertain as to how long she would stay with her cousins in the Cariboo, but she had thoroughly enjoyed Theodor's accounts of his previous ocean crossings and was grateful for the guidance that both he and Joachim provided. She felt some trepidation but knew she could not look back. Her focus was now forward until they reached their destination.

The port of New York, welcome after a voyage of seventeen days, was an introduction to the big cities of America. IMAGE JEW7GK/ALMAY

The *Saxonia* dropped anchor in New York Harbour in sight of the Castle Garden Immigration Depot. Opened in 1855 and operated by the State and City of New York, all immigrants had to pass through this entry point. They were lucky because within twenty-four hours they were carried by small ferry to the depot, their entrance recorded, and their state of health checked. The depot had hospital facilities, quarantine rooms, money exchange services, and an employment service. Since they were only passing through on their way west, their entrance processing was uneventful. They were able to purchase in the depot the railway tickets needed to carry them across the continent.

The depot was Laura's introduction to the immigrant experience. An article describing Castle Garden ran in *Harper's Monthly* in 1870:

PART ONE: LAURA LINDHARD BEEDY DODD

> As we approached the entrance to Castle Garden we found it almost impossible to make our way through, the passage was so blocked up with vehicles, peddlers of cheap cigars, apple-stands, and runners from the different boarding-houses and intelligence-offices that abound in the neighbourhood. However we succeeded in getting through, after encountering an outpouring stream of new arrivals, and being nearly deafened by the repeated shouts of "D'ye want a conveyance?" "Hotel Stadt Hamburg!" "Zum goldenen Adler!" "This way, gents, this way!" etc.[20]

In addition to the crush of people, the article noted the mix of languages heard among arriving passengers, the difficulty of registering names when English was not understood, and the challenge of purchasing train tickets when passengers were uncertain about their destination. Laura was grateful to benefit from the past experiences of Joachim and Theodor, who knew how to negotiate the various checks and service counters efficiently and quickly guided them through the process.

With New York being their first glimpse of America, Laura and Caroline were eager to see some of the city. After an overnight stay and a day to explore, they caught the evening train on the New York Central Line to Chicago.[21] The railways across the United States were new and all efforts were made to provide comfortable and attractive travel. "Hotel cars" that offered in-room dining and all possible services were part of this route. The next day they were in Rochester and then on to Buffalo, where they boarded the Great Western Railway. The Great Western Railway based in Hamilton, Ontario, provided a bridge line between Buffalo, New York, and Detroit, Michigan. Pullman's Palace Cars were added to the train and provided passengers a spectacular view of Niagara Falls as they continued toward Hamilton.

A stop in Hamilton gave Laura her first glimpse of the newly formed Dominion of Canada, then it was back on the train destined

The new railways made every effort to provide comfortable travel and spectacular views across the continent. COURTESY OF THE LIBRARY OF CONGRESS, CPH.3A05486

for Detroit. In Detroit, passengers were transported across the Detroit River to catch the Michigan Central Railroad that carried them to Chicago. At each location where there was a transfer to a new train, there was considerable hustle and confusion to locate luggage and find transport to sometimes an entirely different

PART ONE: LAURA LINDHARD BEEDY DODD

station for the connecting departure. But Joachim had experienced the route and planned well. He wanted his cousins to experience only the best and had secured comfortable berths for their travels on the new railways.

Despite the many transfers to new trains and railways required to reach Chicago, Laura found the journey thoroughly exciting and the scenery spectacular. The route went eight hundred kilometres (five hundred miles) west, from Chicago to Council Bluffs, Iowa, across the Missouri River from Omaha, Nebraska. The Chicago and Northwestern Railroad was the oldest on this section and the one preferred by Joachim and Theodor. Passengers left the train at Council Bluffs and boarded "omnibuses," slowly drawn by four horses to the river's edge, where they were loaded on a flat-bottomed steamer for transport across the Missouri River to the Union Pacific Railroad station in Omaha. This is where the journey on the real transcontinental began!

From Omaha, the Union Pacific Railroad carried them 1,746 kilometres (1,085 miles) to Promontory, Utah. On the way, they made stops in Cheyenne and Sherman, Wyoming, at an altitude of 2,449 metres (8,235 feet), the high point where trains were inspected prior to descending into the Laramie Valley. Past Sherman Summit was a long fast descent across the Dale Creek trestle bridge leading into the valley. Laura was fascinated by the seemingly limitless plains, spring wildflowers, settled farmsteads, antelope, mountain sheep, alkali lakes, and sagebrush everywhere. They stopped at Promontory Summit, northwest of Salt Lake City, where the last spike had been pounded less than one year earlier when the Central Pacific Railroad from the west had

To America

joined with the Union Pacific Railroad from the east, to form the first transcontinental railway across the United States.

The railway passed into Nevada, with its numerous silver mining "cities," including Virginia City, Wells, and Reno. After Reno, the train climbed to the highest point on this section of the line, an altitude of 2,146 metres (7,042 feet), as it crossed the Sierra Nevada mountains. One traveller described the scene in 1869 from this altitude as he gazed at the towering mountain peaks as "one of unprecedented grandeur."[22] The descent from the summit into Sacramento was swift as the train sped through eleven tunnels, over trestle bridges, and into balmy ocean-tempered breezes and a "land teeming with unexpected natural beauties and rare natural delights."[23]

The Central Pacific Railroad delivered the Lindhards right to the Oakland Long Wharf on the east side of the San Francisco Bay, from which a short ferry ride carried them into San Francisco. They might have experienced San Francisco as another traveller described it when arriving at night as a "fairy-like spectacle" that was "enchanting." Beyond enchanting, he was impressed with the potential wealth of the state:

> *There are 65,000,000 acres which can be brought under tillage, and as yet not more than three per cent of the whole has been cultivated ... The soil yields everything human beings require to support and ameliorate existence. All the metals which men value most highly can be procured in abundance and disposed of at a profit. The rivers swarm with fish; the woods are filled with game; the fields are alive with the savoury birds which, in less favoured localities are the luxuries of the rich. The climate is as glorious as that which must have prevailed in those "summer isles of Eden lying in dark purple spheres of sea," which the poet has depicted as the regions of perfect terrestrial beauty and happiness.*[24]

The Lindhards lingered in San Francisco.

An OLDER SISTER DILEMMA

LAURA HAD A PROBLEM. She knew her parents expected her to be a rational, steadying influence on her younger impetuous sister, but while she could advise, she could not control her. Caroline was outgoing, fun-loving, and determined. Laura noticed a mutual attraction developing between Caroline and her cousin Joachim as they travelled across the Atlantic. For Caroline, the train trip across the United States was pure romance.

Joachim was a charmer, full of exaggerated tales of his and his friends' adventures. Caroline found him a funny and captivating companion. He was generous and protective and made her feel confident and secure as they travelled farther into territory unknown to Caroline. In San Francisco, Theodor bid farewell to his companions and returned to his work. When Joachim proposed marriage to Caroline, she readily agreed and did not mention a word to Laura.

On Tuesday, April 5, 1870, Laura, Caroline, and Joachim left San Francisco on the *Active* for the five-day trip up the coast to Victoria. Only when Caroline signed in as Mrs. Lindhard did Laura realize they had married. She was concerned but helpless. She was only more convinced that she could not control her determined, independent sister. She could simply help her in what she chose to do. And it would be up to Caroline to tell her parents. It was not unusual for cousins to marry in the nineteenth century. If both individuals were healthy, it was believed that there was little risk to their future offspring. It was a way to consolidate and keep family wealth within a family line and not at all uncommon for this reason.

The *Active* was a coal-fired, two-masted sidewheel steamer originally launched in 1849. By 1870, it had seen lengthy service on the West Coast transporting miners, was used by the United States Coast Survey, and in 1870 was operated by the North Pacific Transportation Company.[25] After twenty-one years in service, the *Active* was neither glamorous nor luxurious, but it was part of routine travel between San Francisco and Victoria.

Laura soon realized that the journey to the Cariboo began in San Francisco, and now she had to join most of those around her in speaking English. Joachim introduced her and Caroline to many of the fellow passengers that he knew. Some were bound for Victoria, some for the mainland, and some were returning from their winter migration and now heading back to the mining communities in the northern interior of the Colony of British Columbia.

One fellow traveller on the *Active* was Emily Crease (1828–1900), sister of Henry Crease, who was attorney general for the Colony of British Columbia. She was travelling with a servant to Victoria to take a new position as principal of Angela College.[26] From her, Laura learned that Angela College was a girls' school in Victoria created nine years earlier under the direction of Bishop Hills. He believed it was needed to serve the middle- and upper-class parents who wanted an Anglican British education for their daughters. By 1869, it had enrolled over ninety girls, occupied an impressive building endowed by Angela Burdett-Coutts, and taught daughters of upwardly mobile families in the colony. But it was beset by problems of governance, finance, and staffing. Emily Crease remained principal until 1877, when she moved to Lytton to teach at the mission school.[27]

It was Sunday, April 10, when the *Active* pulled into Esquimalt Harbour near Victoria, one month since Laura had left Hamburg. Both Laura and Caroline were eager to explore Victoria because they knew it was the last large town they would experience on their journey to Van Winkle. Joachim busied himself ordering the supplies he would need for summer delivery and getting caught up on news and rumours from the Cariboo. He immediately purchased the *Daily British Colonist,* the local newspaper that would tell him of the steamers and stages running to the interior. They stopped by Barnard's Express on Yates Street to reserve spaces on the Hudson's Bay Company steamer *Enterprise* leaving Victoria for New Westminster and on the steamer *Onward* that would leave New Westminster for Yale on Wednesday. In Yale they would board the stagecoach operated by Barnard's Express[28] that would take them all the way to Van Winkle.

 Laura and Caroline studied the newspaper with great interest and were relieved to know that the *Daily British Colonist,* with its international news coverage, would reach them year-round in Van Winkle. In addition, Barkerville had its own newspaper, the *Cariboo*

Victoria was the last chance to shop before leaving for the smaller towns of the interior.
COURTESY UBC LIBRARY RARE BOOKS AND SPECIAL COLLECTIONS, UNO LANGMANN FAMILY COLLECTION OF B.C. PHOTOGRAPHS, 1-0053338.0014

An Older Sister Dilemma

Sentinel, published during the summer months. From the *Daily British Colonist*, they learned of Victoria's main attractions—lunch at the Adelphi Saloon, good coffee, medicinals, Crosse & Blackwell pickles, sauces and jams, dry goods, and grocery stores. They read about the celebration of the Queen's Birthday planned for May 24, with annual races on Beacon Hill. They caught their first glimpse of the Cariboo landscape through the photographs of Frederick Dally at his gallery on Fort Street. Politics were debated in the newspaper in terms of responsible versus representative government. There was recent news via telegraph from Europe, Portland, California, and the eastern United States. They thought maybe Joachim was right in saying they wouldn't be as cut off from the world in Van Winkle as they feared.

The three spent one night in Yale before boarding Barnard's Express, which would carry them to Van Winkle. They left Yale on Friday, on their first journey up the famous Cariboo Wagon Road that would take about five days. The distance from Yale to Barkerville was approximately 580 kilometres (360 miles) and Barnard's Express had built its reputation on courteous service and keeping to a schedule. Yale to Clinton was the usual route driven by Steve Tingley and he knew well everyone who travelled the Cariboo Road. He had lots of news and all the latest gossip to share with Joachim and was thrilled to meet Laura and Caroline. He offered them the usual courtesies granted to women on Barnard's Express; riding on the box beside him if they chose, sitting to his right at the table when dining, and generally assuring as many comforts as possible. But this was April and riding on the box had little appeal. Steve had married a little over a year ago in New Brunswick and his wife, Elizabeth Harper, had joined him at his home in Yale. He and Elizabeth had little Clarence Harper Tingley, born December 29, and now a few months old. Laura and Caroline saw the joy in his eyes as he talked about his small son.

PART ONE: LAURA LINDHARD BEEDY DODD

Yale was "the gateway to the Cariboo," where the steamers docked and passengers caught Barnard's Express for the remainder of the journey. COURTESY UBC LIBRARY RARE BOOKS AND SPECIAL COLLECTIONS, UNO LANGMANN FAMILY COLLECTION OF B.C. PHOTOGRAPHS, I-0053373.0000

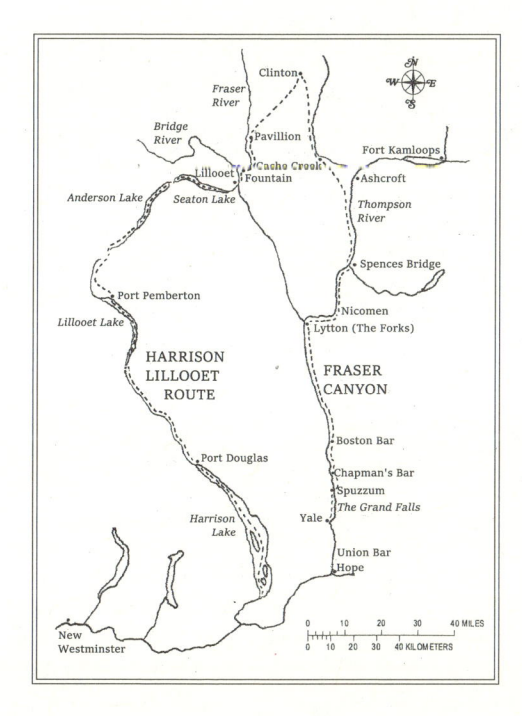

Two routes through Lower BC to Clinton: The original "Douglas Road" connected Harrison with Lillooet on a route of lakes and portages, and the newer "Cariboo Road" connected Yale with Lytton through the Fraser Canyon. COURTESY OF K. MATHER

An Older Sister Dilemma

This early in the travelling season, the stagecoach was not crowded. Confident in their experienced driver and the assistance Joachim provided, they sat back to enjoy the first 161 kilometres (100 miles) out of Yale that they were told was some of the most hazardous and picturesque scenery on the continent.[29] But this was April and with spring break-up, the road could be muddy and deeply rutted the whole way with the stagecoach wheels sinking to the hubs. Or they might encounter steep icy mountain hills that would test all the skill and judgment the driver had in manoeuvring the stagecoach and horses safely. On this last leg of their adventure, they got the first taste of frontier—exhilarating and demanding.

The Cariboo Wagon Road ran 650 kilometres between Yale and Barkerville. Travel by stagecoach was far from luxurious. COURTESY UBC LIBRARY RARE BOOKS AND SPECIAL COLLECTIONS, UNO LANGMANN FAMILY COLLECTION OF B.C. PHOTOGRAPHS, I-0053437.0024

Even at best, conditions of stagecoach travel were barely tolerable.[30] The swinging, swaying, and bumping of the coach created "stage sickness," which was much like seasickness. There were stops about every twenty-nine kilometres (eighteen miles) to change horses and stops at favourite roadhouses for meals. If schedules permitted, there might be overnight stops. Otherwise, they would ride day and night, experiencing spring in British Columbia that could be cold, stormy, and snowy.

In Clinton, they met the other long-time stage driver for Barnard's Express, James Hamilton, who usually drove from Clinton to Soda Creek. Not all roadhouses measured up to the standards Barnard's Express liked for their passengers, but there were stops at 74 Mile House or 83 Mile House, 115 Mile House, and 141 Mile House—all roadhouses with reputations for outstanding meals and clean beds. By the third day, they reached the Exchange Hotel in Soda Creek, agents for Barnard's Express. There at the Exchange Hotel, Laura and Caroline were introduced to Asahel Sumner Bates (a.k.a. A.S. Bates). Asahel had until recently been proprietor and shareholder in the Exchange Hotel, and only months earlier he had sold his share, bought the nearby Deep Creek Farm, and seriously taken up farming.[31]

From Soda Creek, the Cariboo Wagon Road continued to Quesnelmouth (now Quesnel) and on into Barkerville. James's brother John Hamilton drove the last stretch, and it was the most treacherous at this time of the year. Before they reached Van Winkle, the stagecoach was exchanged for a sleigh. In the last forty-eight to sixty-four kilometres (thirty to forty miles) before Barkerville, the road gained elevation and the snowfall was always heavy, the road only three metres (ten feet) wide; by April the sleighs could be travelling one and a half to two metres (five to six feet) above the level of the summer road.[32] The unpredictable weather in April brought frequent fresh snowfalls that added to the remaining winter snow.

An Older Sister Dilemma

Laura and Caroline had come a long way north and their journey had been long. They offered each other grim smiles as they wistfully longed for the warmth of sunny California they had experienced. But there was no turning back now for either of them, and they set about unpacking and settling into Joachim's home in Van Winkle.

By 1865 the Cariboo Wagon Road reached Barkerville. Regular stagecoach runs were made between Yale and Barkerville, with stops in Van Winkle and Stanley. COURTESY OF K. MATHER

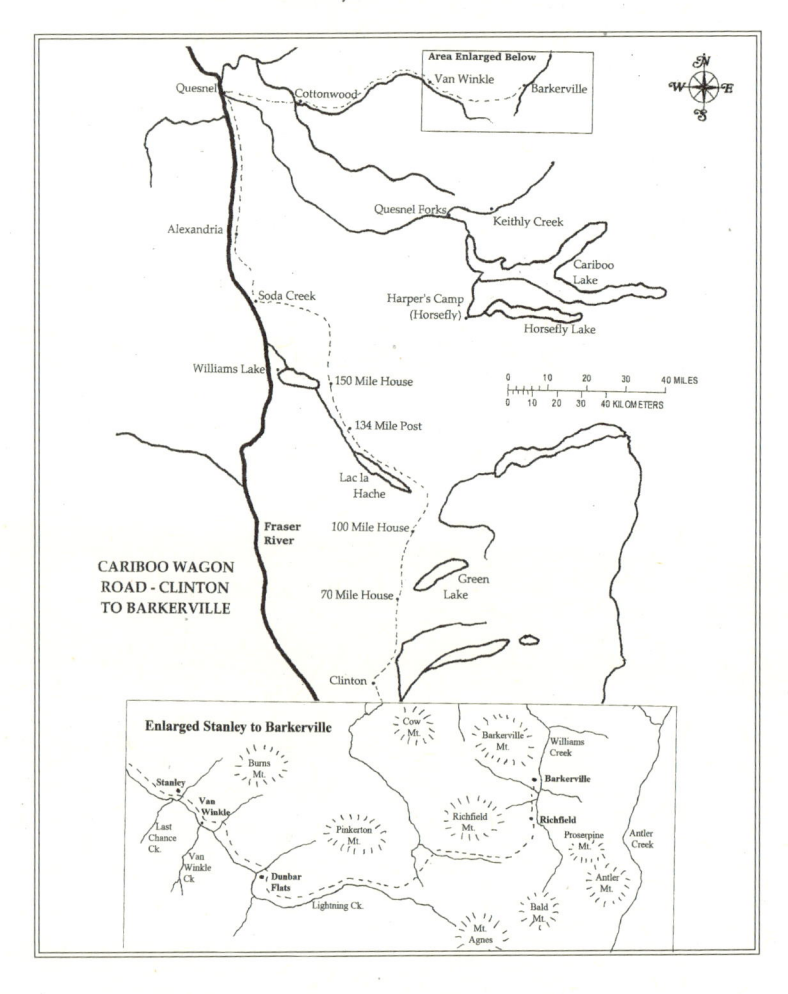

PART ONE: LAURA LINDHARD BEEDY DODD

VAN WINKLE *on* LIGHTNING CREEK

JOACHIM AND HIS PARTNER, Josiah Crosby Beedy, had arrived early in the area where the town of Van Winkle grew. They believed this was where the motherlode of gold would be found. By 1861, prospectors had made their way to the Upper Fraser River in British Columbia and followed the various streams and rivers that flowed into the Fraser—the Quesnel, the Swift, and Cottonwood—searching for the source of gold that had scattered traces throughout the river system. Feeding into the Cottonwood River was a creek that came to be called Lightning Creek, and into it flowed a smaller creek known as Van Winkle. In the spring of 1861, William Cunningham had found gold on Van Winkle Creek and that summer, Ned Campbell found gold on a bench above the creek. In the first season, the creek yielded from $100 to $250 a day per person.[33] These rich finds were the magnet that drew the rush of gold miners that included Joachim and Josiah.

There are several stories of how Lightning Creek got its name. One story involves prospectors in a thunderstorm experiencing severe lightning strikes in the area, and other stories link the idea of lightning to difficult and dangerous conditions in the face of uncertain but great potential reward.[34] Lightning Creek originates on a height of land below Richfield and flows toward the Cottonwood River. Van Winkle Creek enters Lightning Creek about twenty-two kilometres (fourteen miles) southwest of Barkerville. The Van Winkle townsite grew at this juncture. The Rip Van Winkle Bar near Lytton had been prosperous, and the new town was named Van Winkle as a prophetic gesture of similar wealth.[35] Van Winkle was the first town on Lightning Creek and even members of the government believed it would become the main distribution point for all of the mining district. In the summer of 1862, Harry Guillod, a visitor to Van Winkle, described it:

> *Van Winkle lies in a valley, shut in on all sides by high hills, Lightning Creek running through the centre; you have the sun only for a few hours during the day. The town is one street of wooden stores, Restaurant, Bakery, etc. ... On the side of the hill at the right is the Government Encampment consisting of a few tents.*[36]

Towns that sprang up in the Cariboo adjacent to mine shafts were a flurry of activity in summers and then quieted in a rhythm created by the departure of many miners for the winter and their return each spring. In 1861, gold was plentiful and found near the surface on Lightning Creek. Miners became rich. But by the mid-1860s, Van Winkle was quiet; the mid-decade years were not as rewarding. In a letter to his father in the summer of 1869, Josiah described Van Winkle "as a small mining camp that I supply with goods." The bedrock in many places along Lightning Creek was extremely deep, twenty-four metres to forty-six metres (80 to 150 feet) below the surface, and the conditions of water and slum made it almost impossible to reach.[37] Cabins and businesses emptied, and by 1864, the creek was almost abandoned, but Beedy and Lindhard (Josiah and Joachim) believed in Lightning Creek.

When Laura arrived in 1870, Van Winkle was on the upswing, becoming an active mining centre again. Lightning Creek required sophisticated tunnelling, hydraulic mining equipment, and skills, and the mining companies began to acquire these. The Van Winkle

Van Winkle. Photo by Frederick Dally, about 1868. Villages arose near mine shafts and the hills were stripped bare of their timber. Van Winkle Hotel is at centre back. COURTESY UBC LIBRARY RARE BOOKS AND SPECIAL COLLECTIONS, UNO LANGMANN FAMILY COLLECTION OF B.C. PHOTOGRAPHS, I-0053437.0068

Company put in a costly bedrock drain that required a cooperative method using all the miners on the creek. They drained water from the mine shafts by running twelve water wheels simultaneously and pumping approximately 64,000 litres (14,000 gallons) a minute. Within two miles along the creek, many companies began to profit from their claims.

Mining became a year-round underground operation. As mining companies continued their work throughout the winter, the rhythm of seasonal departures and returns that had defined the communities began to change. In the winter of 1869–70, Beedy and Lindhard's store in Van Winkle remained open all winter and supplied a steady stream of mining customers. With this upturn in mining activity, the little town attracted businesses and people from Barkerville, and it grew rapidly. With Van Winkle showing great promise, Beedy and Lindhard became enthusiastic and committed promoters of the community.

Van Winkle on Lightning Creek

BEEDY *and* LINDHARD

JOSIAH CROSBY BEEDY WAS born February 18, 1832, in Cambridge Springs, Crawford County, Pennsylvania, to Samuel Beedy and Elizabeth (Betsy) Crosby Beedy. He was the second youngest in a large family of ten children. His mother died when he was eleven years old. He initially worked as a clerk, living and working with an uncle in Manchester, New Hampshire.[38] Following this experience, Josiah ventured west to California mining territory around La Porte and Oroville in the Sierra Nevada mountains. He may have been lucky in the California gold rush. He was certainly in a mining area that made some wealthy:

> *B.W. Barnes of La Porte states that $500 per day to the man was not unusual pay in the flush days of California. He says that the shipments of gold from Spanish Flat, Warren Hill, LaPorte, and Secret Diggings loaded 30 mules per week. He mentions one instance where he met a train of ten mules all loaded with gold, each mule load averaging 125 lbs. In 1857, two miners left La Porte with $75,000 in gold dust.*[39]

Josiah staked several claims around Warren Hill with partner John Conly before being lured by the promise of greater riches farther north. The Crosby family history describes Josiah as "well educated for business,"[40] and after his experiences in California, he was ready to enter early into the Fraser River gold rush. He lingered for a while in Yale. While searching for gold was a priority, he was an eager entrepreneur with a gambling spirit. He must hold a near record for the number of businesses and business partnerships he created in the time he was active in British Columbia, over twenty years.

In 1860, Josiah Beedy, in partnership with Frank Way, contracted to build the section of the wagon road up the Fraser Canyon from Yale to Spuzzum. That summer he met Francis Jones Barnard, who worked briefly with Frank Way, to locate and lay out the next section of road from Chapman's to Boston Bar.[41] This meeting began a lengthy association with Barnard, who went on to found Barnard's Express.

Josiah was one of the first directors of the Yale Steam Navigation Company, along with Andrew Charles Elliott, Hugh Nelson, William Power, and John Kurtz.[42] They built the sternwheel steamer *Fort Yale*, which launched in November 1860 with much praise as a local product that "the people of Fort Yale are highly delighted with . . . which is a perfect model of beauty and strength."[43] The glory of the steamer was short-lived. In April of 1861, it nearly took the life of purser Barnard, who was on board when its boiler exploded—an accident that claimed several lives and totally destroyed the steamer.[44] The *Daily British Colonist* reported that, "as she is uninsured, the loss will fall heavily upon her enterprising owners."[45]

Josiah's luck may have paid off in other ventures. He was reported as being on Antler Creek in 1860 and arriving in Victoria with a "buckskin filled with coarse gold."[46] The coarse gold of the Cariboo was unlike the fine or flour gold that prospectors panned along the Fraser River. The display of the coarse gold in Victoria was a strategy to stir excitement about the creeks of the Cariboo. He claimed to have worked $75 worth out of a single pan. Josiah was one of the first into Williams Creek in 1861, the richest gold creek in the Cariboo. Four mining claims were registered in 1861 in the names of J.C. Beedy, Thomas Elwyn, E.A. Wadham, and Andrew Hanson.[47]

In December of 1861, Josiah returned to Oroville, California, and his report on opportunities in the Cariboo was carried in California newspapers:

> *Mr. J.C. Beedy formerly of La Porte ... represents to us another and a darker side of those celebrated diggings. The country is one vast swamp of mire. Weather wet and stormy through the whole mining season, the miners having to work continually in a damp condition. Not one sturdy miner in a hundred can endure the exposure. ... A large number of the business men of this far out country are from Sierra County. Beedy says no man with less than $1,000 should venture to Cariboo. Miners there say that if the seasons were as long and the climate as favorable there as here, the mines would then equal those of any part of our own Sierra.*
>
> *Mr. Beedy has been trading very successfully since March last and will return early in the spring. He has no interest to underrate the mines but to the contrary ... It is expected that Lightning Creek will prove one of the most important streams mined next year.*[48]

However, the search for gold was never Josiah's sole venture. When a village began to grow on Antler Creek, he was the first to open a store there.[49] Around the same time he opened a store in Quesnelmouth and another in Richfield.[50] One of his partners at this time was George Eves, but it was a partnership of short duration. Eves, who was on his way back to the Cariboo after conducting business in Victoria, died from typhoid fever in Yale on June 12, 1862.[51] Another partner in Beedy and Company was Robert Magirl.[52] By 1865, Beedy and Company's store in Barkerville was well established, providing the miners with the essentials, such as food and mining supplies.[53] When much of Barkerville burned on September 18, 1868, the store, valued at ten thousand dollars, was destroyed, a significant loss at the time.[54] After the Barkerville fire he chose to move on rather than re-build.

In addition to the stores that Josiah operated and the mines he tended, he operated several mule packtrains that transported goods from Yale to the Cariboo.[55] Packing his own supplies to his stores from Yale took priority, but he also delivered goods for other merchants of the area. On July 3, 1869, he had a day of leisure, "a lonely one," and wrote his father in Cambridge Springs, Pennsylvania, reporting on the weather and his business ventures. It was an extremely hot, dry summer and forest fires raged at nearby Quesnel Lake. Some miners had lost their lives and others were busy fighting the fires. The smoke was so dense that it caused a solar eclipse–like atmosphere when the sunlight was totally blocked by smoke.

Josiah expressed some disillusionment with the Cariboo in 1869: "At one time this place [Quesnel] was the seat of considerable trade but now is on the decline like most other places in the colony."[56] He reported to his father mainly on his business ventures and less on his mining, stating only that he was "somewhat interested in mining about Van Winkle," but that his mining interests had not yet paid. "Claims on either side of mine are paying well but I don't know that it helps me." At this time, Josiah had another partner: C.T. Millard. Millard and Beedy advertised as "importers and dealers in general merchandise" and acted as agents for the Merchants' Line packets from San Francisco, located on Wharf Street in Victoria.[57] He reported to his father that trade in Victoria had been 40 per cent better this year than last, "not as good profits, but larger sales." He expressed caution about the Cariboo markets, stating that he was "curtailing business very materially." But he had yet to reckon with the infectious enthusiasm Joachim Lindhard had for Van Winkle on Lightning Creek.

Josiah's and Joachim's paths may have crossed in California, because their business and mining ventures followed similar routes.

Beedy and Lindhard

When Joachim (a.k.a. Henry in British Columbia) left his home in Stege, Denmark, at age fourteen, destined for California, he was years younger than Josiah. He learned through experience in the mining towns of California. When the miners left California and rushed to what would soon become the Colony of British Columbia in 1858, he knew exactly where he should be in order to benefit from this gold rush. By mid-1858, Joachim was in Yale as proprietor of the California Hotel, a position from which he promoted the abundance of gold to be found in the Upper Fraser River and arranged passage and freight for those heading to and from that area.[58]

In the early years, when the gold rush centred on the Fraser River and before the Cariboo Trail was built, the Harrison–Lillooet route was promoted as an easier route to the gold fields than the Fraser Canyon. By early autumn of 1858, Joachim had partnered with Barnard and advertised an express service from Victoria via Port Douglas at the top of Harrison Lake to the Upper Fraser.[59] Things evolved quickly in the first year of the gold rush, and by November, he was advertising "Lindhard & Co.," a monthly express from Victoria to Port Douglas and as far as the Upper Fraser River and Bridge River, with offices in Victoria at Wells, Fargo & Company.[60]

Joachim saw his financial wellbeing linked to the successful development of roads and mining in the interior. He remained at Port Douglas throughout 1859 and on at least two occasions reported his observations to Governor James Douglas. In February of 1859, he sent a gold sample to Douglas and told him about three active mining camps between Port Douglas and Lillooet Lake.[61] In December of 1859, he again wrote to Governor Douglas, reporting opposition from the packers to a toll being proposed on the Harrison–Lillooet route, opining that local private contractors could be found to build the wagon road if they were granted a five-year charter for the right to charge tolls. The following year, Josiah Beedy and Frank Way received the contract to construct a section of the Yale to Spuzzum wagon road, as Joachim had suggested.

Port Douglas as seen from the waters of Harrison Lake. The toll gate on the road to Lillooet is visible at centre, and a steamer is docked at the foot of the road. COURTESY UBC LIBRARY RARE BOOKS AND SPECIAL COLLECTIONS, UNO LANGMANN FAMILY COLLECTION OF B.C. PHOTOGRAPHS, 1-0053373.0032

Joachim had witnessed the rise and fall of gold-rush towns before, and he knew that the lively boom of Port Douglas would be short lived. Very quickly, Port Douglas could boast having a courthouse, a church, a school, several stores, saloons, and a well-laid-out town plan. Streets were busy and bustling as steamers arrived and stagecoaches waited to transport passengers over the next forty-seven kilometres (twenty-nine miles) to Lillooet Lake. One unimpressed traveller described Port Douglas as "another wooden city among the rocks."[62] However, the town thrived for seven years, until the newly built Cariboo Road up the Fraser Canyon connecting Hope and Yale with the Northern interior became the preferred route.[63] Joachim didn't wait for Port Douglas to decline. His instincts were to follow the miners as they followed the gold trail into the Upper Fraser River and into Lightning Creek by the early 1860s. When Van Winkle sprang to life as a mining town, only twenty-two kilometres

Beedy and Lindhard

from Barkerville but with its own little gold rush in 1862, Joachim was there.

One of Joachim's first ventures was operating a roadhouse in partnership with J.C. Beedy in a location called Dunbar Flats, three kilometres (two miles) east of Van Winkle. In the early 1860s, access to Van Winkle was by a footpath or mule trail that began in Quesnelmouth. Early tourists Cheadle and Milton complained of the rough, muddy, and rocky trail they walked on their way to Williams Creek. On October 21, 1863, they reported seeing about a dozen houses at Van Winkle and two miles later, stopped at "a house where we got a capital dinner, beefsteak pie & beefsteak & onions & pancakes!"[64] The stopping house was one of Beedy and Lindhard's first ventures.

In 1866, Joachim purchased a store in Van Winkle previously operated by Schorling and Company[65] and wrote Colonial Secretary H.M. Ball offering—at the request of local citizens—to operate the post office:

> *Having the welfare of said district at heart and having established myself with permanent intentions, I offer you my humble service for the Post Office here and if accepted think I will be able to discharge the duties of the same satisfactorily as well to the public and to yourself.*[66]

It was common for merchants in small settlements to volunteer to operate the post office. Operating a post office assured them regular clientele and profits from the sale of stamps. Their store usually became the depot for telegraph operations, and often served as the agent for the express and stagecoach companies. Joachim's offer was accepted and by that autumn he operated the post office out of the Van Winkle store.

Joachim regularly advertised the Van Winkle store in the *Cariboo Sentinel*, promising to carry "good stock at lower rates and send orders when accompanied by cash to outlying creeks."[67] In the summer of 1869, Josiah Beedy became his business partner in the Van Winkle store.

MINING TOWN ENTREPRENEURS

WOMEN WERE IN DEMAND in early British Columbia, believed necessary if the men were ever going to settle, form families, and build a future for the province. While white women were welcome for the settling and civilizing influence they could bring to the otherwise homosocial culture of frontier settlements, they were not welcomed on an equal basis with men. Women did not have the right to vote, become citizens, or pre-empt (acquire) land. Their roles were largely circumscribed to the home front; they were considered chattels of men and expected to be unsalaried helpmates to husbands and mothers to children. Acceptable public roles were extensions of the private. Thus, women were encouraged to do community work that supported hospitals, schools, orphanages, and arts and cultural institutions. Women's opportunities to be independent entrepreneurs were limited, and the single opportunity they had to improve their social and economic status was through marriage.

Frontier towns could sometimes be more accepting of unconventional norms than cities. Some women and men found greater freedom in the less established and more fluid social milieu they found. Beyond the frontier town, broader societal changes were afoot, and women were organizing to demand recognition and rights. The *Cariboo Sentinel* reported on the National Woman's Suffrage

Association meeting in New York, chaired by Elizabeth Cady Stanton, in which the discussion focused the question, "If women had the right to vote would they have to be willing to go to war?" It was argued that throughout history women have always gone to war, and Stanton pointed out that if women did go to war, there "could be a division of labor between the sexes, one doing the fighting, the other binding up the wounds."[68] The suffrage debates and demands for equal educational opportunities found their way into newspapers of even remote communities. The *Cariboo Sentinel* reported more on women in the community than the *Daily British Colonist* did in Victoria, which tended to ignore the activities of women in the community, reporting on the ruling class women, if at all. The *Daily British Colonist* was in its eighth year of publishing before it carried an article that even mentioned women and suffrage.[69]

Laura sensed an easy acceptability in Van Winkle and was welcomed by other newcomer families who were all recently arrived in the area. She quickly fit into assisting Joachim with the store and saloon and delighted in the opportunity to practice English. Joachim's partner, Josiah, was immediately attracted, and the couple grew close. He assisted her when sometimes the English words didn't come easily and coached her in understanding the way the store operated. Laura admired the enthusiasm and energy he devoted to his businesses and the community. He loved his life in Van Winkle and was eager to settle there and see the community thrive. Josiah admired Laura's eagerness to learn and her calm, capable demeanour with customers. Josiah's family valued higher education, and several of the women in the family, including his younger sister, Mary Elizabeth Beedy, who was very close to him, was an accomplished educator and advocate for women's rights. Laura saw him as one of the more progressive men in the community.

Entrepreneurial activities in frontier towns of the 1800s were conducted against a backdrop of a short lifespan. In 1871 to 1879, the life expectancy at age twenty for men was forty-one years and for women forty years.[70] When Laura met Josiah, he and Joachim were both in their late thirties. They had been miners and entrepreneurs for almost two decades, but it was only after that length of time that they felt settled and secure enough to add a wife and family to their lives. However, the harsh conditions of mining and frontier life shortened lifespans. Death was ever present in the 1800s. Cholera, smallpox, consumption (tuberculosis), yellow fever, typhoid fever, diphtheria, and scarlet fever were prevalent, and as the populations became more mobile, the communicable diseases followed the transportation routes. These diseases claimed the lives of young children, teenagers, adults, and many Indigenous people, who had never before been exposed to these diseases. Few were immune. Women and men often died in their thirties and forties.

In addition to communicable diseases, mining was a highly dangerous occupation. Many miners were killed in falls, rockslides, and collapses of mine tunnels. Furthermore, the risk of working with mercury was little understood at the time. Mercury was used in extracting minute pieces of gold from slurry, a mixture of water, sand, and soil. Mercury and gold bind together forming an amalgam that sinks to the bottom of buckets and holding ponds where it can be collected. The mercury was then burned off in a crude stove or using a hand torch, leaving the gold behind. Prolonged and high exposure to inhaling mercury vapours damages the immune, digestive, and nervous systems. In addition, the mercury enters the environment, contaminating land and aquatic ecosystems, posing an additional risk to human health.[71] Accidents outside of mining activities also claimed many lives. There were accidents with horses and carriages, drownings, avalanches, and suicides. While marrying in the fourth decade of life was not uncommon, it was with the full realization that the marriage might be of short duration.

Beedy and Lindhard had a busy year in 1870. Josiah's nephew Dixi H. Ross (1852–99), with wife Lucy Birchard Ross and children, arrived from Cambridge Springs, Pennsylvania, to work for Beedy. Celebrations for American Independence Day and Canada's Dominion Day were always large festive summer events in Barkerville, an occasion for people to come into the town from all the nearby mining villages to celebrate. Josiah volunteered on the managing committee for the Fourth of July celebrations, the ninety-fourth anniversary of American Independence. That year he also delved into mining and joined Joachim to become a shareholder in the Van Winkle Company that was mining on Lightning Creek. Later in the summer Beedy and Lindhard consolidated their interests in Van Winkle by moving their hotel and billiard room from Dunbar Flats to Van Winkle. The *Cariboo Sentinel* described them as "enterprising and popular proprietors" and the hotel as a "large and elegant building" that is "very neatly fitted up."[72]

Later in the year, Josiah embarked on his biggest gamble. He and his partner Barnard gave notice that they would be asking the Legislative Council of British Columbia for the exclusive privilege of running road steamers imported from Scotland on the Cariboo Road for three years, beginning October 1871.[73] While 1870 was busy for Josiah, it was only a prelude to the next few years!

Early in 1871, Laura entered her largest gamble. In less than a year after she had arrived, she and Josiah were married by Reverend Thomas Derrick on March 18 at Van Winkle.[74] In addition to the marriage announcement, the *Cariboo Sentinel* announced:

> We have to congratulate our old Caribooites—Mssrs. J.C. Beedy, Charles Oppenheimer, and John Peebles—on assuming the responsibilities of matrimony. These gentlemen have evidently still faith in the country.[75]

Earlier in 1871, Josiah and Joachim had purchased Cottonwood House, and Laura and Josiah moved to Cottonwood to manage it.[76] Cottonwood House was west of Van Winkle and almost halfway to Quesnelmouth, near the junction of the Cottonwood and Lightning

Creeks. Cottonwood House still stands today, having been purchased by the British Columbia government in 1961 and declared a heritage site in 1963. Cottonwood Provincial Park, which surrounds the house, was property first pre-empted in 1863 by John Ferris Ryder (1833–1916), a freight wagon driver.[77] Ryder came from Kingston, Ontario, and for a few years partnered with Allen Smith, who was contracted to build the first trail into Van Winkle in 1862. Their land holding of almost 130 hectares (320 acres) became known as "Ryder and Smith's Ranch" then "Smith and Ryder's" and soon Smith's alone. During several winters, Ryder and Smith helped to transport supplies by sleigh into Richfield from Cottonwood before there was regular stage line service provided by Humphrey, Pool, and Johnston in 1865. Ryder moved on to Cheam in the Fraser Valley where he pre-empted sixty-five hectares (160 acres) in 1868. But he loved the nearby highland, where he purchased land in the area known today as Ryder Lake.[78]

Little is known about Allen Smith. The first roadhouse that he built was a small cabin that operated for a few years while the large two-storey stopping house was being built. Smith took out a short-term mortgage on the property in 1864, operated the large house briefly, and by mid-1865 had lost title to it and moved on.

Laura gained experience operating a household and stopping house at Cottonwood. The house was a large, reputable, and popular stopping place that operated for many years. Ryder and Smith had chosen a strategic location for the house, close to the Cariboo Wagon Road. The front door faced the road, and travellers entered a large room with an almost three-metre (nine-foot) ceiling and a hand-sawn plank floor, dominated by a large barrel heater. A water reservoir sat on top of the heater and dispensed hot water from a tap. Above the reservoir was a second chamber, or oven, heated by the stovepipe that ran through it. This large oven could be used for baking bread, puddings, or cakes. There was never running water in the house, but a supply of water came from the nearby Cottonwood River and

TOP—Cottonwood House, built in 1864–65. The entrance faced the Cariboo Wagon Road. This once large and popular stopping house is today a heritage site within Cottonwood Provincial Park. CA 1890 AM54-S4-:OUT P436 COURTESY OF CITY OF VANCOUVER ARCHIVES

BOTTOM—The efficient stove at Cottonwood House heated the large welcoming room, supplied hot water, and had an oven for baking, visible at the top of the photo.
IMAGE C-07534 COURTESY OF ROYAL BC MUSEUM AND ARCHIVES

a spring that ran on the hill behind the house. A washing station located behind the front door provided containers of hot water from the heater and cold water from outside sources. The water drained through a large hand-carved wooden sink into a bucket.

To the right of the front door in the large entry room was a long counter on which sat gold scales that were used to buy gold and weigh items sold in the small store that was part of the house. The store may have begun during Beedy and Lindhard's time, as an extension of their other stores. It handled staples, such as milk, tobacco, coffee, tea, bacon, rice, beans, and flour. Off the large entry room was the kitchen and a long, large dining room. There were several bedrooms upstairs, some for the resident family and some for guests.

Six kilometres (four miles) east down the Cariboo Road was Cold Spring House, operated by John Boyd and his wife, Janet. Janet Fleming was a young sixteen-year-old bride and a second wife for Boyd, whose first wife died in childbirth in Marysville, California. Boyd was originally from Belfast, Ireland, well educated, a meticulous bookkeeper, and astute businessman. The Boyds married in 1868 and their first son was born the next year.

The many daybooks and cash books used by Beedy and Lindhard and Beedy and Dodd show the same meticulous detail that Boyd was known for.[79] The entrepreneurs either collaborated on bookkeeping practices, were similarly educated, or developed the same skills from years in business. Every transaction was recorded and accounts detailed. The close proximity between Laura and Josiah Beedy at Cottonwood and Janet and John Boyd at Cold Spring was the beginning of a long business association and friendship. In 1871, Laura, her sister Caroline, and Janet all travelled to Barkerville together to enjoy the Dominion Day and Independence Day celebrations at the beginning of July.

It was common for the stopping houses to employ Chinese cooks and it's likely that Beedy and Lindhard followed this practice

Laura Lindhard and Josiah Beedy married in 1871 and managed Cottonwood House briefly before becoming merchants and residents in Stanley. IMAGE G-06710 COURTESY OF ROYAL BC MUSEUM AND ARCHIVES

at Cottonwood. However, the wives of the operators were often the backup cooks, and they usually organized the work of the helpers. The stopping houses that built strong reputations with travellers offered good meals with fresh summer fruit and vegetables. It's reported that Janet Boyd took six laying hens with her to Cold Spring House when she moved there as a young bride. It's likely that Laura also quickly learned the skills needed for self-sufficient living, such as caring for a garden, chickens, and pigs, if she hadn't already had these when she arrived in the Cariboo.[80] Caring for unexpected guests at unexpected hours was also a required skill for stopping house proprietors.

Mining Town Entrepreneurs

During the years that Josiah and Joachim were partners in operating Cottonwood House and the Van Winkle store, their partnership extended to a wide variety of entrepreneurial ventures. They loaned money to miners for the purchase of mining shares. For example, the *Lightning Creek Register of Mortgages 1865–1906* recorded numerous entries from 1870 and 1871:

> March 1, 1871. Harmon Roberts mortgages to Beedy and Lindhard his interest in *The Vancouver Company* as security for the payment of $170 with interest at 2 per cent per month payable on or before July 1, 1871.[81]

Laura and Josiah rode a wave of optimism in 1871. The people of Barkerville were optimistic about British Columbia joining the Dominion of Canada and believed that opportunity and wealth would soon flow into the Cariboo. The start of new businesses and the beginning of their marriage gave Laura and Josiah much personal optimism. At the same time, the first of the road steamers that Beedy had partnered with Barnard to purchase began arriving in British Columbia.

The first two road steamers arrived in Victoria in February. Steam power was the new technology that promised to be faster and more reliable than horses, assuring a competitive edge in the future of transportation. Their arrival was preceded by debate and advertising of the "soon to launch new service." Some citizens complained that if Beedy and Barnard were granted the three-year monopoly to operate on the Cariboo Wagon Road, it would be an unprecedented privilege. But both the *Cariboo Sentinel* and the latter supported the scheme, with the latter calling it "one of the greatest and most important scientific improvements of the age."[82] The *Cariboo Sentinel* believed the road steamers were a plan that would benefit "both merchant and miner" and the colony as a whole. The newspaper based much of its support on the reputation of the entrepreneurs:

> *The names of Barnard and Beedy are sufficient surety of the success of the undertaking; they both from among our earliest pioneers have followed each step of the progress of our new colony and played no small part in each step itself. They are highly respected, and having the confidence of the public in general, will have the good wishes of the population, not of Cariboo alone, but of the whole colony, for the success of their undertaking.*[83]

The Legislative Council approved the bill giving Beedy and Barnard the right to operate the steamers, but it granted the monopoly for one year rather than three. The dream advertised as "Steam to Cariboo!" promised that four Thomson road steamers would operate on the road between Yale and Barkerville beginning the first week of April, or thereabouts. Merchants were encouraged to "be prepared to enter into contracts for the conveyance of freight in eight days to Soda Creek."[84]

The first steamer was transported to Yale, along with Scottish engineers for road tests, and that was where reality set in. The steamers did not perform as expected. They had to stop frequently to take on more wood, roadbeds were damaged, speed was not achieved, and wheel slippage on the rocky roads was a major problem that would have to be solved. At this point, Beedy and Barnard decided to cut their losses and they abandoned the project.[85] All but two steamers were returned to Scotland.

The disappointment the Beedys experienced with the failure of the road steamer venture was set aside in July, as they joined the excitement stirring in Van Winkle and Barkerville, when residents celebrated in anticipation of British Columbia's entrance into the Dominion of Canada. The large presence of Americans in the Cariboo meant that they had from the early days celebrated Independence Day on the Fourth of July. But the Canadians were present in large enough numbers so that beginning July 1 of 1868, one year after the Dominion of Canada formed, residents of Barkerville began an annual celebration of Dominion Day.[86] Throughout the Cariboo there was great anticipation each year for the July celebrations. There was rivalry between the American and Canadian contingents as they tried to outdo each other. Both days generally followed the same pattern of horse races and competitions that included "sports" events for the citizens, such as sledge throwing, tossing the caber, footraces, wheelbarrow races, and jumping.

The Dominion Day celebrations in 1871 were slightly muted when residents learned that British Columbia's entrance to the Dominion would not be proclaimed until July 20, but the celebrations were enough to attract Laura, Caroline, and their friend Janet Boyd from Cold Spring House to Barkerville.[87] They enjoyed the sports events and speeches, cheered on the contenders, and witnessed Jacob Hunter Todd leading the crowd in three cheers for the Queen. The decorations of evergreens and scarlet banners, gilt maple leaves, crowns, wreaths, flowers, ribbons, and flags throughout the town gave a celebratory feel to the day. A royal salute was fired at noon and there were musical performances throughout the day. There was a theatre performance in the evening by the Cariboo Amateur Dramatic Association, a farce titled "The Irishman in London!" and a grand illumination in the evening when all the houses and businesses placed candles in their windows that burned until midnight.

The Fourth of July in 1871 was marked separately in Barkerville and Van Winkle. Inspired by the Dominion Day celebrations, residents of Van Winkle returned home to organize sporting events consisting of races and jumping on July 4. "A Federal Salute was fired at noon. Everything passed off pleasantly and men of all nationalities joined in celebrating America's national day."[88]

An extended family grew around Laura and Josiah. Josiah's nephew Dixi H. Ross, with wife Lucy Birchard Ross, had arrived in the area the previous year from Cambridge Springs, Pennsylvania. Dixi worked with Josiah and was active in the Cariboo Amateur Dramatic

Association. Laura encouraged her cousin Theodor Lindhard to join them in 1871, and he arrived in July. On October 5, Laura and Josiah's first child, Asa Harold Beedy, was born at Cottonwood. Both Laura and Josiah were accustomed to large extended families nearby; they needed employees to help with their businesses, and the extended family network tied them more closely to the community and provided support when needed.

In September, Beedy and Lindhard announced the dissolution of their partnership. In October, James McArthur, one of the Scottish engineers involved in the road steamer project, who sued Beedy and Barnard for three hundred dollars. The court proceedings revealed some disagreement between Beedy and Barnard. Beedy claimed that Barnard had exceeded his authority in the partnership by buying too many steamers and Beedy believed he had paid more than his share of the expenses. Since no partnership had been proved nor any agreement or compromise with the engineers produced, Beedy was granted a non-suit, but the case indicated that Beedy was left with considerable financial losses and bad feelings from this venture.[89]

Josiah had to recover from his financial losses with the road steamer project. Later that autumn after the birth of their son Asa, he and Laura left Cottonwood House and moved to Van Winkle to focus on their next business ventures. Dixi and Lucy Ross took on the job of managing Cottonwood House after Laura and Josiah left.[90]

Laura gave birth to their second son, Ludwig (Louis) Samuel on February 22, 1873, in Van Winkle. She was grateful to have her cousin Theodor's help because Joachim was very ill. Joachim had spent the winter in San Francisco attempting to restore his health, and Josiah and Laura, with Theodor's help, took over operating Joachim's businesses as well as their own. On June 9, at age thirty-eight, Joachim died at home in Van Winkle.

Laura was on her own with her two sons at the time of Joachim's death, while Josiah was visiting his family in Pennsylvania. He remained close to his younger sister, Mary Elizabeth Beedy, an educator and women's rights activist, and his sister Harriet Beedy Ross, who was sixteen years older than him and almost a mother figure in his life. He needed their help. In 1865, he had fathered a daughter with Lora DeLora in Quesnelmouth.[91] His daughter, also named Lora, was now seven years old and he needed to arrange access to schooling for her that wasn't available in Van Winkle. He turned to his sisters for help in working out a solution. Josiah had not been home to Pennsylvania for a very long time, and in addition, his father's health was failing.

With Joachim Lindhard's death, Laura lost a cousin and brother-in-law whose infectious enthusiasm and optimism had drawn her to British Columbia. Josiah lost a former business partner. They now needed to comfort and assist Caroline as she mourned and dealt with Joachim's estate, his many investments and businesses.

In 1873, the Married Women's Property Act was passed in British Columbia. It gave married women the right to own property and businesses. This act appeared emancipatory for women, but it also served the interests of their husbands. It meant that husbands could transfer the title of properties to their wives and thus protect their assets from creditors. This new act may have served both Laura and Caroline as they dealt with legal matters in the following year.

There was another turn of events for Laura and Josiah in 1874. Josiah had experienced several financial setbacks in British Columbia. There was his investment in the steamer *Fort Yale,* which had blown up, then his store in Barkerville that burned, and then the debacle of the road steamers. Each investment had depleted his resources considerably. On March 12, he filed for an adjudication of bankruptcy in the County Court of Richfield. The first meeting of creditors was called for April 16 and a second on May 15. Laura was saddened by this business crisis, but bankruptcy was not uncommon among British Columbia's entrepreneurs. Before the date for the second meeting of creditors, Josiah entered into a new partnership with Alfred Townsend and announced their purchase of the Cosmopolitan Hotel in Van Winkle. The two men took over the "Old Van Winkle Store" that was part of Joachim Lindhard's estate.[92] Undoubtedly, Laura's assistance was paramount in negotiating this arrangement with Caroline and Theodor.

Alfred Townsend was well known along Lightning Creek as the former partner of Henry Roeder and then sole owner and operator of the Beaver Pass Ranch and Roadhouse, about sixteen kilometres (ten miles) west of Van Winkle. He was an ambitious and hardworking partner from 1863 to 1865 but made the mistake of mortgaging the property to local moneylenders, which resulted in his losing the ranch and roadhouse.[93] After this experience, Townsend moved to Van Winkle and began a long association with the Lindhards and Beedys.

In May 1874, Townsend left Van Winkle bound for England, to visit his "homeland."[94] He accompanied Josiah's eight-year-old daughter, Lora, to Cambridge Springs, Pennsylvania, to live with the family of Josiah's sister Harriet Beedy Ross.[95] Townsend continued to New York and purchased stock for the Van Winkle store: playing cards, clocks, books, boots, shoes, and straw hats, all shipped in the care of Charles Oppenheimer of San Francisco. He continued on to England for a visit of some months' duration.

Optimism was high in Van Winkle in 1874, as the mines finally began to produce. The Van Winkle Company often led the way, turning out one to two hundred ounces of gold each week. The "outlook on Lightning has never been better ... there is not at present on the face of the earth a mining camp taking out so much gold ... Everyone has money, and if they have not it is their own fault."[96] Josiah had experienced enough economic ups and downs to realize the newfound wealth might be temporary. He purchased life insurance at this time in recognition of the growing family responsibility he had. He knew that while he was prosperous in the moment, "business was so uncertain in the Cariboo that nobody could foretell how long he would be able to say he was well off."[97] Josiah was now "back

Mining Town Entrepreneurs

on top" and, with new partner Alfred Townsend, was heavily invested in Van Winkle, owning the Cosmopolitan Hotel, the Van Winkle store, a saloon, a butcher shop, and a boarding house.[98]

"Well educated for business," Josiah Beedy rode out the good times and the downturns as an entrepreneur in Stanley. COURTESY OF J. PASNAU

A GROWING FAMILY,
a GROWING COMMUNITY

IN 1874, LAURA AND Caroline made a concerted effort to encourage their sister Christine to leave Denmark and join them in Van Winkle. They missed her company and needed her assistance. They were now committed to living in British Columbia and believed it would be a good move for Christine as well. In April, Caroline had left Van Winkle to live in Victoria, and Laura desperately wanted Christine's company and assistance with her growing family and active businesses. Christine lived in Copenhagen and at age twenty-four her future in Denmark was uncertain.

In addition to the business and mining ventures, Laura's rapidly growing family and the extended family that revolved around the Beedys kept Laura busy. The exact plans that Laura and Caroline had for meeting Christine on her arrival from Denmark in the summer of 1874 are unknown, but they knew she would need them on the journey since her limited English would make it difficult to travel alone.

It was a hazardous summer for travel between Victoria and San Francisco, and Caroline narrowly missed some harrowing and dangerous incidents. Smallpox was prevalent, affecting many travelling by train and ship across the northwest. A case of smallpox turned up on the *Prince Alfred* on the next sailing after Lora Beedy and Alfred

Townsend reached San Francisco in late May. Shortly after, on June 10, the *Prince Alfred* left Victoria for San Francisco with about one hundred passengers on board. On June 14, seven miles north of the entrance to San Francisco harbour and in fog, it struck Duxbury Reef and sank. The passengers and some of the cargo were saved.[99]

Caroline left Victoria for San Francisco on the *William Tabor* in late June, a sidewheeler that temporarily replaced the *Prince Alfred*. Christine arrived in New York on July 8 and on July 27 she and Caroline arrived together in Victoria on the *William Tabor* from San Francisco. Caroline accompanied Christine as far as Yale, where she caught Barnard's Express. Laura, with children Asa and Louis, met Christine in Clinton on August 4 and accompanied her the remaining distance to Van Winkle.

Laura was very pregnant during the summer with a third child. On September 6, 1874, she gave birth to daughter Josephine Caroline at Van Winkle.[100] Jury duty kept Josiah close to home that summer. He served first on the Grand Jury for Supreme Court hearings at Richfield in June and for the Court of Assize at the end of October.[101] With three small children under the age of four, Laura was grateful to have her younger sister Christine with her.

In 1875, three kilometres (two miles) east of Van Winkle, the new town of Stanley grew around the Eleven of England Company's claim on Lightning Creek. Stanley offered a flatter area for the growth of a village. Chief Constable Henry Maynard Ball had a townsite plan drawn up with lots on each side of the road and named the townsite Stanley after Edward Henry Stanley, 15th Earl of Derby and secretary of state for the colonies.[102] Josiah Beedy was the first to turn the sod to begin building a store in the new town.[103] Stanley and Van Winkle became like twin towns built around mining claims. At the height of mining operations, the population of the two towns together was about five thousand people—rivalling Barkerville at one point as the mining centre of the region. The towns attracted all the usual supporting businesses—a number of stores, hotels, saloons, dance halls, tinsmiths, blacksmiths, and other businesses.

Josiah's father, Samuel Beedy, died on April 10, 1875, in Cambridge Springs, Pennsylvania. While Samuel was quite a wealthy man, he had many children, grandchildren, and a wife among whom his wealth was divided. Josiah was willed two hundred dollars, the same amount Samuel granted to all his children, except two daughters who had helped him more.

As their family grew, Laura and Josiah did not often travel outside the communities of Van Winkle and Stanley. They quickly became old-timers on Lightning Creek. The outside world came to them through the regular stagecoach drivers and passengers who stopped in, the newspapers they sold, the telegraph office, and the miners who came from the outlying camps for supplies. Their businesses and mining activities held them to the area year round. Unlike others who annually migrated south, they seldom left the area, becoming a constant presence in the mining community.

The Beedys lived a self-sufficient lifestyle in Stanley. It was common for most families to have chickens for meat and hens for fresh eggs, often a milk cow and even a pig or two. In small villages of the time, the livestock ran freely. Free roaming pigs were a problem as they destroyed other people's property, and Josiah was named as one pig owner who should be called to task when citizens of Stanley asked people to keep their pigs penned. Families rounded out their diet with garden produce and wild berries picked and preserved in the summer.

Laura and Josiah's family continued to grow. On January 9, 1876, a third son, Winslow Lindhard, was born at Stanley. Laura now had four small children and she was appreciating Christine's help with the family. However, in the spring of that year Christine married James Hamilton in a small private ceremony in the Beedy home. While she would not be far away and on the regular stagecoach run, she would live with James in Soda Creek for the next while.

A Growing Family, a Growing Community

Both Laura and Josiah valued education for their children and worked toward opening a school in Stanley to serve the children of the town. The Welsh Mining Company offered their assembly hall rent free for a schoolhouse. The school opened in 1877, the Beedy children enrolled, and Josiah served as a school trustee along with John Peebles and Frederick Rose.[104] The Beedy store became a central meeting place in the community, and both Laura and Josiah became closely identified with the Stanley community. By 1877–78, both Stanley and Barkerville were prominent towns in the Cariboo district, "maintained by mining operations of the surrounding country."[105] Josiah has been rightly called one of the founding fathers of Lightning Creek, and Laura was at his side, both totally dedicated to building their community.

In the spring of 1878, family obligations called Laura away. She had not been away from Van Winkle for several years, but Caroline needed her. Caroline was now married to Asahel Sumner Bates and lived during winters in San Francisco and summers in British Columbia. Caroline's two-year-old daughter was gravely ill in San Francisco with malarial fever. Laura took her two younger children, Winslow and Josephine, and in mid-March went to be with Caroline.

While Josiah maintained his many businesses, he knew they would only thrive if mining in the area also thrived. He held shares in the Van Winkle Company, the Ross Company, and the Rock Dale Company on Chisholm Creek among others. While Joachim Lindhard had not lived to see the Van Winkle Company mine produce significant amounts, in 1875 the tide turned. That summer the Van Winkle Company mine produced over four thousand ounces of gold. In 1877–78 the excitement on Lightning Creek shifted to quartz mining. Josiah had a mine on Perkin's Ledge on Burns Mountain. The quartz had to be crushed to separate out the gold and silver. In July 1878, mining engineer Riotte publicized extraordinary results from Josiah's Burns Mountain mine—forty-five dollars' worth of gold from each ton of rock.[106] Josiah was reported as saying, "All we require are stamps and quicksilver."[107] He was one of the first to invest in and build his own small quartz mill, with a capacity equal to five ordinary stamps.[108]

Always a promoter of the community and mining interests, in March 1879 the *Daily British Colonist* announced that a gold bar valued at about fifteen hundred dollars from Josiah's quartz mine on Burns Mountain was received by the Bank of British North America in Victoria: "The rock grows in richness as he sinks on the ledge. There is plenty of latent wealth in Cariboo, which sooner or later, will find its way into circulation."[109]

While things were looking very positive for Josiah in the spring of 1879, Laura gave birth to the couple's fifth child, Josiah Crosby, on March 14. By late summer of 1879, Josiah was not feeling his usual energetic self, but always the upbeat promoter he dispatched notes to the *Daily British Colonist* about the mining riches of the Cariboo. His faith in the riches of Lightning Creek never wavered. By August,

The young Beedy family in 1879. Josiah III is in the arms of his father, Josiah, and left to right are Josephine, Winslow, Louis, and Asa, with Laura behind Louis and Asa.
IMAGE G-06711 COURTESY OF ROYAL BC MUSEUM AND ARCHIVES

he knew he was seriously ill and drew up a will. In early winter the *Daily British Colonist* wrote that, "Mr. J. C. Beedy is very ill at Van Winkle."[110] His eventual cause of death was registered as apoplexy (or stroke). He died on January 27, 1880, at age forty-seven, and was buried in the Stanley cemetery.

Laura was thirty-three and had five little children under the age of eight when Josiah died. His estate was complex. He left a will prepared on August 16, 1879. Creditors had until March 5, 1881, to register claims on the estate with District Registrar John Bowron at Richfield.[111] Hector McKenzie of Stanley, brother-in-law James Hamilton of Clinton, and Laura were executors for the estate, the estimated value of which was under $6,752.00.[112] A life insurance policy paid $11,060.[113] Laura remained in Stanley for the summer. She sold many of her possessions to friends and neighbours, and in late November she and the children sailed on the *Dakota* from Victoria to San Francisco.[114]

In March 1881, a dispatch from the Cariboo stated, "The tunnel in the Beedy claim—now the property of Mr. James Reid—Burn's Mountain, has reached the ledge. It proves to be rotten quartz, rich in gold and easily worked. The telegram says that it is the greatest and most important strike ever made in Cariboo."[115]

Laura settled with her children, not far from Caroline, in Oakland, California. The three oldest children enrolled in Lincoln Elementary School. Over the next two years, she purchased property in Oakland from the guardian of Caroline's stepson, Otis Bates, and properties in San Francisco and Berkeley. The Lindhard sisters were now separated by a vast distance, with Laura and Caroline living in Oakland, and Christine feeling very alone, with her family in Clinton, British Columbia. Christine did not enjoy the separation from her sisters and with her children she chose to spend most of 1880 with her sisters in Oakland. With both sisters nearby, Laura had lots of support in making her transition to Oakland. The young cousins and sisters-as-mothers got to know each other well.

Built by Josiah Beedy in 1875 in Stanley, the provision store was operated by W.W. Dodd from 1880 to 1888. Laura Beedy Dodd ran the store and post office from 1888 to 1899. This photo is from circa 1900s, when the store was operated by the H.J. Gardner family.

COURTESY UBC LIBRARY RARE BOOKS AND SPECIAL COLLECTIONS, UNO LANGMANN FAMILY COLLECTION OF B.C. PHOTOGRAPHS, I-0053384.0015

When Laura left Stanley in 1880, William Wright Dodd purchased the store that contained the post and express offices. He had been in the Barkerville area for almost twenty years and came to Stanley in 1874, when he purchased the Vulcan Saloon. In 1880–81, he sold many of his mining shares and in May, announced a partnership with Walter Budd and the takeover of Beedy's store. The new "Dodd, Budd and Company" advertised:

> *Importers and dealers in dry goods, clothing, boots & shoes, mining tools, hardware and crockery, groceries, wines, liquors & cigars—and also—General Commission Merchants and Butchers. All kinds of produce purchased and sold on commission.*

A Growing Family, a Growing Community

Hay and Grain constantly kept on hand. Orders solicited. Stanley B.C.[116]

The partnership lasted almost a year before Dodd, Budd and Company announced the dissolution of their partnership.[117] It was advertised as:

W.W. Dodd (Successor to Dodd, Budd & Co.) Commission Merchant, Butcher, Importer and Dealer in Groceries, Provisions, Hardware, Clothing, Hay and Grain, Stanley, B.C.[118]

William Dodd had learned well from Beedy and Lindhard that the merchants of the Cariboo had to promote the mining potential of the area whenever and wherever they could. Positive reports created excitement in the area and were good for business. In March of 1884, he travelled to Victoria and checked in at the *Daily British Colonist* with news from the Cariboo. Most of the mining companies were "taking out pay." There was "great confidence felt" in the Burns Mountain Quartz Company's mine.[119] In May, he advertised the Stanley store for sale. Described as a "rare opportunity to buy a flourishing business," he offered:

His entire stock-in-trade, together with buildings, live stock, wagons, sleighs, etc., if applied for promptly. Location at Stanley in the centre of the Lightning Creek gold mines and near the Burns Mountain quartz lead. Easy terms to responsible parties. W.W. Dodd, Stanley, B.C.[120]

Laura and William stayed in touch after she left Stanley. William visited his brother William Henry Harrison Dodd in San Francisco occasionally and he also visited Laura. She enjoyed hearing about her old friends in Stanley. She missed them and her children missed their old friends and the freedom they enjoyed in the small rural community.

When William visited Laura in 1884, he had a proposal for her, but she needed time to think it through.

The following April, William travelled again to Victoria and reported to the *Daily British Colonist*. Mining reports were again positive, and this time he carried a piece of gold and quartz taken from the Burns Mountain tunnel that was a "very rich and pretty specimen."

> *He has still unbounded confidence that the final result will handsomely pay the plucky promoters of this novel mining scheme ... The health generally of the district has been good, and the prospects are remarkably bright for good pay during the season ... Mr. Dodd believes that Cariboo in the next few years will see brighter days than those of the gold excitement of 1861–62 in the development of the numerous rich quartz deposits that abound.*[121]

William may have thought the gold and rich quartz he carried would help convince Laura in case she changed her mind about his proposal. But she was ready for her second big gamble. On May 1, 1885, Laura married William Wright Dodd. One account claims they married in Josiah's hometown of Cambridge Springs, Pennsylvania, but they may have married in Oakland and travelled to visit Cambridge Springs and points east after marrying.[122] It was important to her to cement her and her children's relationship with the Beedy family since she would need their assistance as her children grew.

The *Daily British Colonist* announced Laura and William's wedding, noting, "Both bride and bridegroom are well and favorably known in this province [BC] where they have many friends."[123] Their return to the province was announced in August with the added note, "There is no more popular gentleman than Mr. Dodd in the upper country, and rumour connects his name with a seat in the legislature next session."[124]

RETURN *to* STANLEY

THE TRAVEL ROUTES BETWEEN British Columbia and the United States shifted in 1885–86 as the transcontinental railway across Canada neared completion. Travel through Victoria and San Francisco was no longer the only route. By 1886, the first train travelled from Montreal to Vancouver and Ashcroft replaced Yale as the new "gateway" to the Cariboo. This meant that people living in Stanley were connected to eastern Canada by stagecoach to Ashcroft where they could catch an eastbound train that would connect into the eastern United States. For Laura's family, and the children particularly who needed to travel somewhere out of British Columbia for higher education, they now had easier access to the family in Pennsylvania.

Laura's return to Stanley could work for her with the assistance of her sisters, the Beedy family, her children, and a supportive partnership with William. Her oldest child, Asa, was fourteen and the youngest, Josiah (Si), was six. All were of school age. The school they had left in Stanley five years earlier only provided elementary level education, and it had closed when the Beedy children left. She knew the children would have to travel away to larger towns that had boarding schools, collegiate level, or preparatory schools if they wanted to continue their education beyond elementary. She had to find ways to help them get the kind of education they wanted.

Laura also had to earn an income, since the resources left her in 1880 were rapidly diminishing. William Dodd's commitment meant she could return to a community she knew well and have an income from operating the store and post office, a job she had done before.

Laura had known William since she arrived in Van Winkle in 1870. She first saw him perform that summer with the Cariboo Amateur Dramatic Association in Barkerville as part of the Dominion Day celebrations. He was born in 1831 in Liverpool, England, to Thomas Steward Dodd and Jane Wright Dodd. He arrived in California in 1849 and in 1862 he took out his first mining licence in Barkerville. He was a partner in the Vaughan and Sweeney Company mining that year on Lowhee Creek. In addition to mining, he was at times a

W.W. Dodd (1831–88), miner, merchant, saloon proprietor, and entertainer.
P-0011 BARKERVILLE HISTORIC TOWN ARCHIVES

Return to Stanley

merchant, saloon keeper, and postmaster at Stanley. He held shares, along with several other Barkerville businessmen, in the Read and Cora companies on Conklin Gulch and the Ballarat Company,[125] the Two Sisters Claim on Jack of Clubs Creek, the Foster Gold Mining Company, and the Huntingdon Company on Valley Mountain.[126]

In September 1868, most of the town of Barkerville burned. Many shops and businesses were rebuilt, but fire was a constant threat in the villages and towns where all the buildings were constructed of wood and built close together. The most common threat was from stovepipes conducting sparks up the chimney and onto the roof of a nearby building, igniting it. William was noted for taking fire protection into his own hands by building a narrow platform along the ridge of the roof of his saloon, where he placed barrels of water.[127]

He was acclaimed for his singing ability when he debuted with a local adaptation of the song "Billy Barlow" during the second intermission of the Theatre Royal on New Year's Eve 1871 in Barkerville:

It is to be regretted that the gentleman ... has so long allowed his light to be hid under a bushel, as his acting and singing on this occasion showed him to possess talents of no mean order, calling forth from beginning to end the rapturous acclamations of the entire house.[128]

He partnered briefly with Joseph Z. Hough to operate the New Eldorado Billiard & Dancing Saloon in Barkerville in early 1871.[129] The partnership lasted only months before William became sole owner and operator of the saloon. Some of his quirky sense of humour is shown in the creative "reverse psychology" he used in advertising the Eldorado Saloon.

In late 1872, William Dodd formed a new partnership with Llewellyn Jones and together they "opened this old and favourite stand in a new and improved form" and renamed it "The Eldorado Club Rooms."[130] This partnership again lasted only a few months

> **NOTICE.**
> **GENTLEMEN ARE CAUTIONED NOT TO VISIT**
>
> **THE ELDORADO,**
>
> although it is generally conceded that the
>
> **LIQUORS and CIGARS**
>
> are of the FIRST QUALITY, and the
>
> **BILLIARD TABLES**
>
> are not the most inferior in Barkerville. And further, the proprietor,
>
> **WM. W. DODD,**
>
> endeavors to make his patrons as comfortable as possible by furnishing a great number of the most interesting NEWSPAPERS, and studying their other comforts.
>
> Yet as the times are so dull and money scarce, it would be well for all his old patrons and friends in the community not to visit the Eldorado.
>
> Barkerville, August 31, 1872.

William Wright Dodd's quirky sense of humour was evident in his advertisements for the Eldorado Saloon. CARIBOO SENTINEL, AUGUST 31, 1872, P. 2

before William became sole manager of the club. In June 1873, William advertised the Eldorado Saloon and his mining claim on Jack of Clubs Creek for sale. He reduced prices at the Eldorado Saloon:

> *Liquors are now sold at Dodd's Eldorado Saloon at 12½ cents per glass and the figure for a game of billiards has been reduced to 25 cents. The proprietor calls attention to the advantages of his saloon as a place of resort, it being supplied with the best reading matter in the shape of English, American, and Canadian newspapers and periodicals.*[131]

In 1874, Benjamin Edwards bought the Eldorado Saloon, dismantled it, and moved it to Edwardsville.[132] William Dodd's

Return to Stanley

withdrawal from business in Barkerville enabled his move to the growing community of Stanley, where he bought the Vulcan Saloon.[133]

Laura and William knew each other well as long-time business operators and residents in Stanley. Laura saw that her two oldest sons, Asa and Louis, were interested in business, and she knew they could gain valuable experience working in the Stanley store. And the younger children could benefit from another adult in the household. Laura and William wrote the provincial secretary and began organizing to re-open the school for the children in Stanley.

While residing in Oakland, Laura's heart had never totally left the Cariboo. She had been in Van Winkle and Stanley for ten years and for some old-timers, that was the turning point after which it became harder to leave and one was more likely to remain. Thomas Nichol once said, "If you want to get out, get out before ten years . . . after ten years, you start to grow horns and you have to stay in the Cariboo to shed them."[134] Laura may have suffered from the same malady experienced by British Columbia historian Art Downs, who termed it "Caribooitis . . . The most noticeable symptom . . . is an unsettled feeling when the victim is anywhere else except the Cariboo."[135] *The British Columbia Directory of 1887* enumerated the advantages of life in the Cariboo: "The climate is cold but healthy. The population is intelligent and social. Fare by stage from Barkerville to Ashcroft, nearest railway station, 280 miles, $42.50"[136]

Pioneer towns relied on the resourcefulness and participation of their citizens. Laura had enduring friendships with families such as the Boyds and Peebles, who were long-time residents in the Stanley area. Often humour and friendly fun prevailed in relationships as revealed in the anecdote of "Paddy the Milkman" as told in the *Daily British Colonist*:

> Amongst the good things told of this person, who is a character at Cariboo, is the following: One of his best customers on Williams Creek was a clergyman at whose door every morning

Paddy was in the habit of leaving a can of milk. One morning after Paddy had gone his rounds, some of the boys dropped a small fish into the clergyman's can. The next day Paddy was confronted by his clerical customer with the fish. "Fots that?" asked Paddy. "It's a fish I found in the milk yesterday. When next you water your milk be sure you don't patronize a trout stream." Paddy thinking himself fairly caught, dropped on his knees and confessed that times being hard he was compelled to "lingthen the milk wid wather to make a wee bit of profit."[137]

The five years in Oakland had been a welcome interlude for Laura. They were years busy with caring for her young children. In proximity to her sisters, she realized they had all matured and changed. She and Christine had children who took top priority in their decisions. Caroline was happy with her new husband and social life among San Francisco's nouveau riche. Christine, though, was not happy with life in the Cariboo, nor in Oakland, and was searching for a place she could feel at home.

Laura had found William an easy working partner. In 1886, a travelling correspondent described his road trip from Clinton to Barkerville and his observations of Stanley. On his way into Barkerville, he stopped at "W.W. Dodd's store" (Provision Store) where William served as express agent, postmaster, telegrapher, and trader. He observed "deserted shaft-houses, broken over-shot wheels, broken sluices, piles of tailings, and every evidence of hydraulic and deep mining." He described Stanley as a "deserted place with but small population, nearly all composed of those still engaged in mining."[138] On his way back to Quesnel the correspondent had to remain at Stanley overnight, "a not very desirable haven, though we were met with kind hospitality from Mr. Dodd, who, like most of the Argonauts, possesses a generous heart."[139]

In June 1887, William suffered a stroke that left him partially paralyzed. That summer, a new widely advertised attraction in

Return to Stanley

British Columbia were the Harrison Hot Springs on Harrison Lake. It promoted its "Mineral Baths," where the medical profession was now sending patients who suffered from a wide array of medical conditions, including paralysis, stating, there is "no better tonic to restore tired or tried nature." At the end of September, William checked into the St. Alice Hotel at Harrison Hot Springs, seeking an improvement in his health. After his stay at the Hot Springs, he continued with Laura and family to Oakland, California, for the winter, hoping that the warmer climate would bring improvements. He died March 9, 1888. He was described as a "genial, kindly man," with many friends left to mourn him.[140] He was buried in the Bates/Beedy family plot in Mountain View Cemetery, Oakland.

MERCHANT *and* POSTMISTRESS

LAURA WAS THE SOLE beneficiary of the Dodd estate, and the provision store in Stanley was now hers. The estate was settled quickly with probate in May. She signed the British Columbia Supreme Court documents in Portland, Oregon. Laura had several reasons to be in Portland. William's brother Charles Henry Dodd (1838–1921) resided there. He was president and an active member of the Board of Trade of Portland. He operated Charles H. Dodd and Company, a hardware merchant and farm machinery enterprise that extended across Washington and Oregon states.[141] In addition, Laura's youngest brother, William Laurist Lindhard (1860–1948), had arrived in the United States in 1877 and lived in Portland. Recently married to Belle Malarkey, he was partner in Malarkey and Lindhard, operating the Cleveland Oil and Paint Manufacturing Company.[142] Portland was a city that appealed to Laura more than Oakland. She bought a house in the city and hoped to move there. She respected the business acumen of both her brother and brother-in-law, and they helped her think through the options she had.

In July, Laura advertised the Stanley store as a "Rare Business Opportunity" and part of an "Administratrix Estate Sale." She described the business as an "old and well known establishment" and offered stock and fixtures at a very low price and on most reasonable terms. The stock was valued at over $8,000 and the building, warehouse, butcher shop, and outhouses, with the lots, were offered "low to wind up the estate."[143] The advertisement ran only a short time before her sons Asa (now seventeen years old) and Louis (fifteen) proposed that they help her run the store and post office. They were both old enough that they would continue to study and at the same time gain some business experience in the store. Stanley and Barkerville were in difficult economic times and there was little interest from potential buyers. Things would not be easy but with determination and cooperation the store could help Laura and her family get by.

In 1886 when the railway reached Vancouver and the east–west route became the dominant transportation and travel corridor in British Columbia and across Canada, the Cariboo, including Stanley, became more connected to the east but cut off from the political and business centres of Vancouver and Victoria. One report from Ashcroft described the heavily laden bull teams and pack trains that could be observed all summer long travelling the "one government wagon road" from Ashcroft supplying "the large population of Cariboo . . . The amount of freight that goes each year to this mysterious faraway region is something surprising to a stranger."[144]

In 1888, a letter in the *Daily British Colonist* elaborated the problem for the Cariboo mining sector in being so far from their base of needed supplies and called for "a railway into the heart of the mining district." While the unrealized wealth of the area still held great promise, a railway to the faraway region was needed now to "give renewed life to the province."[145]

Stanley had fallen into a slumber. *The British Columbia Directory of 1891* stated:

> Owing to the want of capital several large shaft houses containing some fine steam power are allowed to remain idle and rusting. Lightning Creek, running through Stanley, has been imperfectly washed, owing to the same cause. The settlers are

living in hopes of times improving and returning once more to the prosperous times of ten years ago.[146]

By the mid-1890s, the mines in the Stanley area saw renewed activity and Laura could ride out the good and bad turns that she had experienced before. There was hope that a railway might soon reach into the north. In 1893, Stanley was described as having a population of about 150 people, with two hotels, five general stores, and no churches or schools. It was served by the BC Express Company that ran stages twice a week from Ashcroft to Barkerville. When Laura held the express and post offices, she successfully retained clientele from the outlying mining camps, as well as many locals.

In the 1891 Canadian Census, Laura recorded all her children as residents with her in Stanley although they began to seek education opportunities and work elsewhere. In 1889, Josephine had enrolled for one year of preparatory studies at Oberlin College, Ohio, while Asa attended Oberlin Business College. Books held in Barkerville Archives inscribed with "Asa H. Beedy, Oberlin, Ohio," include ones on Latin prose and grammar, commercial law, business math, and physics. His aunt, Mary Elizabeth Beedy, gave him "Thoughts for a Young Man," by Horace Mann, a lecture delivered before the Boston mercantile library association on its twenty-ninth anniversary and inscribed it "Christmas '91."

Mary Elizabeth Beedy, Josiah's sister, had completed a master's in education from Antioch College where Horace Mann had been the first principal. She became a noted educator and advocate for women's right to education and had an interest in guiding the Beedy children's education. After Josephine completed one year at Oberlin, she studied at the Girls' Collegiate School in Chicago where Mary Elizabeth was co-principal with Rebecca Rice. From there, Josephine attended Stanford University and graduated in May of 1897. She was described as "a brilliant Latin and Greek scholar graduating near the top of her class of 117 students."[147]

Asa worked as a bookkeeper and express agent with his mother in the Stanley store.[148] In 1892, he worked for Malarkey and Company in Portland before returning and becoming an active member of the Stanley and Barkerville communities. In 1891, Louis was described as a miner living in Stanley and then as a clerk working in Stanley in 1893. By 1894, he had enrolled in a pre-law program at Stanford University, California.[149] He graduated with a law degree in 1898 and began a practice in San Francisco. While studying and working in California, the children often lived with their aunt Caroline and her husband, Commodore Harrison, in Sausalito.

When Winslow was fifteen in 1891, he enrolled for two years at Titusville High School in Pennsylvania, close to his uncle, Asa Beedy, in Cambridge Springs. He followed this with studies at the Eastman Business College in Poughkeepsie, New York, and one year at Stanford University.[150] He spent some years in Stanley assisting Laura and by the end of the decade was an accountant employed and living in San Francisco and often living with his aunt Caroline in Sausalito.

Josiah was six when his mother had returned to Stanley and nine when she was widowed for a second time. It's unclear where his elementary schooling was attained. The Beedy family history records that "when he was old enough, he was sent to Marin County to the Selborne Academy (now Tamalpais Boys' School)." He used to relate to his children the stories of his "adventure south from boat to boat with a money belt around his waist. From Barkerville he took the stagecoach to Yale . . . Then down the river by steamboat to Vancouver on an ocean-going steamer. They made a stop at Seattle. The entire trip took about a month. He was about fourteen the first trip." The month duration would be an exaggeration for the 1890s, done for the sake of narrating a good story for his children, and it probably did seem that long through the eyes of a child. By the end of the decade Josiah was living in Sausalito and working as a clerk.

Laura understood the mining community and their needs. Day books that she kept reveal the diverse streams of retail she operated. Gold dust was a legitimate tender at the time, and she regularly sent amounts of gold dust—sometimes exceeding a thousand dollars each time—to the Bank of British Columbia in San Francisco. She deposited similar amounts of cash to the Bank of Victoria. She purchased live pigs that provided meat for the butcher shop. She sold shovels, shirts, pants, underwear, overshoes, stamps, pink pills, tobacco, whisky, gum boots, candles, flour, bacon, nails, and butter. She sold hay on commission that John Boyd had grown. She bought and sold fur pelts from local trappers. She sent cheques of usually less than one hundred dollars to her children Louis and Winslow in California, and cheques often for several hundred dollars to her sister Caroline Harrison.[151] In addition she retained her house in Portland and realized monthly rental income from it.

With old friends, Laura maintained an interest in the mines on Lightning Creek.
Left to right: Fred Tregillus, Mrs. John Fraser, Watkin Price, Laura, Harry Jones.
P-0011 BARKERVILLE HISTORIC TOWN ARCHIVES

Laura had lasting friendships with other families of Stanley who had been in the community as long as she had. Janet and John Boyd owned and operated Cold Spring House before buying Cottonwood House from Beedy and Lindhard in 1874. Janet's brother John Fleming managed Cottonwood until 1886 when the Boyds finally moved in. Laura's business records show a continued business relationship, as well as a friendship with the Boyds. On May 24, 1886, when John's daughter Mary Ann, from his first marriage, was married to Alfred Carson of Quesnel at Cold Spring House, Laura was one of the few chosen friends who witnessed the wedding.[152]

The usual practice for Stanley merchants was to run accounts for purchases by individuals and mining companies throughout each month with the account being due after thirty days. Unpaid accounts at the end of each month would be charged interest, and if still unpaid after a certain length of time, merchants would take the account to County Court. Considering Laura was a long-time merchant, she

Picnics were popular with all ages. Photo taken about 1896. *Left to right:* Mrs. Fred Laird, Mrs. H. Flynn, Laura, Mrs. Hobart Flynn, Kathleen Laird.
P1318 BARKERVILLE HISTORIC TOWN ARCHIVES

W.W. Dodd, General Dealer and Butcher, bill of sale, dated December 1, 1897, included in the paperwork lodged in the County Court. Merchants regularly went to County Court to settle unpaid accounts. G-0570 PLAINTIFF & PROCEDURE BOOKS 1864–1896, VOLUME I, COURTESY OF ROYAL BC MUSEUM AND ARCHIVES

took comparatively few customers to court. However, she did use the court to satisfy some claims. In 1896, she had a court summons served on the Van Winkle Creek Company for $177.13 and in 1897 on E.A. Bradley, L.M. Bardo, and Thomas Nam for $247.29. In both cases the proceedings dragged on into the next year and resulted in claims against employers to garnish wages of the debtors.

Unlike male entrepreneurs who often could not hold business and family together, Laura managed as a single parent by relying on extended family members to assist in occasionally housing her children and providing support as needed. She relied on her children to assist each other and assist in running the businesses. Anecdotes from the family history offer a glimpse of the relationship that developed among the children. As told from the perspective of Josiah, the youngest of five children, he felt he was often given the "short end of the stick."

Merchant and Postmistress

There was the time that he saved his favourite floating island dessert so that he could eat it with his big brothers when they came home later in the evening. A dessert called floating island sounds exotic and special to a young child, as it was to young Josiah, who wished to make it more special by sharing the treat with his brothers. The dessert is a sweet mixture of custard and meringue created from milk and eggs—readily available ingredients in rural households. His older brothers, however, had a different notion of sharing because instead of awakening him so they could share the experience of eating together, they let him sleep and ate his dessert!

Another memory that Josiah held of life in Stanley was when the older boys came to bed on freezing cold Canadian nights, and they would often pass poor Si from one bed to the other as a sort of convenient warming pan![153] While there were trying times, as viewed by the eyes of the youngest family member, warm relationships developed among the children that continued through the rest of their lives.

Asa remained the longest in Stanley, assisting his mother, as needed, in the store with the post and express offices and with bookkeeping throughout much of the 1890s. Louis, Winslow, and Asa developed close friendships with long-time Stanley resident Fred Tregillus. They exchanged letters in 1900 when Fred was travelling the world. Asa wrote him a letter in April, in which he described the warmer winter than usual that they had just had. He detailed the activity in all the mines and in town:

> Both hotels are full and Stanley has been lively all winter ... Ogden bought a pipe and is putting it on his claim at Dunbar Flat. I think Seymour Baker bought McAlindens claim on Grouse Creek. Jas Deacon is working on it now. Pat Carey has several men working on Beecher's claim on Grouse Creek. Lottie Bowron is to be bookkeeper there this summer ... Mr. Yolland has bought Ah Fung's ranch near Quesnelle and has moved his family there ... I have turned miner now and have bought St. Clair's interest in Coffee Creek.[154]

The tone of the lengthy letter indicates a well-established friendship. Asa detailed who had lost their heart to whom and that three young women had recently arrived in town. "There have been no deaths or marriages . . . I hope to see you in a couple of months and then I will give you all the news. I will say good night. Kind regards to yourself and brother."

Asa remained in the Barkerville area until 1905. Having spent more than thirty years in the area, he was regarded as a "Cariboo pioneer." He was well known as "the manager of the S.A. Rogers store in Barkerville, where his personality and popularity were greatly responsible for the success of the business."[155] Asa and Fred Tregillus remained in touch and exchanged letters and postcards for many years. Following his move to California, Asa worked as

Barkerville pioneers, the next generation, circa 1899. *Left to right, standing:* Winslow Beedy, Willie Bowron; *seated:* Hugh Cochran, Asa Beedy, William McArthur.
IMAGE C-07534 COURTESY OF ROYAL BC MUSEUM AND ARCHIVES

a clerk, bookkeeper, and accountant. He never married and lived much of his life with brother Winslow and family, and often lived at his aunt Caroline's home in Sausalito.

Winslow worked with Laura for several years in the 1890s. He and Lottie Bowron established a friendship that involved exchanging letters of reminiscences and news every summer for years. Lottie returned each summer to Barkerville from her home and work in Victoria to live and vacation with Tregilluses. Her last letter to Winslow was in 1963 in which she reflected on the emptiness of the house since Fred Tregillus had died the previous summer. She reported on the restoration of Barkerville that was underway. Both Lottie Bowron and Winslow died in the next year, in 1964.

RETIRING *to* CALIFORNIA

THE GOLD MINING TOWN of Stanley during the 1890s and into the 1900s was described in the memories of William Hong.[156] It boasted three hotels—the Stanley, the Grand, and the Lightning. In the lower end of town were three saloons, while at the upper end there were four Chinese operated stores. The town also claimed four gambling houses, a shoemaker, and a town jail. Lightning Creek had yielded an estimated twelve to thirteen million dollars' worth of gold.[157] In 1905, there were more people living in Stanley than in Barkerville, about five hundred in the summer, over two hundred of whom were Chinese. The Slough Creek and LaFontaine Mines and the Willow River mine at the mouth of Red Gulch caused a small mining boom that employed the people who shopped, gambled, and drank in Stanley.

In 1899, Laura was fifty-three, and her children were between twenty and twenty-eight years old. All the children except Asa were living and working in California. She resigned as postmistress and left Stanley. It was time for an easier lifestyle for sure! Ellen Dickie Peebles and John Peebles bought the store when she left. They were already area merchants and Ellen Peebles became postmistress and agent for the BC Express.[158]

Laura's participation in the Stanley community spanned twenty-nine years. She, like others who invested far fewer years in the area, left with mixed emotions. The people, the land, and the community of the Cariboo had become part of her. As mentioned earlier, the Cariboo has a way of holding people and bidding them to return after they leave. Some miners only stayed one season and never returned. As in other resource-based communities, people often arrived with no intention of staying long term. They came for the opportunity to improve their personal wealth and with plans to move on to a larger city or less remote area. Laura stayed longer than she had probably intended, and yet Stanley provided her and her children with a livelihood and they forged strong attachments.

Many have bid farewell to the Cariboo and many poems of farewell have been written. It is unclear who the author W.L.F. was, but the following poem was clipped from an unidentified newspaper and found among Lottie Bowron's collection in the Royal British Columbia Archives. The poem captures the mixed emotions of leaving a community that one is attached to. It provides a feeling of the past dynamism of the area; the people that came from all over the world and many who filled the cemeteries from the 1860s to 1930s:

"GOOD-BYE TO CARIBOO," BY W.L.F.

If at Barkerville's old graveyard you cast a friendly glance
You'll see tombs of men from Germany, from England and from France,
From Denmark, Norway, Sweden and from Alsace and Lorraine;
From Austria and Hungary, from Portugal and Spain.
All men of different languages, by God's will once dispersed—
Surely the camp at Barkerville was Babylon reversed
Here Judge Begbie gave his "dictum"—"Killers will surely rue"
"For those who slay in this Northland, there will be hanging too."
If miners covet all the gold, they'll take the people true.
For gold is in the hearts of those who toil in Cariboo.

Good-bye! Good folks of Cariboo, I leave you with a sigh,
My heart aches as I say it, but "Klahowya"[159] and "Good-bye."

> *Farewell now to the "Mountain" drear, I'll never traverse more*
> *And struggle to "The Hundred Mile," or south to "Seventy-four."*
>
> *For each of us the time's arrived, to go a different way*
> *I leave you, and I love you—that is all that I can say;*
> *I'll never meet more kindly folk, wherever I may dwell;*
> *Good-bye! Good-bye! Old Cariboo! Klahowya and farewell.*
> *Where careless of the winter and, comparatively few*
> *The warmest-hearted people dwell—the folks of Cariboo.*[160]

Today there are few signs of where the mining town of Stanley stood. The old Lightning Hotel, unoccupied and neglected for years, is still there but the main marker is the cemetery where J.C. Beedy and other early adventurers lay.

Back in California, Laura moved in temporarily with her sister Caroline in Sausalito before securing a flat for the family on Washington Street in San Francisco. During these years, Caroline's home with Charles Harrison was home for many nieces and nephews. Laura joined her sons Winslow and Josiah and nieces Helen Lindhard and Olive Hamilton, who were also living at Caroline's.[161] In 1901, Laura travelled to Europe with Asa. They enjoyed days in Paris and a visit with family in Denmark.[162] Laura had not seen Denmark since she had left thirty-one years earlier.

Laura remained in touch with friends and financial interests in Stanley, while Asa continued to work in Barkerville. In 1900, she prepared a handwritten will leaving all the property she possessed to her five children "to share and share alike." Asa and Louis were appointed executors and her sister Caroline Harrison and niece Olive Hamilton witnessed the document.

Laura and Caroline were together for a Christmas family reunion in 1905 at Caroline's home in Sausalito. They were joined by their children, nieces and nephews, and Laura's first grandchild, Mary Elizabeth Beedy, Louis's daughter born earlier that year. By 1905,

ABOVE—Josephine, Asa, Caroline, and Winslow Beedy at a giant sequoia tree in Yosemite Park, 1913. COURTESY J. BEEDY YOUNG

OPPOSITE—Caroline Lindhard Bates Harrison (1852–1913).
IMAGE G-06712 COURTESY OF ROYAL BC MUSEUM AND ARCHIVES. DETAIL FROM ORIGINAL

Louis, Winslow, and Josiah had all married and established their own homes. After a brief marriage, Winslow was widowed and left with his baby daughter Caroline. In her final years, Laura returned to Sausalito to live with her sister Caroline, children Asa, Josephine, and Winslow, and grandchild Caroline.[163] Laura died suddenly at age sixty-four on May 30, 1910.

PART ONE: LAURA LINDHARD BEEDY DODD

— *Part Two* —

CAROLINE LINDHARD BATES HARRISON

FOR EVERY OUNCE OF Laura's calm steadfastness, Caroline matched her with impulsiveness and determination. Laura was the older sister by six years and Caroline was the outgoing, romantic, fashionable, and flighty younger one. She was eager to experience the "new country" that her cousin Joachim described. She was enthralled by all that was new and anxious to test her abilities in a setting where women might be afforded new opportunities. Growing up in Stege, she watched the ships come and go from the harbour and listened to the stories of their far destinations. She longed to travel and experience the places they had been.

Born Caroline Serine Josephine Lindhard on February 28, 1852, in Stege, Denmark, Caroline was the youngest daughter and fourth child of Joachim Lindhard and Josephine Margrethe Rasmussen Lindhard. Seven months later she was baptized in the Lutheran Church, as was customary in Denmark, and confirmed in the church at age fourteen. She had graduated from school but was uncertain about the future she could build for herself in Denmark. She was captivated by the restless tempo of social buoyancy simmering around her.

In December of 1869, when her cousins Joachim and Theodor returned home for Christmas, she listened intently to the stories they told of the people they knew and the adventures they had in California and the Colony of British Columbia. Joachim had left Stege for California when he was fourteen and Caroline had not yet been born. Joachim had seen a lot of life in British America. He told of the mines he had invested in, the steamer routes he took, and the stagecoaches that ran up the Cariboo Road to Van Winkle and into Barkerville. He talked of the women who made a living operating boarding houses, laundries, restaurants, shops, and pack trains. Some partnered with men to operate stopping houses and others invested in and participated in mining. He said there were many opportunities for everyone. He told of the people on Lightning Creek and Barkerville area who came from all around the world. There were Americans, British, Europeans, Chinese, Mexicans, South Americans, and people indigenous to British Columbia.

Joachim loved Lightning Creek, where he now lived, and he was an enthusiastic supporter of the community. If she could learn English and some Chinook, he could use her assistance in the store, saloon, and hotel he operated. He was a great promoter, but it didn't take much convincing. Caroline shared the determination of well-loved author and suffragette Louisa May Alcott, who as a child reportedly shook her fist at the universe and declared, "I *will* do something by-and-by. Don't care what, teach, sew, act, write, anything to help the family; and I'll be rich and famous and happy before I die, see if I won't!"[1] Caroline may well have shaken her fist at the universe and declared, "Give me a chance! I'm ready!"

Caroline's youthful energy and resolve made her think of nothing else than returning with Joachim to Van Winkle on Lightning Creek. Her parents, however, were skeptical and worried that Caroline might make some wrong decisions unless Laura, with her more reasoned influence, accompanied her. An agreement was made. Joachim knew he could entice Laura with the promise that there were many potential husbands in the colony—after all, she was twenty-four years old and should be getting on with marriage soon! He imagined having his cousins as capable workers to help him with his businesses. Laura agreed and all four Lindhards were booked to sail March 9, 1870, on the *Saxonia* from Hamburg to New York.

To the NEW COUNTRY

MARCH 9 WAS THE most exciting day for Caroline. She felt secure and confident in the company of her cousins and Laura. Her whole future lay before her open for discovery. Caroline and Laura seriously took to learning English. After studying and practising every day of the two and a half weeks it took to cross the Atlantic, they were remarkably proficient. Caroline's excitement diminished with the processing delays and the crush of people encountered in the Castle Garden Immigration Depot in New York. However, Joachim did his best to speed them through the various checks and line-ups and secure the tickets they needed for the cross-continent train travel.

It was a romantic scenic journey for Caroline as they left New York behind. She was thrilled by the majesty of Niagara Falls, the wide expansive prairies, and the stunning snow-capped mountains. She loved the new trains, the luxuries of the Pullman cars, and the efforts made to provide exceptional food and comforts to the passengers. She also found herself totally charmed by Joachim. They had time in San Francisco to explore the city that Joachim knew well. When he proposed marriage to her, it felt like the logical outcome of their adventurous travels. He was wealthy and generous. She felt secure and protected by him. What could go wrong?

When Caroline, Joachim, and Laura left San Francisco on April 5, aboard the *Active*, Caroline was very happy to sign in as Mrs. Lindhard. On board the *Active* were many fellow travellers also heading to a variety of places along the Cariboo Road. Joachim introduced her to David Oppenheimer (1834–97) who had left Germany in 1848 with most of his ten brothers and sisters for the United States. Their journey had taken them to New Orleans, California, and now Victoria, Yale, and Barkerville. David was travelling to Yale where he currently managed the wholesale and retail company and various real estate interests for Oppenheimer brothers. Joachim had known David for a long time, as many of their entrepreneurial interests paralleled: operating pack trains, buying and selling land, and sticking together as a family.[2]

Through these fellow passengers, Caroline was introduced to life in the Colony of British Columbia. She recognized that many of the successful entrepreneurs were highly dependent on family members as they worked together to run successful businesses and move up the social ladder in this new society. Caroline understood now why Joachim had encouraged Theodor, Laura, and her to join him. He needed the larger family network and missed the extended family he had in Stege.

On the *Active*, Caroline met another newly married couple heading to their home in the Sumas/Chilliwack area. George Chadsey had just married Eliza Jane Thorne at Hilton in Brighton Township in Ontario, and she was making her first trip to George's home, accompanied by his sister Laura and her husband, David Miller. Three other brothers, Chester, William, and James Chadsey, had moved from Ontario in the early 1860s, and Joachim knew them as dairy producers who sold butter in the Cariboo area. Laura Chadsey Miller had been in the colony for almost ten years and she, her husband, and her brothers worked closely together under the name of Miller and Company. The families had several young children and were active in settlement life. Recognizing the agricultural potential of the area, the families pre-empted land on the Sumas Prairie, first renting it out for winter pasturing of horses and pack train animals from the Interior. Then they built their own herd of cattle, started growing grains and vegetables, and by 1865 had begun the first dairy farm in the Sumas Valley. James and William Chadsey had innovated by packing the butter they produced in airtight cans that enabled them to sell thousands of pounds to merchants in the Cariboo, including Joachim.[3]

Some apprehension overtook Caroline as the steamer docked in Yale where she would transfer to the stagecoach for the remainder of her journey to Van Winkle. The stagecoaches were small, crowded, and uncomfortable. Fortunately, there were not many others travelling this early in the season and the drivers were competent and courteous. Sensing this apprehension, Joachim kept a steady narration of his past experiences in each of the places they stopped and some they passed.

He explained to the sisters the changes he had seen in British Columbia since he arrived in 1858. There had been many in the Colony of British Columbia, and it was on the verge of many more. In 1850, the Colony of Vancouver Island had been created and James Douglas was installed in the dual role of first governor of the colony and chief factor of the Hudson's Bay Company in the Columbia district that extended west of the Rockies and north of the forty-ninth parallel. His authority as governor of Vancouver Island did not extend to the mainland, but his authority as chief factor did. In England, Sir Edward Bulwer Lytton was appointed colonial secretary in 1858. His interest in reducing the control of the Hudson's Bay Company and opening the area to "free trade" coincided with Douglas's angst about the twenty thousand miners heading north to the Fraser River gold rush. In August 1858, Queen Victoria created the Colony of British Columbia on the mainland. In September, she appointed James Douglas as governor of both colonies and Matthew Begbie as judge of the Colony of British Columbia. Begbie was given the authority and proclamations to establish the Colony of British Columbia, to appoint Douglas as governor, to revoke the exclusive trading licence of the Hudson's Bay Company, and to declare the Law of England to be the Law of British Columbia. He arrived at Victoria on Vancouver Island on November 16, 1858.

The two British colonies on the West Coast lasted until 1866, when they were joined to become the United Colony of British Columbia. Frederick Seymour, who had been governor of the Colony of British Columbia beginning in 1864, after Sir James Douglas retired, served as governor of the United Colony from 1864 to 1869. Anthony Musgrave succeeded Seymour as governor and was given the mandate to move the colony toward union with the Dominion of Canada.

A second wave of apprehension overtook Caroline when Van Winkle came into site. The dreary little village was still in the grip of winter. The hillsides were barren of trees, all having been cut for the new cabins and buildings scattered throughout the village. Tall leafless trees and fields of tree stumps loomed large all around when she stepped from the stagecoach and Joachim welcomed her and Laura into his home and store.

PART TWO: CAROLINE LINDHARD BATES HARRISON

FAR *from* FASHION

CAROLINE'S CURIOSITY AND ADAPTABILITY were called upon as she gradually settled into a rural mining village life. With energy and determination, she set about learning what she needed to assist Joachim with his businesses. Caroline was eighteen and Joachim thirty-five when they began their married life. He was enchanted by her bright energy and youthful ways. He knew she would succeed in whatever she chose and set about helping her learn some basic business practices. Neither Caroline nor Laura was about to sit on the sidelines. They doffed their ornate chapeaux and busied themselves sewing some practical cotton work dresses from the fabric Joachim encouraged them to buy in Victoria. He had a plan that they would only recognize as it unfolded.

Every day new people came into the Van Winkle store and saloon. In the evenings, the saloon filled with miners, exchanging stories of the day's work and happenings over an evening meal and drink. Caroline listened and tried to figure out the different opinions of those who strongly supported the colony joining the Dominion of Canada and those who didn't. She listened to speculation on who would return this spring to the mines and the businesses they had left in the fall. She listened to the usual complaints about the condition of the road and the weather. She saw that families who stuck together and worked together were the ones that prospered. She was grateful that Laura was with her, for together they would support each other and figure things out.

The Van Winkle store was a busy place. Advertisements at the time appeared:[4]

> **VAN WINKLE STORE**
>
> LIGHTNING CREEK
>
> MINERS AND TRADERS will find it to their advantage to purchase at this Store, where there is
>
> **A LARGE ASSORTMENT OF GOODS**
>
> Of the very best description on hand, and the Stock constantly replenished by new arrivals. The proprietors will sell Goods
>
> AS CHEAP AS ANY IN CARIBOO
>
> Orders promptly filled and forwarded with dispatch.
>
> Van Winkle   BEEDY & LINDHARD,
>   Proprietors

Ad for the Van Winkle store. *Cariboo Sentinel*, May 28, 1870, p. 4

People dropped in constantly for their mail at the post office and to pick up a copy of the *Cariboo Sentinel*. Barnard's Express made regular stops on its way into Barkerville. Caroline and Laura both quickly became absorbed in the work needed to operate the store, post office, hotel, and saloon. Ah Fung was the trusty cook who turned out the delicious food that kept the saloon customers returning night after night.[5]

In 1870, Van Winkle and the Barkerville area teetered between dull boredom and renewed excitement; people were pondering every idea for exploiting the gold that was tightly held in the bedrock beneath the streams. Some miners continued to move north to the new gold discoveries in the Omineca region, and a quiet summer settled. As Joachim was major shareholder in the Van Winkle Company, the anxious waiting felt in the mines spilled into their home. The mining report from Lightning Creek read:

> On this creek all eyes are anxiously turned toward the Van Winkle claim which is being pushed forward as fast as money

and labor can accomplish. The company had many obstacles but have overcome all and are now drifting in the rock at a level of 70 feet below the water in the creek. They are running three shifts and are in about 45 feet; they expect to reach the channel by the end of next week. A large iron pump is being prepared to go in and the machinery having been repaired, there is no doubt that it will succeed in testing the channel, on which we may say the whole country anxiously looks to, as one of the main sources of wealth, and as each foot is excavated the interest increases, and all other interests are absorbed in the one, "how is the Van Winkle getting on?" And no wonder, for if success is attained there, it is certain the whole creek, for a distance of twenty miles will be worked the coming season, so let us all hope for success.[6]

Life in the community moved in its own rhythm of deaths, births, accidents, thefts, robberies of sluice boxes, and court cases. The long days of summer were a flurry of activity and unexpected events. On May 31, 1870, Mr. Chartres Brew, gold commissioner and stipendiary magistrate for the Cariboo district, died at age fifty-nine. In 1858, he had come to the Colony of British Columbia as chief inspector of police. In 1867, he began his work in the Cariboo and was highly regarded by miners and citizens.[7] In late August, Mrs. Allan, also known as "Scotch Jeanie" of the Hotel de Fife on Lightning Creek, was driving a buggy through the canyon between Barkerville and Richfield. In this dangerous stretch of road, with barely room to pass, she met a wagon, lost control of her buggy, and was thrown into the canyon, sustaining serious injuries that took her life.[8] The Grunbaum brothers opened a branch store at Van Winkle, selling groceries and supplies to the miners, creating new competition for Beedy and Lindhard. In November, Joachim went to court charging Yee Kee with theft of merchandise from Beedy and Lindhard's warehouse. After some of the hottest summer days on record, snow arrived on October 15. In mid-November, Barnard's Express announced it would only bring the mail every two weeks during the next five months. Fortunately, the *Cariboo Sentinel* continued to publish every Saturday throughout the winter, and Joachim Lindhard was its agent in Van Winkle.

Many changes were afoot in the colony. The Land Ordinance Act of 1870 allowed any male British subject eighteen years old or over to pre-empt 320 acres east and north of the Cascade Mountains or 160 acres elsewhere.[9] While the governor could grant exemptions and permissions, this act excluded the Lindhards and certainly excluded women from any hope of land ownership. Even the editor of the *Cariboo Sentinel* protested, arguing that there needed to be fewer conditions and restrictions in order to promote settlement.[10] The Common School Ordinance Act of 1869 encouraged residents to petition the governor for a school district, when it appeared that the number of children likely to attend the school might exceed twelve or the amount likely to be collected for the teacher might be more than three hundred dollars per annum.[11] The number of young children in the area was increasing and residents of Williams Creek organized to open a school. By early January, it was announced that the telegraph was up between Barkerville and New Westminster. This broke community isolation by bringing news of the world quickly to the *Cariboo Sentinel*, so it could print and dispatch news to all readers.

There was always time for entertainment, dances, and fun, especially in winter. Small remote communities are good at creating their own entertainment and Barkerville was no different. The Fire Brigade Ball was held in mid-December. On New Year's Eve at the Theatre Royal, the Cariboo Amateur Dramatic Association offered a farce in two acts—"Who Killed Cock-Robin?" with a musical interlude at intermission. On New Year's Day, a good dinner, including wine, liquor, and cigars, could be had for $2.50 at the New Dominion Dining Rooms. Harry Wilmot had a new light sleigh he ran regularly between Barkerville and Van Winkle and encouraged all his friends to give such a pleasant ride a try.[12] Joachim's saloon became the Van Winkle centre for lectures and meetings. In January, the saloon was packed to listen to Reverend Thomas Derrick

PART TWO: CAROLINE LINDHARD BATES HARRISON

Caroline Lindhard and Laura Lindhard Beedy in Stanley, circa 1875.
IMAGE G-06712 COURTESY OF ROYAL BC MUSEUM AND ARCHIVES

lecture on "The Past, Present and Future of British Columbia."[13] The appreciative crowd invited a second lecture in February on "Enthusiasm in Relation to Art, Science and Human Progress."[14]

Caroline was delighted when Laura and Josiah Beedy married in March of 1871. It meant that Laura would be close, and they could continue to support each other. But the partnership between their husbands didn't last. The investment in road steamers that year caused a significant financial setback for the Beedys and the Beedy Lindhard partnership was dissolved. Joachim's brother Theodor arrived that summer with plans to remain in Van Winkle and open a tinsmith shop.[15] Caroline was overjoyed in October of 1871 when Laura and Josiah welcomed their first child, Asa Harold, born at Cottonwood. Caroline loved children and was thrilled with a new baby added to the family. Soon after, Laura and Josiah left their residence at Cottonwood House, and the job of managing it. They returned to live in Van Winkle and focused on Josiah's many investments.

Joachim needed Caroline's help after the Beedy Lindhard partnership ended and he had to manage the store and saloon on his own. The seasonal rhythm of September departures became evident in late August through advertisements in the newspaper. Merchants planning to leave for the winter called for payment of outstanding accounts by a certain date or else the claim would be referred to the courts. It was Caroline's second winter in Van Winkle, and it was busy. With work in the mines continuing all winter, Joachim was preoccupied with the Van Winkle Company and together they kept the store and saloon running. In addition to the Van Winkle and Union Jack companies, Joachim held shares in the Halliday Company on Peters Creek and the Rock Dale Company on Chisholm Creek.[16]

The following year continued to be busy for Caroline and Joachim, as their saloon frequently served as a community centre for Van Winkle. Caroline admired Joachim's enthusiasm for the community and eagerly assisted him with all community events. In June they hosted a community meeting to hear from Mr. Walkem, area representative to the legislature, who reported on the proceedings of the last legislative session. He described the bills passed by the legislature and the route that the Canadian Pacific Railroad would likely take. He received unanimous support from those at the meeting.[17] The saloon was also a place for voting registration and was a polling station for the provincial election held in early 1872.[18]

A summer highlight for Caroline and Joachim was to attend the July 1 and 4 celebrations in Barkerville in 1872.[19] Dominion Day was celebrated in the tradition of previous years, with speeches, three cheers for the Queen, the singing of "God Save the Queen," horse races and human races, and an evening theatre performance. American Independence was more sombre this year because two men had been killed the day before when a mine in the McLaughlin Company claim caved in. The day began with a funeral and then followed with games and horse races, an evening concert, and fireworks.

Joachim had long been opposed to what he described as a beef monopoly in the Barkerville area. The Harper brothers were ranchers who supplied Van Volkenburgh's butcher shops in Barkerville and Van Winkle with beef and other livestock. Joachim had operated a butcher shop for years and now local ranchers and farmers had surplus beef to sell into the market. Working in partnership with the Pioneer Line of Stages, he advertised to supply beef daily to customers in Barkerville, Richfield, and places on the road between Richfield and Van Winkle. He promised greatly reduced prices and delivery to those ordering through the stage drivers of the Pioneer Line.[20]

Caroline had been in Van Winkle for over two years. The fashionable dresses she enjoyed had rarely been worn. The evenings in the company of powerful and influential people were rarer than she wished. Joachim was well connected, and his business was the hub of Van Winkle, but the mining village was not fashion central compared to San Francisco or even Victoria, as she had experienced them. She was younger than many of the women in the town. She felt isolated and began to feel stuck in a mining outpost while all that was exciting and new was happening somewhere else.

Far from Fashion

A SECRET REVEALED

I T HAD BEEN A busy year in 1872 and by summer's end, Joachim was not well. Caroline was worried. He tried to allay her fears but had to admit that he had not been well for some time. At the beginning of September, he left on Barnard's Express for Yale and Victoria. Caroline encouraged him to go to San Francisco for medical advice and to take the winter for recovery there. She followed later in September and joined him in San Francisco. It had been over two years since she arrived in Van Winkle, and she was eager to experience San Francisco again. Like many Cariboo residents who needed a break during the winter, they remained in San Francisco, hoping that rest and an easier warm climate might aid in recuperation. Their respite lasted until the end of April, when they were back in Van Winkle.[21]

Joachim quickly resumed business and became the agent for Barnard's Express in Van Winkle in May. However, on June 9, 1873, he died at home. The official cause of death was Bright's disease.[22] Joachim was thirty-eight years old. Caroline was shattered by the sudden loss in her life. She had depended on Joachim for so much and now a giant chasm had opened under her feet. She relied on the consoling presence of Laura and Josiah.

Joachim Lindhard had lived intensely, and the *Cariboo Sentinel* paid tribute to its well-regarded citizen:

> Mr. Lindhard came to this province in 1858 and during his long residence in the country acquired the esteem and goodwill of all with whom he came in contact. To his indomitable pluck, boundless faith, and untiring energy and liberality are the people of Lightning Creek indebted in no small degree for the success which has lately attended their efforts in opening up the mines of that district; and it will be a source of regret that Providence has seen fit to call him from his labors before he had the satisfaction of seeing his hopes fully realized and reaped the full share of the reward of his enterprise and energy. Mr. Lindhard's death will be felt as a public loss throughout this section of the province. His large heartedness and liberality have been experienced by many and his memory will survive and continue to live, while the fruits of his untiring energy and enterprise will benefit the inhabitants of Cariboo.[23]

The same article noted that Joachim's death "leaves a disconsolate widow to mourn his early death." A "Tribute of Respect" from a Lightning Creek miner followed the newspaper article and reported on the funeral held on June 11. The miner noted that all mines on Lightning Creek were silenced and stores closed, as over five hundred people attended the funeral and burial in Stanley. He wrote:

> The death of Mr. Lindhard will leave a void which I am afraid will hardly if ever be filled. It is to his exertions more than to any other man that Lightning Creek is today prospected. Not only did he help us with his means, but he was always first and foremost in every enterprise for the benefit of this creek and the country in general.[24]

The newspaper tributes spoke of the high regard in which Joachim was held by community members. He was buried in the Stanley cemetery. The pain of loss Caroline and his family felt was sharp because he had been a leader and an inspiration for them all. Joachim came to be acclaimed, along with Josiah Crosby Beedy and John Evans, as one of "The Fathers of Lightning Creek."[25]

Harry Jones reminisced, "Mr. Lindhard was one of the finest men I have known. Kind-hearted and generous, he would always help those who were willing to work; but the shiftless and the idle quickly learned that it was useless to go to him for credit."[26]

Caroline was twenty-two and the sole beneficiary of Joachim's estate. Theodor Lindhard and Alfred Townsend were executors, and shortly after his death, a notice ran in the newspaper that those indebted to or who had claims on the estate were requested to settle. Caroline stayed in Van Winkle throughout the summer, finding comfort in being close to Laura and keeping a close eye on her inherited assets, as Joachim had counselled her. She was consoled by Laura's second son, Louis, born that February, and in being with little Asa as he became a toddler. She soon learned of the shares that Joachim held in the Van Winkle and other mining companies, an interest in Cottonwood Ranch, and the store, saloon, and properties in Van Winkle. The estate was valued at approximately $40,000. It was near the end of 1874 before she settled with the Van Winkle Company. They bought her two shares for $14,000 and reduced the total shares in the company to ten.[27] It had been an optimistic year for the mines and she was able to realize a very good price for her shares.

Caroline remained in Van Winkle throughout the fall and winter and into 1874. Josiah Beedy and Theodor assisted with operating the store and post office. She decided that she would stay in British Columbia near Laura even though Joachim was gone. Theodor planned to show his commitment to British Columbia by applying for citizenship. Caroline and Laura's sister Christine was living in Copenhagen, and they all agreed that Christine should join them. They offered to meet her in New York and accompany her on the land and ocean journey from there to Van Winkle. In April, Caroline was exhausted and tired of the long winter. She believed Victoria

PART TWO: CAROLINE LINDHARD BATES HARRISON

would be good for her and give her a place to think about what she would do next and where she could await Christine's arrival. Josiah Beedy helped move her belongings and accompanied her to Victoria to see her suitably settled. With Caroline's departure, Beedy and Alfred Townsend became partners in operating the Van Winkle store.

In Victoria, Caroline reconnected with old acquaintances and made new friends. The warmer weather and emerging spring cheered her, and she began to look forward to Christine's arrival in June or July. She felt more closely connected to the outside world, enjoyed the daily newspaper with its news of the world, and the abundance of social events, concerts, and Theatre Royal performances that gradually drew her out of her sadness. Her friendship with Lizzie Munro[28] flourished. She connected with the social life of Victoria, replete with teas, picnics, and other social benefits that dominated the women's lives. She had occasions to again wear her beautiful gowns and hats. She became a supporter of Victoria's Protestant Orphan's Home, by donating fabric, food, and cash to their operation.[29]

Caroline reflected on her four years in Van Winkle, years that had been full and busy. She was grateful for the past winter she and Joachim had spent in San Francisco. They fell in love with the city again and had time to explore the nearby communities of Oakland and Sausalito. Caroline imagined that one day she would like to follow in the footsteps of many other Cariboo residents and spend the harshest part of the winter in such a pleasing place. In late May, a visit from Asahel Sumner Bates in Victoria began the next chapter in her life.

A Secret Revealed

A NEW GAMBLE

IN VICTORIA, CAROLINE LEARNED from her friends that many of them kept homes in San Francisco—where their children could be educated and the mothers could enjoy more hospitable winters. Some entire families spent their winters in California and returned each summer to their business ventures in British Columbia. While Caroline enjoyed Victoria, the idea of winters in San Francisco appealed greatly.

Shortly after Caroline settled in Victoria, Asahel Sumner Bates came to call. She had met Asahel in 1870 when she first came to British Columbia, at the Exchange Hotel in Soda Creek, a stop for Barnard's Express on their way to Van Winkle. Asahel was a well-known farmer and rancher near 150 Mile House, Williams Lake, and Soda Creek, approximately two hundred kilometres (124 miles) southwest of Van Winkle. He occasionally travelled to Barkerville and stopped in Van Winkle to reconnect with Josiah Beedy and Joachim, who were old acquaintances. She read often in the newspaper about his successful farming and ranching activities. He had witnessed Caroline's love and enthusiasm for young children. He knew she was now on her own, as he was also, and he had his son Otis, now seven years old, to care for.

For Asahel, 1874 was a turning point. He had been almost fifteen years in the Cariboo, and he was ready for some changes. That summer would be his first as captain of the *Victoria*, a steamship built

> **STEAMER VICTORIA**
>
> WILL COMMENCE HER REGULAR Trips on the 18ᵗʰ June, running as follows until further notice:
> Leaves SODA CREEK on THURSDAYS, at 12 o'clock, noon.
> Leaves QUESNELMOUTH on SUNDAYS, at half-past 3 p.m.
>
> A.S. BATES.
> Soda Creek, June 12, 1874.   je20

In the summer of 1874, A.S. Bates took over operation of the steamer *Victoria*, running between Soda Creek and Quesnelmouth. CARIBOO SENTINEL, JUNE 6 AND JUNE 20, 1874, P. 4

in Quesnel by James Trahey and launched in 1869. The steamer operated between Soda Creek and Quesnelmouth on the Upper Fraser River, and in June, it was announced that it was under A.S. Bates's control.[30]

It's unclear if Asahel purchased the *Victoria*, but he captained the steamer during the summer season that extended from May to October for the next five years.[31] The steamer had been built for Gustavus Blin Wright and Edgar Marvin. It was built using the boiler and engines from the *Prince of Wales* that had sailed on Lillooet Lake. But little else has been written about the *Victoria*.[32]

Asahel was in a position to make an offer to Caroline. They could spend summers in the Cariboo and be near her sisters while he operated the *Victoria* and spend their winters in San Francisco. This sounded like a lifestyle that would work for them both. At the same time, he would assist her in investing her inheritance in California properties. He was an experienced investor who had become wealthy from his British Columbia properties. Asahel could see that the railway promised to British Columbia after joining Canada would be very slow in coming. There was a downturn

A New Gamble

in the market for beef as mining activity declined, and he saw it as the right time to sell the ranch lands he had accumulated. He had already begun to shed some of his assets and move his investments to Oakland and San Francisco. His mother had recently died, and he had inherited a farm and half a woodlot in Massachusetts that she had held since his father had died many years before. Both Caroline and Asahel were ready for a new start.

PART TWO: CAROLINE LINDHARD BATES HARRISON

FREIGHTER, FARMER, STEAMBOAT CAPTAIN

WHEN CAROLINE MARRIED ASAHEL Sumner Bates, he was twenty-four years her senior—more than twice her age of twenty-two years. He came with a past of sixteen years in British Columbia. He had been born November 18, 1828, in Webster, Worcester County, Massachusetts, the youngest child of Alanson Bates and Levina Brown Bates. He attended Nichols Academy in nearby Dudley, Massachusetts.[33] The Bates family lived close to a Nimpmuc reservation, a tribe of Algonquins in Massachusetts. As wards of the state, the Algonquins experienced similar treatment to the Indigenous people of British Columbia. When the state needed money, it used Indigenous lands as a source of revenue. From an early age, Asahel had witnessed the settler–Indigenous relationships prevalent in Massachusetts.

His father died when Asahel was thirteen years old, leaving him a small cash inheritance. The more valuable family assets that he inherited were held by Asahel's mother until she died in 1874. Asahel's first job was as a retail clerk in Hartford, Connecticut. At age twenty, in 1848, he left the eastern states for California.[34] He ventured into northwest California and gained experience observing and participating in the activities common to mining areas—building roads, packing, freighting, and supplying miners with needed goods.[35]

Freighter, farmer, miner, rancher, stopping house proprietor, steamship captain, "Yankee trader"— A.S. Bates played many roles. IMAGE A-01085 COURTESY OF ROYAL BC MUSEUM AND ARCHIVES

Asahel may have arrived in the Colony of British Columbia as early as 1858.[36] By 1861, he was working as a packer in the Savona and Bonaparte areas.[37] Jack Splawn told of meeting him in a group of packers that included John Cluxton, Louis Campbell, and others who were wintering on the Thompson River in 1861–62. Splawn encountered Asahel again in 1863–64 as a roadhouse proprietor about forty-eight kilometres (thirty miles) below Quesnel Forks. Splawn was on his way home to Oregon via Victoria after having delivered a pack train of bacon to merchants in Barkerville. Splawn described Bates's roadhouse as "full of lawless men, drinking, gambling, swearing, and fighting. With all my worldly possessions in my pocket, I felt uncomfortable." Splawn didn't linger but left Asahel's roadhouse and continued to Thomas Menefee's place thirty-two kilometres (twenty miles) down the road, where he felt more secure. Menefee had been a neighbour of Splawn's mother in Missouri.[38]

Dan Drumheller recalled meeting Asahel, who he described as a "shrewd Yankee trader," in the Ashcroft area in the winter of 1862–63, when Drumheller was overwintering cattle he had driven from Washington and Oregon that spring.[39] Asahel purchased Drumheller's cattle in the spring of 1863 and paid him for the winter care of cattle belonging to Spokane Jackson, a mutual acquaintance.

Thomas Menefee reappeared in Asahel's story in 1866. Described as a Williams Lake rancher, Menefee charged Asahel in court with having knowingly purchased eighty-one head of breeding stock cattle from his partner Francis Marion Woodward at their Mission Ranch while Menefee was away delivering cattle to Barkerville. This was a sensational case presided over by Judge Begbie that revealed Woodward's planned swindle of Menefee, and a background story of a love affair, assault, murder, imprisonment of a pregnant woman, and debtor's law. All these enticing background details are beyond the scope of Asahel's involvement and have been detailed by Marie Elliott in her recent book *Gold in British Columbia*. Asahel testified he had paid Woodward $4,600 for the cattle. Judge Begbie's decision was to order him to pay Menefee an additional $2,500.[40]

Asahel's enterprises in British Columbia were varied. He was an ambitious farmer and rancher and continued to operate pack trains for at least a decade. One of his first ranching ventures was near Savona, and it was there in the mid-1860s that he had formed a relationship with an Indigenous woman, Tlopelkey (a.k.a. Tlapelkey and Tlopelken) from the Bonaparte Band in the Cache Creek area.[41] She accompanied him to the Williams Lake area, and they had two children: Ellie, born about 1866, and John (a.k.a. Otis), born in 1867.[42] "Country marriages" with Indigenous women were common among newcomer men in this era and were encouraged in earlier decades by the Hudson's Bay Company for the traders they employed. There were few white women in the area and such a marriage was a path to positive relationships with Indigenous neighbours. These familial relationships were crucial for the success of many ranchers in early British Columbia. The early entrepreneurs and miners who ventured into the harsh climate of northern British Columbia often relied on the knowledge of the Indigenous people who had survived on the land for centuries. The Indigenous people had mastered survival skills, medicine, and nutritional knowledge. They knew the landscape, the trails, and the weather. Indigenous women often served as midwives for the newcomer women. And there is at least one story of a rancher who, once married to an Indigenous woman, moved the stakes from the edge of his ranch farther onto Indigenous lands.[43]

Both Ellie and John were baptized at the St. Joseph's Mission at Williams Lake on June 23, 1867.[44] It is unclear what happened to Tlopelkey and Ellie, but when Asahel visited Caroline in 1874, it appears that only the care of Otis was in his hands. This suggests that Tlopelkey may have died and possibly Ellie also. A common pattern in Indigenous–white newcomer marriages was that when the relationship ended, the care of the children reverted to the mother's family. It is also possible that Asahel and Tlopelkey split, each taking one child. Whatever happened, Asahel was responsible for Otis at this point.

In 1865, Asahel had written to H.W. Ball at Quesnelmouth, requesting pre-emption of a parcel of land consisting of 1,058 acres at the head of Williams Lake and the adjoining pre-emption that had been made by Royal Engineer John Grant at Quesnelmouth. In the previous year of 1864, Sir James Douglas had retired as governor of the Colony of British Columbia and was replaced by Frederick Seymour. While the Indigenous people often pleaded with Seymour to protect their land, his chief commissioner of Lands and Works, Joseph William Trutch, began to reduce the size of the reserves that had been allocated by Douglas's government. Thus, it was under

Trutch's tenure that Asahel began to acquire extensive land holdings around Williams Lake.

Preference in granting land pre-emptions was given to British and Canadian citizens (men) or those willing to become British subjects. This stipulation could have disadvantaged Asahel, but it was a policy that could be by-passed through special requests. At that time, the colonial administrators were interested in "industrious cultivators" who would settle and become producers of food for the colony. Local food production was important in the Cariboo because it was extremely difficult and costly to transport food from the Lower Mainland and Vancouver Island into the north. The transportation routes were poor and costly to maintain. Thus, the government officials looked with favour upon anyone interested in farming. As a result, Asahel's requests for land met with approval. He also acquired much of his land by purchasing failed or abandoned pre-emptions that would have been purchases made from mortgage holders or banks. By the early 1870s, Asahel was seriously farming, and the productivity of his crops was frequently reported in the *Cariboo Sentinel*. In 1870, he was reported as having one hundred acres under cultivation at Deep Creek.[45]

While Asahel invested in several ranches and businesses around Williams Lake, like most in the area, he also dabbled in mining. He held a mining licence as early as 1865. In 1870, he organized a company of Williams Lake farmers in an active mining operation on Black Bear Creek.[46] In 1866, he had leased Deep Creek House from the Bank of British Columbia after it had foreclosed on the property formerly held by Frank Way. In a letter written at Beaver Pass, September 10, 1867, "travelling correspondent" Captain Bumsby reported in the *Cariboo Sentinel* about a stop at Deep Creek House:

> Mr. Bates, proprietor of the hotel at Deep Creek, being a shareholder in the concern (mining company), was so highly delighted with Captain Bilks' good news that he invited all hands to dine

Freighter, Farmer, Steamboat Captain

with him that afternoon, which was unanimously accepted. We had a splendid feed and lots of lush; about 12 p.m., everybody appeared to have their cargo on board. Bates was called on for a song, he rose to his feet, made an eloquent and telling speech, in which he expressed the happiness it afforded him to accommodate his friends, and sung two verses of "My Old Aunt Sally," broke down and started on the "Woodpecker," forgot the second verse, sat down and commenced to whistle "Yankee Doodle." At this point all left the room unperceived and turned in, leaving Bates still whistling the same old tune. At six next morning I got up and had an eye-opener, and on looking into the room we occupied the evening previous I saw Bates in the same position we had left him. After a good breakfast, I bid my worthy host goodbye and got under weigh in company with Captain Bilk for Soda Creek where we arrived in a few hours.[47]

In 1868, Asahel added to his holdings an interest in the Exchange Hotel at Soda Creek, and early in the year, an advertisement announced his proprietorship. This was a partnership with Peter Curran Dunlevy, but by September of 1869, the partnership was dissolved.[48] He continued to hold the lease on Deep Creek House and advertise its services. His partnership in the Exchange Hotel was brief as he prepared to buy Deep Creek House and Ranch in 1870.

In 1869, Asahel operated a wagon team, carrying freight from Yale to Deep Creek, delivering supplies of up to 8,618 kilograms (19,000 pounds) for his operations and freight for others further into the Cariboo. In 1872, he operated a bull team, packing supplies from Yale to 150 Mile House.[49] He purchased additional ranches and in 1871, purchased the 150 Mile Stopping House and Ranch from the Davison brothers. He moved to 150 Mile House shortly after purchase to become proprietor of the stopping house and operator of the post office from 1874 to 1879. While under Bates's tenure, 150 Mile House was often referred to as Bates's or Mr. A.S. Bates's. The house

> ## EXCHANGE HOTEL
> ### SODA CREEK, B.C.
>
> THE UNDERSIGNED PROPRIETORS OF THE above well known and popular establishment, beg to inform their numerous friends and the public generally, that they are now prepared to afford every accommodation to the travelling community, at the most reasonable rate of charges. Good clean, airy bed-chambers.
> The Bar is stocked with the very best brands of Wines, Spirits and Cigars.
> The Table is supplied with all the substantials and luxuries the country affords, and meals are served at all hours.
> The Stables are spacious, comfortable and attended by first-class hostlers, and a constant supply of the best provender of all kinds.
> In short, every convenience and facility conducive to the comfort of man and beast, will be found, and the proprietors will spare no effort in order to give entire satisfaction to all who may patronize their establishment.
>
> A.S. BATES & CO.
> Soda Creek, B.C., March 19, 1868.   my1 6m

From 1868 to 1870, A.S. Bates was a partner in the Exchange Hotel in Soda Creek, prior to his purchase of the Deep Creek House and Ranch. CARIBOO SENTINEL, MAY 25, 1868, P. 4

became the setting for hearings of local court cases by travelling judges and the place for registering voters for upcoming elections.[50] Around the stopping house, a small village grew that included a store, a hotel, and blacksmith shop. The house had a reputation as a place of entertainment where travellers could always find a poker game, play a billiard game, or place their bets on horse races and dog fights.[51]

It's uncertain if it was during Asahel's residency at 150 Mile House that "The Home of the Dead Waltz" originated, but it is one of many stories that remain about the lively roadhouse. During winter, a favourite pastime of those in the Cariboo was for groups to travel from roadhouse to roadhouse for a dance every night. These dances were the chief social activity and usually lasted until dawn. At 150 Mile one man was an outstanding dancer and no celebration

Freighter, Farmer, Steamboat Captain

was complete without him. Unfortunately, after one series of parties, he contracted pneumonia and died. As was the custom, a three-day wake was held. The first night was solemn and quiet, with all proprieties observed. The second night things livened up. On the third night a dance was held in his memory. Since the man had been an outstanding dancer of the waltz, most of the music consisted of his favourite waltzes. At dawn the event broke up, but someone suggested that since the deceased was particularly partial to waltzes, they should give him one last fling on the floor. This was done and so was born the nickname.[52]

By 1872, Asahel had gained a reputation throughout the colony. The *New Westminster Mainland Guardian* reported on his movements:

> Mr. A.S. Bates, of Williams Lake, went down on the Enterprise yesterday on his way East. Mr. Bates has been in British Columbia since '58 and has distinguished himself by his enterprise and perseverance. He owns some of the most valuable property, north of the Cascades, in the province.[53]

A pack train leaving 150 Mile House for the north, 1880s. Strategically located on the Cariboo Wagon Road, 150 Mile House was a popular stopping house and social centre.
IMAGE C-01198 COURTESY OF ROYAL BC MUSEUM AND ARCHIVES

On this occasion, Asahel travelled as far as New Orleans and other points east, with stops in Oregon.[54] On his travels he made purchases for his Cariboo operations and checked on mining and other business interests in the United States. When he returned at the beginning of May to 150 Mile House, he brought with him a large boiler and the machinery for a grist and sawmill.[55] By October, the flour and sawmill were operating. The *Cariboo Sentinel* reported:

> *Everything worked satisfactorily. The stones which are the best French burrs, are said to be the largest in the colony. The sawmill capacity is estimated at about 10,000 feet per day. No expense has been spared to render the whole plan perfect.*[56]

In July 1874, a Canadian Pacific Railway surveyor's account of the Cariboo Wagon Road and the Chilcotin described Asahel's home and business at 150 Mile House where he lingered on a stop for several days:

> *The view from Bates' hotel stoop is very grand; a valley to the right for about ten miles in length and 1 mile wide, which encloses Williams Lake; in front another valley of considerable extent partly cultivated, dotted here and there with trees.*
>
> *The timothy here was 4½ to 5 feet high, new potatoes small and watery, onions well advanced, peas in blossom, turnips and cabbages growing large and healthy. Mr. Bates has a saw and grist mill here run by steam, sells boards at $25 per thousand feet; grinds flour for toll ... returns 65 lbs per 100 lbs wheat or purchase, grain at 1½ to 3 cents per lb according to quality. The altitude here is 2,300 feet above the sea. Thermometer 40 deg. below zero in winter, 100 in summer. Cattle are often frozen; several were seen with short stumpy tails which I was told was from being frost bitten.*[57]

Freighter, Farmer, Steamboat Captain

It may have been this experience with steam power that led Asahel in 1874 to his next venture as captain of the *Victoria*. Some claim that steamboat captains were usually men of "substance and probity."[58] Others characterize them as colourful adventuresome characters, gregarious and entertaining of their passengers. Asahel had honed his skills as a genial host of stopping houses and applied these in his new role of steamboat captain. In August 1874, he was assisted in entertaining passengers by a small black bear that dared to cross his path:

> QUEER ADVENTURE—*From the deck of the steamer Victoria, on the Upper Fraser, when near Alexandria, a few days ago, was discovered a black bear swimming across the river. The boat was put about, the bear headed off and lassoed from the guards. He was then hauled up and dispatched with an ax. The passengers pronounce bear steaks good eating.*[59]

> BEAR STEAKS
> *Rub bear steaks with sliced onion and spread with butter (generously). Sprinkle with salt and pepper. Broil in a hot oven turning once while cooking. Bear should be young and tender. Venison may be done in the same way.*[60]

Caroline was attracted by Asahel's easy-going fun-loving nature and his gregariousness and wealth—all characteristics her previous husband Joachim had. In addition, he was well connected, worldly, and had business experience from which she could benefit.

SISTERS REUNITED

CAROLINE COMMITTED THE SUMMER of 1874 to meeting sister Christine in New York and accompanying her to Yale. Christine did not speak English well, nor would she have the coaching that Caroline and Laura had during their cross-Atlantic journey. Christine arrived in New York on July 8 and Caroline had planned a stop of several days in New York. She had heard of the Museum of Art and the Natural History Museum that were new and ready to explore. And it would be perfect to explore with Christine the new department stores that everyone had been talking about. Macy's and Lord & Taylor department stores were turning New York into an enviable city for shopping. Caroline thoroughly enjoyed their time in New York before boarding the train that carried them across the United States to San Francisco. She felt like an experienced traveller as she guided Christine on her way through various train stops and connections across the country. They had several days in San Francisco that Caroline had to admit was beginning to feel like home. They visited all of her favourite places and on July 27, left on the *William Tabor* for Victoria. Caroline accompanied Christine to Yale and saw her onboard the stagecoach for Clinton, where Laura met her. Caroline stayed in Victoria for the remainder of the summer and pondered the options she had for her future. Should she marry again or remain a widow indefinitely?

In 1873, the British Columbia legislature passed an act that allowed married women to own real estate and transact business, free from any supervisory or controlling power of their husbands. The act had the potential to allow women greater legal and economic autonomy, but its interpretation by judges occurred within a conservative Victorian climate. At the same time, British Columbia granted municipal voting rights to property-owning women regardless of their marital status.[61] These changes sparked debate over women's role and status in society, but the judges who interpreted the law and many of the legislators who approved it could not imagine that a society could be stable and marriages "harmonious" if men were not head of the household. Most could not imagine equal partnerships with women in marriage. Women, however, including Indigenous women, did increasingly turn to the courts for settlement of claims from business dealings and within common-law relationships.[62]

Though there were not many newcomer women in British Columbia, they did increasingly take on visible social roles. This was true in 1860s Barkerville, where Emily Edwards Bowron and Florence Wilson helped found and regularly acted in the Cariboo Amateur Theatre productions. Mary Clunes organized the Miner's Ball and Concert to mark Queen Victoria's birthday[63] and others, such as Fanny Bendixen, Elizabeth Thurber, and Elizabeth Ord, were businesswomen, operating saloons, restaurants, boarding houses, and investing in mining ventures. Mrs. Gannon of Richfield sold and delivered milk.[64] In Victoria, some women were business owners and entrepreneurs. Upwardly aspiring and entrepreneurial class women, however, mainly limited their public participation to charity work in support of the Protestant Orphan Home, the library, schools, and hospital, and were active in the temperance movement.

With her friend Lizzie Munro in Victoria, Caroline began to follow the activities of the provincial legislature more closely. They talked about the ongoing struggle for suffrage and the property rights of women inside and outside of marriage. Caroline realized she had significant financial decisions to make. She trusted Asahel's guidance and plan to invest in properties in the San Francisco area. The proposal seemed almost perfect. She could be in San Francisco for the harshest parts of the year and then close to her sisters in the summer months while he captained the *Victoria* and they lived either in 150 Mile House or Soda Creek.

On September 18, 1874, Caroline married Asahel in Victoria. Their witnesses were Caroline's friend Lizzie Munro and W.G. Bowman, livery stable operator. Despite Asahel's promise of winters in San Francisco, it was not to be during their first winter together. They settled into 150 Mile House for one more winter that turned out to be a winter to remember.

Winters at 150 Mile House could be brutal, and the winter of 1874–75 was especially cold. While ranchers ranged large herds of cattle, if the snow was deep or there was extreme cold, they could not shelter them from prolonged killing temperatures. In late January of 1875, the temperature at Bates's was recorded at fifty-nine degrees below zero Fahrenheit, "colder than ever known before."[65] Asahel's herd sustained heavy losses, with 45 mules and 150 beef cattle succumbing to the extreme weather. The steamer *Victoria* sustained damage when late-season ice lifted it and carried it down the Fraser River. In addition, the spring floodwaters damaged about half of the 32,000 kilograms (70,000 pounds) of flour Asahel had stored at the steamboat landing in Soda Creek.[66]

In April, as the brutal cold lingered late into the spring, Caroline and Asahel escaped with Christine for a month in Victoria and San Francisco. Despite the cold, Caroline was delighted to be pregnant with the couple's first child. Exira (Ex) Sumner Bates was born August 24, 1875. Christine arrived at 150 Mile House to be with Caroline throughout September. Christine had been in the Cariboo for over a year, and she discussed with Caroline the attention she had been receiving from James Hamilton. He met with the approval of both Caroline and Laura, who believed they would make a good match. Caroline refused to spend another winter in the Cariboo so as soon as she felt able to travel with her new baby she set off for Victoria and San Francisco.

Caroline had another mission to accomplish in San Francisco for herself. She visited the recently opened Palace Hotel in the city. The *Daily British Colonist* had regularly reported on progress in the lead-up to the opening of the Palace Hotel in the fall of 1875. It was setting the standard for elegant Victorian living:

> *In less than a week the doors of the Palace Hotel will be thrown open to the public, and visitors will then have the opportunity of enjoying the comforts of the largest, best-appointed and most favorably-located caravansary on the face of the Globe.*[67]
>
> *The silverware for the Great Palace Hotel, at San Francisco cost $60,000, and among its features is quite a novelty in the shape of silver tea caddies, with four compartments for as many different kinds of tea, which will be set before the guests at the table, with scalding water at hand, that they may help themselves to the leaf and make their tea after the Chinese fashion.*[68]

The lower floor of the Palace contained offices and dining, breakfast, and reception rooms. The kitchen contained everything that could facilitate the speedy and artistic cooking of food. The sixth floor was the "aristocratic" storey and already had some rooms filled. The *Daily British Colonist* reported, "Many citizens of wealth and position have located in the Palace and have their meals served in their rooms." With elegant and tasteful finishes throughout, the paper noted that grand central court would be "as comfortable and enjoyable almost as was the Garden of Eden."[69] With these superlatives and grand detail, Caroline was most intrigued to investigate further. The Palace apartments consisted of a drawing room, one or two spacious bedrooms, a dressing room, a bath, and buzzers to summon servants.[70] Guest rooms could be joined together to create suites or to make large

When the Palace Hotel in San Francisco opened in 1875, it set the new standard for luxurious and genteel living. IMAGE KWDJN2/ALMAY

apartments for long-term residents. The parlour of each guest room featured a large bay window overlooking the street below.

The Palace Hotel had cost five million dollars to construct. William Ralston was president of the Bank of California and a promoter of business and progress in the city. The Bank of California financed the hotel, but the bank failed a few months before the hotel opened in 1875. Ralston was asked to resign, and within hours he drowned in an act of suicide. But the hotel was larger than those who financed it. It was the largest hotel in the western United States, with 755 guest rooms, and at 37 metres (120 feet) in height, it was the tallest building in San Francisco for over a decade.

The grandeur of the Palace Hotel far surpassed any hotel in Victoria at the time and Caroline was impressed. She began to think of a plan to live there one day—or at least it would be a great place to spend the winters. Asahel realized he had to put 150 Mile House behind him, and so by the autumn of 1875, he had leased the stopping house and post office to Welsh miner James Griffin.[71]

During their winter in San Francisco, Asahel looked for investment opportunities in the area, focusing on land and real estate investments in Oakland. He invested the money Caroline had acquired from Joachim's estate. Unfortunately, she lost control of her inheritance at this time because Asahel invested in the properties under his name and not hers.

For the first two years of her marriage, Caroline was immersed in building her small family and enjoying every moment with her children. When in California, they settled into a lavish home that Asahel had built, "cosily situated among the foothills lying between Temescal and Berkeley."[72] In later property disputes, the home was referred to as the "Claremont Estate." During winter they spent several months at the Palace Hotel in San Francisco, and they resided at the Temescal estate in the more favourable months. Asahel's son Otis was with them most of the time and the little family found much happiness in watching the new baby

PART TWO: CAROLINE LINDHARD BATES HARRISON

grow and develop. Their second daughter, Theodora Levina, was born February 25, 1877, in Oakland.

Theodora Levina was not a healthy baby and both parents were concerned. At the end of April, Asahel returned to Victoria on his own to prepare for taking charge of the *Victoria* again on the Soda Creek to Quesnel section of the Upper Fraser River. Asahel returned to San Francisco a month later and in early July, Caroline with their two daughters accompanied him back to British Columbia. They based themselves in Soda Creek that summer and anxiously awaited the arrival of sister Christine's first baby. Christine had married James Hamilton the previous year and now all three sisters were focused on their own growing families. Olive Daghmar was born on August 6, Christine's first daughter.

Caroline began to find that it was not easy to move between Soda Creek and San Francisco with three children sometimes accompanying her. The family returned to Oakland in mid-November of 1877. On December 26, baby Theodora Levina died.

FAMILY LOSS

CAROLINE AND ASAHEL ADORED their daughters and were deeply saddened by the death of Theodora Levina. She was ten months old when she died of a condition identified as cerebral anemia. Four months later, their first-born daughter Exira Sumner died from malarial fever on April 26, 1878. She was two years old. When their second child died, Caroline and Asahel purchased a family burial plot in Oakland's Mountain View Cemetery. They arranged for burial of both their daughters in the family plot before returning to Soda Creek for the summer.

For Caroline, the loss of her daughters was devastating. However, the loss of a baby or infant was much more common in the 1870s than today. In 1830, the mortality rate for children under age five in Canada was 333 deaths per 1,000 births. This meant that one-third of all children born in 1830 did not make it to their fifth birthday. Child mortality remained above 25 per cent throughout the nineteenth century.[73] By the mid-nineteenth century, attitudes toward children began to change. In the early part of the century, infant deaths were commonly accepted as a part of everyday life, a reflection of the natural order in which the strong outlived the weak. By the second half of the century children came to be viewed differently. They were seen as important to the future of the society and deserving of better protection. Many infant deaths became preventable and high infant death rates were no longer considered acceptable. Public officials were pressured to improve conditions that would prevent high child death rates. While attitudes began to change, families in all economic strata experienced frequent losses of their infants and young children.

Early in 1878, it was announced that Asahel had partnered with John Irving to purchase the steamer *Wilson G. Hunt* that would work coastal British Columbia. It arrived and began to operate semi-regular sailings between Victoria and New Westminster. It was chartered for special excursions and for hauling freight. Competition developed between it and the Hudson's Bay Company *Enterprise* that ran regular passenger trips on the Victoria to New Westminster route. Several times during the summer the two steamers raced between the cities. Usually, the *Enterprise* won and on October 12 it was only by five minutes.[74] Asahel soon divested himself of the *Wilson G. Hunt*, selling his share to Thomas Briggs.[75]

Caroline was consoled during the summer spent close to Christine and baby Olive, who became a replacement daughter for her. By the end of 1878, Asahel had sold 150 Mile House to Gavin Hamilton for a reported $35,000 and shed many of his other investments in British Columbia.[76] The stopping house included a well-developed farm and ranch running four hundred head of cattle, and an emerging town site with a blacksmith, telegraph, post office, store, and saloon. On November 11, Caroline and Asahel sailed on the steamer the *Alaska* from Victoria to San Francisco. It was a surprising and glorious send-off in Victoria when the tug pilot pulled alongside with the New Westminster Brass Band on board. They "serenaded the passengers, and as the steamship moved off encouraged them with several enlivening airs."[77]

As winter approached, Asahel conceded to Caroline's wishes and purchased a suite in the Palace Hotel. They settled in and Caroline was much happier during the winter months in the middle of

San Francisco, close to the social life that attracted her, rather than in more suburban Oakland.

On New Year's morning 1879, Asahel suddenly died of heart failure at his home in the Palace Hotel. His death announcement in the *Daily British Colonist* noted, "In every portion of the mainland his influence has been felt and his enterprises have generally been crowned with success . . . British Columbia can but ill afford to lose men of his stamp."[78] The *Ottawa Daily Citizen* described him as "one of the wealthiest stockraisers of British Columbia" who "had acquired great wealth during a twenty years' residence in the Pacific province, and although an American by birth, had become thoroughly identified with his adopted country."[79]

Within one year, Caroline's life had changed dramatically. She had lost all members of the small family that she held dearly and gave her life meaning. She had her home in California that she loved. But she was on her own once again, left to care for her stepson, Otis, who was now eleven years old.

PART TWO: CAROLINE LINDHARD BATES HARRISON

An ESTATE UNSETTLED

Asahel was fifty years old when he died, and he did not leave a will (intestate). He held extensive properties in British Columbia and California. Was dying without a will intentional or neglectful for a seemingly shrewd businessman? Perhaps death came too suddenly and silently for a man preoccupied with business and family events. Whatever the case, Caroline was left with a complex estate that would preoccupy her for the next decade and become her prime lesson in entrepreneurship.

In 1877 the British Columbia government, at the urging of Judge Begbie, had amended the Intestate Estates Act. Begbie had heard a recent case in which an Indigenous common-law wife had brought a case against her deceased common-law white husband's estate to recover wages for the years they had spent together. He recognized the need to provide for the women partners of the Indigenous–settler relationships and the offspring of these unions. The amended Intestate Estates Act provided allowances to common-law wives and children of $500 or 10 per cent of the total estate, whichever was larger.[80] The only people who had a claim on the estate were declared to be Caroline and Asahel's son, Otis, which suggests that his Indigenous wife Tlopelkey and daughter Ellie may have died some time earlier.

Shortly after Asahel died in 1879, a famous letter by Chief William of the Williams Lake Indian Band was published in the *Daily British*

Colonist. Chief William was a highly regarded and peaceful chief. He had travelled that year with other Indigenous leaders to a meeting at New Westminster for treaty talks with the government. He wrote:

> *I am an Indian Chief, and my people are threatened by starvation. The white men have taken all the land and all the fish. A vast country was ours. It is all gone. The noise of the threshing machine and the wagon has frightened the deer and the beaver. We have nothing to eat. We cannot live on the air, and we must die. My people are sick. My young men are angry.*
>
> *All the Indians from Canoe Creek to the headwaters of the Fraser say "William is an old woman. He sleeps and starves in silence."*
>
> *I am old and feeble, and my authority diminishes every day. I am sorely puzzled. I do not know what to say next week when the chiefs are assembled in council. A war with the white man will end in our destruction, but death in war is not so bad as death by starvation.*
>
> *The land on which my people lived for five hundred years was taken by a white man; he has piles of wheat and herds of cattle. We have nothing—not an acre. Another white man has enclosed the graves in which the ashes of our fathers rest, and we may live to see their bones turned over by his plough! Any white man can take three hundred and twenty acres of our land and the Indian dare not touch an acre.*
>
> *Her Majesty sent me a coat, two ploughs and some turnip seed. The coat will not keep away the hunger; the ploughs are idle, and the seed is useless because we have no land.*
>
> *All our people are willing to work because they know they must work like the white man or die. They work for the white man. Mr. Bates was a good friend. He would not have a white man if he could get an Indian. My young men can plough and mow and cut corn with a cradle.*

Now, what I want to say is this—THERE WILL BE TROUBLE, SURE.

The whites have taken all the salmon and all the land, and my people will not starve in peace. Good friends to the Indian say that "her Majesty loves her Indian subjects and will do justice." Justice is no use for a dead Indian.

They say, "Mr. Sproat is coming to give you land." We hear he is a very good man, but he has no horse. He was at Hope last June and he has not yet arrived here. Her Majesty ought to give him a horse and let justice come fast to the starving Indians.

Land, land, a little of our own land, that is all we ask from her Majesty. If we had the deer and the salmon, we could live by hunting and fishing. We have nothing now and here comes the cold and the snow. Maybe the white man thinks we can live on snow. We can make fires to make people warm— that is what we can do. Wood will burn. We are not stones.

William, Chief of the Williams Lake Indians (Williams Lake Indian Band)[81]

Chief William's letter drew several responses and discussion that followed in the *Daily British Colonist*. Indian Superintendent Israel Powell responded with concern about the inaction of the British Columbia government on Indigenous people's issues and stated that Asahel's land was within the traditional territory of the Williams Lake Band and was appropriate land for the Band to occupy. The *Daily Colonist* took a stand and wrote in an editorial:

Poor William and his people have long in the land of their forefathers been without a home to call their own, as the tract, originally for residence, pastoral purposes and burial ground, occupied as their headquarters, has for years been legally owned and highly improved by a farmer of the white race.[82]

In the same issue of the newspaper Archibald McKinlay addressed Chief William directly in a letter having an apologetic tone and admitting that the Indigenous people of Williams Lake had no land and that land needed to be purchased from white settlers. He called on James Lenihan or Israel Powell to do something to assure that starvation would not result.[83] A settler from Kamloops chimed in:

> I know these Indians of Williams Lake and their complaints are true to the letter. They have been swindled out of all their land; they have not an inch left and, what is worse, there is no land fit for cultivation left to give them.[84]

McKinlay wrote directly to Chief William, assuring him that he was working in his interests and attempting to regain his trust. He encouraged the authorities to purchase Asahel's land "at the end of Williams Lake and known as Sugar Cane." Since Asahel had died intestate, "[the land] will go cheap either at auction or otherwise."[85]

In January of 1880, Asahel's lands in British Columbia were listed for sale by the chief justice of the Supreme Court of British Columbia: The Sugar Cane Ranch, about 944 acres of which had been a Crown grant; Deep Creek Farm, about 1,880 acres; the Young pre-emption of 320 acres; the Meason Ranch of about 360 acres; and property known as the Carpenter Ranch of unstated acreage. Together the properties exceeded 1,416 hectares (3,500 acres).[86]

By March 1881, Israel Powell had arranged purchase of these lands on behalf of the Government of Canada.[87] There was an initial payment of $5,000 to the A.S. Bates estate and a final settlement and payment of $1,345 to the estate in 1886.[88] The final payment was for the purchase of 1,464 acres for the Xat'sull (Soda Creek) Band that was agreed to in 1884.[89]

In addition to investments and land holdings in British Columbia, Asahel held mining properties in the Arivapai mining district, Pima County, Arizona Territory. These investments included the whole of the Oakland Mine and a quarter interest in six additional mines and two mill sites. Like his other properties, a year after his death the Arizona mining properties went to public auction.[90] The settling of his estate dragged on.

For anyone counting on wealth from California real estate, 1879 was disappointing. The *Daily British Colonist* reported on "California's Dullness," as the economic downturn of 1879–80 was termed. While Asahel's estate was unsettled, Caroline had to wait out the dullness and hope that more buoyant economic times would return soon.

> *"Dull times" seem to have settled down like a pall on every interest in California. The depression is universal. Merchandise, real estate, mining stocks, manufacturing and farming, are all in a desperate condition and serious misgivings as to the near future of San Francisco are freely expressed. In May only 158 sales in real estate were made in that city of the unusually small value of $626,677. Lots at $1,500 to $2,000, and houses and lots at $4,000 to $6,000 were the most inquired for.*[91]

The dull times that California experienced extended to British Columbia, and the *Daily British Colonist* commented that "the world is passing through a season of unprecedented dullness ... When all the rest of the world is dull, how can British Columbia hope to be prosperous?"[92] British Columbia held onto the hope that the nearly two hundred kilometres (125 miles) of transcontinental railway construction promised for that summer in the province would provide the economic stimulus needed.

Caroline needed time to recover from the many deaths in her family that had left her shattered. Her father had also recently died in Denmark, and she needed time away. She left her younger brother, William Laurist Lindhard, who was now resident in California, in charge of any urgent matters and returned for several months to her family home in Denmark.

When Josiah Beedy died in January of 1880, Caroline could not remain in San Francisco. She and Otis travelled together to Stanley to be with Laura. They sailed on the *Dakota* to Victoria from San Francisco and continued on the *Enterprise* to New Westminster in the company of Caroline's old friend G.B. Wright. Travel to Stanley in the midst of winter was an adventure. The weather was extremely cold with plenty of snow and the adjustment to the harsh conditions was extremely demanding. When Caroline returned to San Francisco a few months later, Christine and her children Olive and George accompanied her, and Christine awaited the arrival of her third child during the summer of 1880 in Oakland. In November, when Laura and her children arrived in Oakland, all three sisters were together again.

In September of 1880, the A.S. Bates estate went into probate in California.[93] While his financial affairs in British Columbia were unsettled, related court cases in California began. In November of 1881, Joseph Foster Hixon,[94] who had been a trader residing at 150 Mile House at the same time as Asahel, opened a suit in California Superior Court against Otis Bates to recover $2,295 "for services rendered in hunting up testimony in a contest" between Caroline and Otis as heirs to the A.S. Bates estate. While this case brought Caroline into the proceedings, the decision made in December that year dismissed the action against her and made Otis alone responsible for the $2,550 owing to Hixon.

At the same time, the first recorded sale of property by Caroline was described as a lot on the "northeast corner of Pagoda Place and Ross Street" in Alameda County, which she sold for five dollars.[95] The next spring she sold several lots in the Vernon Park area of Oakland for fifteen thousand dollars. The next year she invested $10,500 in a lot at the corner of Pinkney Place and Hinckley Street in San Francisco.[96] She was on her way as a property investor!

By the spring of 1882 Caroline realized she had to fight for what was her share of the A.S. Bates estate and thus began a series of court cases. She brought a suit against Otis for partition of lands in Oakland County.[97] This was granted in the fall, and she was able to sell additional Oakland County lands. Later she came to regard the 1882 decision as unfair and in May of 1883 she brought a suit against Otis, "to have the Superior Court ascertain the extent and value of her separate estate" now claimed as part of the A.S. Bates estate.[98] As part of this court proceeding, she revealed that she had brought $40,000 from the estate of her first husband and given it to Asahel to invest in real estate in Oakland County and that amount should not be considered part of the estate in 1880. She asked for a new trial, her case being that,

> *After the husband's death [she] besides being unacquainted with her husband's investments, was prostrated with grief, and unable properly to instruct her counsel, who, having to make the best of her imperfect instructions, brought this action for partition in her name, assuming the property left by the husband was common property of the widow and the heir.*[99]

She argued that additional evidence and affidavits from British Columbia that had not been considered earlier were now available and they proved that she had inherited a fortune from her first husband that was rolled into the estate. Her request for a new trial was denied and she took the case to California Supreme Court. It was 1886 before the court heard her case and her request for a new trial was denied.

By this time Charles Henry Harrison, a successful businessman and shareholder in the Sausalito Land and Ferry Company, was part of Caroline's life. He had been widowed over five years and they quickly became steady companions. He advised her on the business and family challenges she faced. He had no children from his marriage, and he delighted in getting to know Otis and the nieces and nephews that frequently stayed with Caroline. Twenty-seven years her senior, she trusted his expertise and advice on financial and business matters.

An Estate Unsettled

Harrison was a professional bay pilot and skipper of the ferry *Princess* that carried people across the bay from San Francisco to Sausalito. Otis was a restless youth and Harrison encouraged him to go to sea. It was not unusual for fourteen-year-old boys to go to sea as a way of gaining work experience and falling into the disciplinary hands of the ship's captain. Otis set off for Australia and for the next seven years had no contact with Caroline. The court cases continued, however, and because Otis was a minor during this time, the courts had to choose a guardian for him. In 1883, it was announced that Judge A.M. Rosborough had been appointed his guardian.[100] When Caroline didn't hear from Otis for seven years, she and others began to assume he was dead.

While Asahel's estate remained unsettled and Caroline continued to press her case in the courts, she married Charles Henry Harrison on September 7, 1883. It was a quiet ceremony in the suite of Mrs. and Mr. Alban Nelson Towne at the Palace Hotel.[101] Following the ceremony Caroline and Harrison travelled to Lake Tahoe and British Columbia. Their immediate plan was to remain resident at the Palace Hotel. Harrison was described as "an English gentleman" who had been a long time captain of the San Francisco Yacht Club and was known by the title of Commodore.[102] He was fifty-eight years old, and Caroline was thirty-one.

The post-wedding plans were altered when Christine's husband, James Hamilton, died on October 3, 1883. Caroline and Charles, along with Laura and her children, sailed to Victoria to be with Christine. On their return to San Francisco in mid-October, they all checked in to the El Monte Hotel, Sausalito, for rest and recuperation. The stable core of the family now shifted to Caroline and Charles. By the end of the year, Christine and her children were resident in Oakland, close to Laura and her children. Caroline and Charles welcomed having eight nieces and nephews nearby that they could dote on and who would in exchange enliven their lives and tie them closely to the social scene of Sausalito.

PART TWO: CAROLINE LINDHARD BATES HARRISON

SOCIAL PACESETTERS *of* SAUSALITO

C AROLINE RELISHED THE SOCIAL and physical climate of San Francisco. The friends she enjoyed in British Columbia frequently travelled to San Francisco and some of the mothers and children resided in the area part time. She could count among her friends some of the well-known British Columbia families—the Rithets, the Wrights, the Munroes, and the Dunsmuirs. Thirty years after the California gold rush, the San Francisco population was sorting itself into the property-owning established wealthier class and the not so wealthy newcomers.

The *Elite Directory for San Francisco and Oakland*, published for the first time in 1879, recognized and celebrated the emerging elite society in the city. The introduction to the book conveyed the tone of the times in San Francisco society:

> *The lines that divide its different classes are not yet distinctly drawn. The different sections overlap at the edges ... It is changing rapidly. The lines are year by year more tightly drawn ... It has been remarked by eastern visitors that in no hotel in the country, excepting perhaps those of the fashionable watering places, can there be daily seen so well dressed and self-possessed an assemblage of people as gathers every evening in the dining-room of the Palace.*[103]

Permanent guests listed at the Palace Hotel and published in *The Elite Directory* in 1879 were "Mr. and Mrs. S. Bates." In the United States, Asahel Sumner Bates usually used Sumner Bates as his name. Caroline and Sumner had achieved recognition as part of San Francisco's elite class.

The Elite Directory gave instructions to the elite and aspiring elite in San Francisco and Oakland through a large section on etiquette that included topics such as "Introductions," "Visiting and Visiting Cards for Ladies," "Dinners and Dining Out," and "Theatre Etiquette." This directory was followed in 1884 by *The Social Manual of San Francisco and Oakland*. The manual included the usual listings of elite citizens, clubs, and their members and a section entitled "Rules of Good Breeding" that replaced the section on etiquette. The topics covered in the "Rules" section included "Riding and Driving," "The Toothpick," "Smart Sayings," "How to Please," "In the Carriage," and "Etiquette in Church."

Caroline found both *The Elite Directory* and *The Social Manual* to be important guidebooks in determining what mattered in the Oakland and San Francisco societies. *The Elite Directory* was explicit in describing the society founded in the pioneer frontier gold-rush era and having earlier Spanish and Indigenous roots. In the 1840s, "The city was full of bright, intellectual, energetic people. Most of them were young, hopeful and romantic. Their social intercourse had the polish of older communities, mingled with the dash and freedom of the frontier."[104]

During the "second epoch" of social history in San Francisco, "there lived several ladies of superior accomplishments who would have adorned the society of any city in the world . . . Manners were becoming more formal, though they still had a freedom not usual in eastern cities." *The Elite Directory* described the many new neighbourhoods, the wealth being accumulated by some families, the splendid homes being built, and "every part of the city has a tinge of gentility." It cautioned, "Fashion should never aim to exist for itself alone, and it always has at hand the means of uniting polite social intercourse with mutual improvement and the amelioration of the ills that afflict humanity."[105] Both books were implicitly directed at women and provided explicit instruction for the elite and aspiring elite on the essential practices for a cultured and civilized society in San Francisco.

Caroline's marriage to Charles assured her a secure position among the nouveau riche of the San Francisco area. Charles was born June 1, 1825, in Manchester, England. He arrived in California at age twenty-four in 1849 and became a citizen of the United States in 1853. For twenty years he lived in San Francisco, where he married Alithea Rose and worked as a bay pilot, merchant, and ferry skipper. In 1868, he and Alithea became one of the founding families of Sausalito when a consortium of nineteen San Francisco businessmen pooled resources to buy 471 hectares (1,164 acres) of the Rancho Sausalito and create a townsite. He was an original investor and president of the Sausalito Land and Ferry Company. Charles and Alithea constructed a modest cottage in Sausalito that they named Hazel Mount. He became general manager of the first ferry line between Sausalito and San Francisco. He sold this business in 1875 to North Pacific Coast Railroad Company. In the same year, his wife Alithea Rose died.

In the 1880s, Harrison became commodore of the San Francisco Yacht Club, whose anchorage and clubhouse were in Sausalito. Newspaper reports on his marriage with Caroline implied he married a "wealthy widow" whose wealth exceeded his. However, Harrison had slowly accumulated considerable wealth from his various business ventures. In the 1870 US Census he reported holding $164,000 in real estate and personal wealth of $5,250. While commodore of the Yacht Club, he enjoyed his own yacht, the *Frolic,* that he regularly took into races. He and Caroline enjoyed entertaining friends on the *Frolic* on weekend outings in the Bay area.

Harrison was not unknown in British Columbia. He made several trips to the province, including one in early 1883, prior to marrying Caroline, and several later in the year to Victoria. Caroline

Charles Harrison, as commodore of the San Francisco Yacht Club, and Caroline enjoyed leading club outings and sailing with friends.

IMAGE 1980.84C COURTESY OF THE SAUSALITO HISTORICAL SOCIETY

and Commodore Harrison attended the opening of the Legislative Assembly in December of 1883 before accompanying Christine and children back to San Francisco.

Caroline and Charles joined the trend in the 1880s among the San Francisco wealthy to display their wealth by building large, splendid homes. They planned to replace Hazel Mount Cottage with a large home in Sausalito. While it was being built, they left in July 1885 for more than a year of travel in the eastern United States, England, and Europe to gather ideas, furniture, and adornments for their new home. The house was completed at 86 San Carlos Avenue in 1889, described as an

> *elegant residence, commanding a fine view of the bay. It is furnished with the result of the Commodore's recent European trip, and contains many choice specimens of art and bric-a-brac, some of it being what was purchased at the sale of the Tuileries collection, being marked with the Napoleonic "N." The name of the new home was Hazel Mount.*[106]

PART TWO: CAROLINE LINDHARD BATES HARRISON

Completed in 1889, Hazel Mount hosted many social events in Sausalito and was home for nieces and nephews over several decades.

IMAGE 1980.91 COURTESY OF THE SAUSALITO HISTORICAL SOCIETY

Hazel Mount became their year-round home in the 1890s "away from the dust and fogs of the metropolis" of San Francisco, although for a number of years the couple continued to spend winters at the Palace Hotel. The large home became a base for their extended family. Many nieces and nephews lived with their aunt Caroline while they attended school and post-secondary education. She oversaw their "proper" introduction to San Francisco and Sausalito societies and assisted in finding suitable marriageable partners. Laura's and Christine's children became known as the nieces and nephews of Commodore and Caroline Harrison and tied Caroline closely to the social scene of Sausalito.

Social Pacesetters of Sausalito

Caroline and Charles revelled in the social swirl of life in San Francisco and Sausalito. In San Francisco, Caroline was part of the Grand Hotel Club, a group of women who organized dances by invitation at the Grand Hotel.[107] She actively sponsored dances and social events among the Sausalito young people and assisted with debutante balls and special social events of the community.

The Harrisons were highly visible in Sausalito's social scene. Their activities were regularly reported on in the local newspaper:

> *Commodore and Mrs. Harrison make life enjoyable for themselves and their friends in their elegant home on the hill, far above anyone else. They entertain in the way of yachting and driving parties and quiet little dinners, that are said to be revelations in the art of cookery. It is said on the quiet that the genial Commodore is always pleased when he can mix a half dozen cocktails for his friends and serve them in the delicate glasses once the property of Napolean.*[108]

Other social events on the Harrison's yacht, the *Frolic*, registered in the social columns of the newspaper:

> *A jolly crowd sailed from the San Francisco Yacht Club's wharf at Sausalito Tuesday afternoon of last week on board the yacht Frolic, owned by Commodore C.H. Harrison with the genial Commodore himself at the wheel. Party: Mrs. Wm Hamilton, Mrs. Wm. Keeley, Mrs. John Jackson Jr., Mr. and Mrs. Graves of New York, Misses Kittridge and Barnett, Mr. Sherwood, Mr. Biethen, Dr. and Mrs. Macdonald. In less than three hours the Frolic had touched Fort Point, circled Yerba Buena, Alcatraz and Angel Islands.*[109]

Caroline enjoyed some of her happiest years with Charles H. Harrison.
IMAGE 1980.86H COURTESY OF THE SAUSALITO HISTORICAL SOCIETY

A STEPSON'S RETURN

IT WAS SENSATIONAL NEWS in November 1888 when Otis Bates, at age twenty-one and no longer a minor, returned to San Francisco to claim his inheritance. Caroline and Charles Harrison were crafting a reputation as part of the San Francisco and Sausalito elite and had recently returned from an "elegant and leisurely trip of a year's duration in Europe." So, the "family dispute" made tantalizing headline news.

The *San Francisco Examiner*, Victoria's *Daily British Colonist*, and newspapers in Washington State, Arizona, and Kansas carried versions of the story with exaggerated and embellished details. The newspapers tended to construct a "schadenfreude" account for their readers. A wealthy society couple were now facing lawsuits from a presumed-dead stepson that could destroy their wealth and social status. The newspapers offered headings and subheadings, such as, "An Unexpected Heir, Young Otis Bates' Strange Return After Many Years, After a Fortune, The Trouble he is Causing 'Commodore' Harrison and Others." They wrote enticing bylines and opening accounts for what they hoped would be a long saga that would assure continuing newspaper sales. The newspaper article headlined above commented: "The young man seems to have so clean a claim to dispossess the Commodore and Mrs. Harrison out of a big fortune which has been hitherto known as theirs."[110] The reality was considerably different.

Shortly after Asahel died, Caroline's court struggles had begun. The first case brought to court was by J.F. Hixon against Caroline and Otis for payment for services rendered. Since the services were for Otis, Caroline escaped any financial consequence of that case. Being a minor, Otis had a court-appointed guardian who oversaw financial affairs related to transactions impacting his inheritance.

When Asahel's estate went to probate in California, Caroline went to court to ask for a partition of lands in Oakland County. In 1883, the value of lands in Oakland City and Township held in the estate of A.S. Bates was $11,500. This ranked him among the wealthy landowners. In 1885, Otis was listed as holding lands valued at $5,850 and Caroline's holdings were valued at $5,000.[111] The partition of lands enabled both Caroline and Otis to sell some of the holdings. Caroline sold some properties and bought others.

When Otis arrived at the Palace Hotel in the autumn of 1888, he was described as "tall and sunburned and wore a broad white sombrero." During his seven-year absence he had been a sailor and a cowboy, and a "wanderer . . . visiting most parts of the globe."[112] It's unknown how much his father's estate was worth or how much Otis had already received from it. In sensationalizing the story, newspaper reports estimated the value at between $90,000 and $200,000, but Caroline claimed it was much less. The dispute between Caroline and Otis on his return concerned "the valuable Claremont estate near Oakland." A settlement was reached, and the newspaper stories subsided after reporting that Caroline paid Otis three thousand dollars.[113]

Asahel's dying without a will had caused Caroline and Otis considerable losses. There were lawyer and court costs, and the properties in Arizona and British Columbia were handled by public trustees at public auction, which meant they usually sold at lower than market value. The financial and business lessons had an impact on Caroline.

Now an adult, Otis made his way independently. He served as a private in Company G Infantry during the Spanish–American War of 1898, a ten-week war carried out in both the Caribbean and Pacific.[114]

A Stepson's Return

The brief war resulted in the United States temporarily gaining control of Cuba and gaining a longer lasting control over Puerto Rico, Guam, and the Philippines. Otis continued service in the Philippines after the war and remained there until 1900.

Otis returned to Oakland, lived there for several years, and worked as a night watchman. He died March 13, 1904, at age thirty-seven.[115] The recorded cause of death was cerebral embolism. Despite their differences, Caroline had kept in touch with Otis. When she learned of his death, she extended the large family tent to include him and arranged his burial near his father in the Bates/Beedy family plot in Oakland's Mountain View Cemetery.

The FAMILY BRANCHES

FINALLY, BY THE 1890S, Caroline had settled Asahel's estate with Otis, the court cases were behind her, and she and Charles settled into their large new home, Hazel Mount, in Sausalito. Laura continued to live in distant Stanley, British Columbia, where she operated the provision store and post office. Her two oldest sons, Asa and Louis, and at times Winslow, frequently worked with her. Christine lived near Caroline, in Oakland, with her three daughters. Hazel Mount provided Caroline and Charles with space to accommodate many of their nieces and nephews, and this they did.

Caroline provided a home for Laura's daughter Josephine Beedy from 1893 to 1897, while she studied at Stanford University, and for Josephine's brother Louis while he studied law at Stanford from 1894 to 1898. Caroline had a very close bond with Christine's daughter Olive, who lived most of her life with the Harrisons. Olive continued to live with her aunt Caroline after Christine moved with her two younger daughters to Chicago in 1892. Laura's son Winslow began living with Caroline in 1898 when he attended Stanford for one year and continued to live with her almost constantly until he married, developing a close bond that led to naming his first child Caroline. Laura's youngest son, Josiah, was about fourteen when he first ventured south on his own to live with his aunt Caroline.

In addition to Laura's and Christine's children, Caroline had her brother William's daughter, Helen Lindhard, live with her for several years after the child's mother died in 1896. In 1900, Christine's two younger daughters, Minerva and Linda, moved to Sausalito and lived with Caroline. As a result, the house was constantly abuzz with young people.

While Caroline provided a home for the many nieces and nephews, she also took a parental interest in them, guiding their future and setting expectations for their careers and conduct. She employed a helper, as well as a Chinese cook, for many years, and later a maid. As matron of her large home and part of the social set in Sausalito, she opened doors and facilitated social connections for her nieces and nephews. In exchange, she expected upstanding behaviour and academic achievement. They did not disappoint. Rather, the Commodore and Mrs. Harrison's nieces and nephews often met with praise and recognition among Sausalito citizens. Their names appeared regularly in the society column of the *Sausalito News*.

Caroline was wealthy and frugal. She enjoyed fine expensive things but had also witnessed how money could be easily lost or squandered. She expected the children to pay their way. She regularly received money from Laura when Laura's children lived with her. One nephew recalled how when living with Caroline, "He was sent to school with a lunch of left-overs and dry bread, which so mortified him that he chose to dine alone." It would likely have been the thrifty cooks that Caroline employed and not she herself who prepared lunches, but thrift and frugality were central values.

Caroline was particularly protective and supportive of her nieces. She was especially bonded with Olive Hamilton and served as a surrogate mother in Christine's absence. Olive and her cousin Josephine helped host teas and receptions, and they were frequently guests at Sausalito's parties and dances. The question of women's right to vote first surfaced in California in 1871, when Ellen Van Valkenburg sued the Santa Cruz County Clerk for refusing to include her name in the county's Register of Voters. At the 1879 Constitutional Convention in the state, there were hopes that the state constitution might be changed to permit women to vote. However, that didn't happen, and a vote held during the 1896 general election also failed.

Despite these setbacks, the women of California were undefeated in their efforts and continued to organize, creating women's suffrage clubs throughout the state. In October 1896, Susan B. Anthony and Kate Tupper-Galpin of Los Angeles spoke to a crowd gathered in the Sausalito Hall on the question of woman's suffrage. Caroline and Charles attended, and Charles was elected chairman of a temporary organization formed at the end of the meeting. The plan was to call another meeting in the near future to form a permanent organization. It's unclear if the permanent organization ever formed, since there were no further newspaper reports on the meeting's outcome.

In 1901, the Sausalito Women's Club formed under the name Las Amigas and Caroline and Charles were directly involved. The club met and held events at the San Francisco Yacht Club in Sausalito. Three years later they initiated the "Women's Exchange" that opened in rooms of Hazel Mount Cottage two afternoons each week. The exchange offered for sale items from sixteen consignors: "homemade bread, pies, cakes, pickles, jams, candy, plum pudding, flowers, kitchen aprons and fancy work of every description ... The Exchange hopes to branch out in every direction, thus reaching all classes ... The main thing is to encourage and help the needy."[116]

Caroline and Charles were involved in many activities that contributed to the growth and prosperity of the community. Charles focused on town politics and was elected a town trustee. He also derived great pride from his nieces and nephews. They shared his interest in sports and sailing. He developed a particular bond with Josiah Beedy, who was with him to celebrate the opening of the new San Francisco Yacht Club in Sausalito in 1899.[117] Josiah's genial nature was similar to Charles's, and he had talent that Harrison admired. When Constance Borrowe gave a baby party and everyone came dressed in a baby costume, Josiah was described as "by far the funniest man in the room."[118] On March 14, 1900, when Josiah turned twenty-one, Charles flew the flag atop Hazel Mount in his honour.

As the turn of the century approached, Charles's health began to fail, and true to the astute business person he was, he and Caroline devised a plan for disposing of the estate they had built together. He transferred all properties over into Caroline's name. As a result, when a property issue that had been simmering in Sausalito for several years came to a head, it was Caroline versus the town that went to court. The issue concerned a discrepancy between the official town map that had laid out roadways sixty feet wide but had been reduced to thirty feet wide as survey stakes were lost or removed and people built their homes according to where they believed their properties to be, rather than conforming to the official map. The revised town map drawn up in 1895 affected the Harrison property and the couple protested. The dispute was over a strip of land situated along the east side of San Carlos Avenue. Others in the town had similar disputes with the town and the outcome of the case had implications for many. The case went to Superior Court in February of 1902 and the decision in April was made in Caroline's favour.

The 1890s were a happy, busy time for Caroline, but health issues that arose for her and Charles signalled it was time to slow life's pace. Harrison had sold the *Frolic* in the early part of the decade, and they focused their business dealings on acquiring building lots in San Francisco. On June 18, 1902, Charles succumbed to heart issues at his home in Sausalito. He was seventy-seven years old. Caroline had had almost twenty years as his partner, and she was bereft. At the age of fifty, she was widowed for the third time. She had enjoyed her happiest years with Harrison. He had totally adored her, and they both found immense pleasure in entertaining friends on their yacht and in their beautiful Sausalito home, and enjoying the company of their many nieces and nephews.

PART TWO: CAROLINE LINDHARD BATES HARRISON

Tributes for Charles spoke to the person he was:

> *The Commodore was a man of genial disposition; fond of company, he enjoyed the association of his friends. His home life was ideal. There still remained much of that old-fashioned courtesy, that unceremonial sociability, that dignified and kind hospitality. . . . He treated all alike if he thought them deserving and drew no hard line along the ascents of worldly prosperity above which his friends were chosen . . . his spirit was democratic and he recognized the humble as readily as the great and resented that which he did not approve in the great as readily as in the humble . . . He was possessed of exceptional physical and mental force which he retained until overtaken by the illness causing his death.*[119]

FORWARD *on* HER OWN

A FUNERAL SERVICE WAS HELD for Charles Henry Harrison at Christ Church in Sausalito and burial was in the Bates/Beedy family plot of Oakland's Mountain View Cemetery. Caroline grieved and turned inward to focus on her home and family. She was now in charge of the family business, and she continued each year to buy and sell lots and properties in San Francisco. Her nieces and nephews didn't allow her much time to withdraw from the Sausalito social scene. In the next year, 1903, the first of Caroline's nieces and nephews married, on June 24: Laura's son Louis to Mabel Elizabeth Hosmer of Palo Alto.

Every wedding involved a lengthy round of social events that Caroline enjoyed. There was first an engagement party, then several teas and receptions hosted by friends. Finally, there was the wedding itself. Caroline hosted many of these events for family members and friends.

In 1904, Hazel Mount was the setting for a party honouring Charlotte Henley of Berkeley and Lawrence Sutton Ainsworth on their approaching wedding. The party was hosted by Caroline and her niece Linda Hamilton and was an occasion for Linda to announce her engagement to Charles Albert Wright, Lawrence's cousin. "The Harrison home was beautiful with cut flowers and greens, and its gracious mistress, Mrs. Harrison, with whom Miss Hamilton resides, assisted her niece in receiving her guests with the charming cordiality that has made her home famous for its hospitality."[120]

When Caroline wasn't hosting parties and teas, she was attending them. A 1907 society report described the tone and atmosphere:

> *A very beautiful tea was given in Sausalito on Wednesday afternoon by Mrs. J.E. Shoobert, complimentary to her daughters Mrs. Robin Dunsmuir of Victoria B.C., and Mrs. Frederick Bancroft of New York. Her attractive cottage was decorated with beautiful flowers and on the veranda and through the grounds the guests in light summer gowns enjoyed their refreshments. Among the guests were Mrs. Rodman Pell, Mrs. Robert Greer, Mrs. Leonard Chenery, Mrs. Watkins, Mrs. Robbins, Mrs. Bonny, Mrs. Wheeler, Miss Helen Wheeler, Mrs. C.H. Harrison, Mrs. Godley, Mrs. Cantwell, Mrs. William Merry, Mrs. Bryant and a number of army people from the posts around the bay.*[121]

In addition to her social obligations, Caroline now had control of a portfolio of properties she and Charles held as investments. Records show that she bought holdings, added to them, and sold.[122] She was not averse to taking risks in her investments. She mortgaged properties when she needed to. In 1895, jointly with Charles, she took out a loan from California Title Insurance and Trust Company for $76,000, using her Pinkney Place property as security.[123]

Caroline was exceedingly busy with family events in 1905. In February, Louis and Mabel Hosmer Beedy's daughter Mary Elizabeth was born, the first child of the next generation and Laura's first grandchild. In April, Laura's son Winslow married his cousin Olive in Sausalito; the wedding was "one of the most important social events in the resort this spring."[124] In May, Caroline's niece Linda Hamilton married Charles Wright, the son of Gustavus Blinn and Julie Sutton Wright, some of Caroline's best friends from

British Columbia days. In October, Laura's youngest son Josiah married Elizabeth Callender, daughter of a well-connected New York family. In the same year, Asa decided to leave his position as manager for S.A. Rogers in Barkerville and join the rest of the family in California.

Asa and his mother Laura arrived in November for an extended stay with Caroline and this led to a large family reunion at Hazel Mount for Christmas. Caroline and Laura were together again and were now with all of Laura's children, Christine's children, new spouses, and the first grandchild. The family reunion marked a transition to the next generation with four of the young cousins married and beginning to establish their careers and families. Laura was enjoying retirement and some international travel with Asa. Caroline was ready to enjoy her large extended family, but fate had other plans in store.

The celebratory days of 1905 took a devastating turn for Caroline the next year. In the early morning of April 18, 1906, an earthquake that registered 7.9 struck San Francisco, leaving over 200,000 people homeless, and as many as three thousand dead:

> *The terrible earthquake which visited us on the morning of April 18th resulted in reducing the greater part of San Francisco to ashes—fires started simultaneously in all parts of the city, caused by the breaking of electric wires and various other causes due to the wrenching of buildings.*
>
> *It is generally estimated that the San Francisco fire is the greatest conflagration known to history, but the western spirit will soon clear away the ruins, and a greater, finer, more beautiful city will rise from the ashes.*[125]

The homes of Sausalito had been badly shaken, and few chimneys were left standing, but families were safe. The community sprang into action, setting up an emergency hospital, public kitchens, and spaces to accommodate the refugees, mostly women and small children.

PART TWO: CAROLINE LINDHARD BATES HARRISON

The fires in San Francisco burned for days and Caroline and family watched from the balcony of Hazel Mount.

Caroline's home was not unscathed, and the *Sausalito News* reported,

> "Hazel Mount," the beautiful home of Mrs. C.H. Harrison perhaps suffered more serious loss than any other, for, in addition to the plastered wall being badly cracked, the upsetting of a tank resulted in serious damage by water. It is estimated that five thousand dollars is the extent of the Harrison loss.[126]

Less than three months later, Caroline was overjoyed when her favourite niece, Olive Hamilton Beedy, gave birth on July 1, to a daughter that Olive and Winslow named Caroline. The joy was muted when Olive remained in hospital and a deep sadness descended when she died on August 17. Olive had a special place in Caroline's heart and her death was almost too much for Caroline to bear. Olive's sister Linda had given birth to a daughter on July 30, and Linda took on mothering of both babies. Caroline provided a home for baby Caroline who along with her father, Winslow Beedy, lived at Hazel Mount for most of the next decade.

The new baby and new responsibilities injected new energy into Caroline. San Francisco had to be rebuilt and there was a dire need for housing. Before the end of the year, Caroline had contracted to build a three-storey frame building on Chestnut Street. At the beginning of 1907 she started construction of a larger more expensive structure on Hinckley Alley. The following year she had a two-storey brick building built on Kearny Street, downtown.[127]

While Caroline didn't hesitate to jump into the re-building of downtown San Francisco, family events continued to unfold. Her mother, Josephine Margrethe, died in 1909 in Denmark. Her family at Hazel Mount focused on raising baby Caroline. Other family members who lived with her and assisted were her sister Laura, Laura's children Asa, Josephine, and Winslow, and niece Minerva Hamilton. Suddenly, on May 30, 1910, Laura died of a heart attack.

Caroline grieved another loss, this time that of her older sister who had been with her throughout her life. She hearkened back to forty years earlier when together they had ventured to Van Winkle. Much had unfolded since, but the forty years had been good for her and Laura. Despite the different decisions they made in life, they remained close and supportive of each other. Laura's children were like her own. She adored them, admired their accomplishments, and now relied on their assistance and advice. Caroline was now on her own, the family elder among the many nieces and nephews and their young families. She found sustenance among her community of friends and continued to host social teas with the help of her nieces. She opened the doors of Hazel Mount to host a benefit lecture for the Arbor Society—a talk on Leo Tolstoy.

Caroline encouraged her nieces to be supportive of women's suffrage, although she had never been an open activist for change. In 1911, the passing of Proposition 4 in California amended the state constitution to give women the right to vote in state elections. It had been a long struggle and was narrowly approved by 50.7 per cent of the voters. Marin County where Caroline lived did not support expanding the franchise to women. The county clerk therefore had to design a creative strategy that would reach Sausalito women and have them register to vote. The clerk appointed "a number of well-known women registration clerks" and found women to host "registration teas," a strategy described as "an original, high class plan" that could make Sausalito women feel once again that they were powerful community leaders. Consequently, Mrs. C.M. Gunn hosted a tea and invited twenty-five friends. Josephine Beedy and Fannie Shoobert acted as registration deputies and were in a room adjacent to the tea ready to register the women as voters. All twenty-five friends who attended the tea registered, including Caroline.[128]

PART TWO: CAROLINE LINDHARD BATES HARRISON

After her sister Laura's sudden death, Caroline began to think of her own estate and the conversations she had with Charles when he first became seriously ill. It was time to pass her assets on to the next generation. She had three empty lots in Sausalito that she gift-deeded, one each to Louis and Josiah Beedy and Linda Hamilton Wright. In 1912, she drew up her will naming Asa and Winslow Beedy as executors. She left something for all her nieces and nephews and for Charles Harrison's nephew and nieces living in England.

Caroline died on February 7, 1913, in Sausalito. Death notices indicated she had been ill for some time. "The Harrison home immediately became the center of social and charitable association. She was loved and respected by everyone who knew her and the regrets at her death are heartfelt and general." She was also described as "one of our most highly esteemed and pioneer charitable women ... She belonged to the Civic League of San Francisco, the Women's Auxiliary to the California Pioneers and was always active in everything for the betterment of the community."[129]

Caroline's estate was large and complex. She left lifetime annuities for Laura's daughter Josephine Beedy and for two of Charles Harrison's nieces in England. This meant that the estate residues established a family trust that paid annual amounts to the three nieces until their deaths. Fortunately, the executors could call on brother Louis Beedy, who was a practising San Francisco attorney to handle the legal matters. The estate was valued initially in the range of $225,000, approximately a value of six million in today's dollars. Its value changed over the years and the trust finally closed in 1960 after the death of Caroline's nieces. The remainder on closure of the estate trust was willed to her great-niece, Caroline Beedy, Winslow and Olive's daughter.

Caroline did something in her life. She helped her family and her community. She was rich and famous and happy before she died.

Forward on Her Own

OPPOSITE—Christine Lindhard Hamilton (1850–1922).
IMAGE KOR1097 COURTESY STATE ARCHIVES OF FLORIDA.
DETAIL FROM ORIGINAL

Part Three

CHRISTINE LINDHARD HAMILTON

CHRISTINE LINDHARD TURNED TWENTY-FOUR in 1874. Like her older sister Laura four years before, she was unmarried, finding few opportunities in Copenhagen, and turning that crucial age in Denmark when women were considered spinsterish. She needed to get out and experience the world now if she was going to do it. Her sisters needed her. Laura was married and living in Stanley with her third child expected in the fall. Caroline was in Victoria recovering from the death of her husband Joachim and planning to remain either in British Columbia or California. Both Caroline and Laura wrote Christine to encourage her to join them. They needed her help and companionship. They were even planning an early introduction to one of the most eligible bachelors in the province.

Like Laura, Christine was a serious young woman who loved to read about the latest social and economic theories and talk about philosophies and lifestyles. She loved her times with the large extended family she had in Stege and occupied herself with the domestic arts of sewing, cooking, and needlework. She was, however, in no rush to marry and have children of her own. She enjoyed music and there was always a piano in her home that provided entertainment.

Christine Emilie Constance Lindhard was born on April 30, 1850, in Stege, Denmark, the middle daughter and third child of Joachim Lindhard and Josephine Margrethe Rasmussen Lindhard. She was four years younger than Laura and two years older than Caroline. Like her siblings she was baptized three months after her birth and confirmed in the Lutheran Church at age fourteen. She had been close with her sisters as they grew up. They had been encouraged as children to help each other, and she missed both Caroline and Laura after they went to North America. In the letters they wrote, they seemed happy enough in their new homes. When her young brother, William, announced he planned to move to the United States when he turned seventeen, Christine was convinced she should also try her luck.

Christine arrived in New York on July 8, 1874, on the *Silesia* that had sailed from Hamburg, Germany. Since she was travelling alone, Caroline met her in New York. Christine was not fluent in English and Caroline and Laura knew it would be difficult for her to find her way alone across the United States on the transcontinental railway. She needed a companion and they agreed to accompany her on the journey as much as possible.

PART THREE: CHRISTINE LINDHARD HAMILTON

A MOST UNPLEASANT JOURNEY

CHRISTINE AND CAROLINE LEFT New York, bound for San Francisco. On the long journey together, Caroline began some coaching in English that hopefully would ease Christine's adjustment to life on this new continent. She recalled only four years earlier the lessons that Joachim and Theodor had provided as they crossed the Atlantic and the United States together.

Following a brief stop in San Francisco, on July 21, Christine and Caroline boarded the steamship *William Tabor* destined for Victoria. It was a rough introduction to North American ocean travel on a voyage that took five and a half days, about two days longer than normal. Captain Bogart described it as "one of the unpleasantest [trips] ever made on the coast. The wind blew steadily from the northwest and the sea was very rough."[1]

Even though the ocean trip from San Francisco to Victoria was a difficult one, Christine and Caroline had time to talk, practise more English, and plan their lives. They had been close and good friends growing up together. Caroline looked up to Christine and found comfort in being near her. Christine was older-sister protective, far more serious and calmer than her younger, impulsive, and ambitious sister.

The year following Joachim's death had been difficult for Caroline as she struggled with settling his affairs and deciding what to do next. Caroline confided that Asahel Sumner Bates had proposed marriage and that she was considering the offer. It was a proposal that was tempting, since he had agreed they would spend winters in San Francisco, a proposal much more to her liking than enduring the dreary long winters of Van Winkle or 150 Mile House.

Once in Victoria, Caroline assured Christine that she was almost in the "home stretch" of her journey and that July in British Columbia was wonderful. The warm sea breezes and abundant growth of fruits and flowers in Victoria brightened Christine's outlook. Caroline knew that her friends would be attending the talk that evening by Mrs. Pinkham, "a Quaker lady," who was giving a lecture on the leading characteristics of her sect.[2] She knew Christine would be interested in the new social ideas, but she would have to translate most of it for her to understand. They settled for an evening walk through Victoria and Caroline showed her the familiar and favourite

The steamer *Onward* on its way to Yale on the Fraser River.
COURTESY UBC LIBRARY RARE BOOKS AND SPECIAL COLLECTIONS,
UNO LANGMANN FAMILY COLLECTION OF B.C. PHOTOGRAPHS, UL_1001_0007

PART THREE: CHRISTINE LINDHARD HAMILTON

spots that she enjoyed. They had much to think and talk about as they boarded the *Enterprise* the next day for New Westminster and then the *Onward* from New Westminster to Yale. Caroline accompanied her until she could place her in the confident hands of Barnard's Express[3] and know that Christine was on her way to Clinton where Laura would meet her.

As Caroline had hoped, Steve Tingley, the usual driver from Yale to Clinton, was in charge, and Christine was comfortably settled in the stagecoach before Caroline boarded the *Onward* for her return trip to Victoria. The stagecoach in early August was hot and stuffy, but the river and tall trees afforded cool oases on the trail as they climbed and turned on the Cariboo Wagon Road out of Yale. The 220 kilometres (136 miles) of spectacular mountain and river vistas from Yale to Clinton totally enchanted Christine. The mountains were spectacular, the steep ravines, rivers, and waterfalls both soothing and frightening. At Clinton, Tingley turned the north-bound stage over to partner and veteran stage driver James Hamilton, who regularly drove from Clinton to Soda Creek.

Laura and her two young sons, Asa and Louis, met Christine in Clinton. Laura was eager to introduce her to her friend and stagecoach driver James Hamilton. At times, James drove the stagecoach all the way to Barkerville and made regular stops at the Stanley store and express office. James was delighted to meet Christine and quickly extended the usual courtesy of the stage line, inviting her to the seat of honour on the box next to the driver. By this point in the journey and having endured the rough voyage from San Francisco to Victoria, she was ready for a little more excitement and ready to prove to Laura she could handle everything the frontier had to offer. With Laura's encouragement and James's promise that it was one of the gentler sections on the wagon road, she accepted his offer and climbed onto the box beside him as the stage left Clinton for Soda Creek.

The stagecoach was soon into the Green Timbers section of the Cariboo Wagon Road, where the lush dark forests, lakes, and glimpses

Christine was ready to prove she could handle frontier challenges and accepted the invitation to ride on the box. IMAGE A-09775 COURTESY OF ROYAL BC MUSEUM AND ARCHIVES

of wildlife kept Christine enthralled. The summer days were long and with daylight from five in the morning to nine at night, Christine experienced the Cariboo at its best. The 70 Mile, 100 Mile, and 150 Mile stopping houses offered some of the best meals with fresh fruit and vegetables from the local gardens and plenty of fresh meat and dairy. James was very attentive and helped orient her to the offerings at each stopping house along the route and assisted by introducing her to the English words she needed.

Since it was summer, the steamer *Victoria* ran from Soda Creek to Quesnel on the Upper Fraser River and this year the captain was Asahel Sumner Bates. Laura recommended they take it because it offered a more comfortable and faster journey than by stagecoach. Being well along in a pregnancy, she sought comfort. She was also eager to introduce Christine to Asahel, especially since she heard that he may soon be their brother-in-law.

James Hamilton's brother John often drove the last section of the stagecoach run into Barkerville from Quesnel and he was their driver for the final part of the trip. Christine, Laura, Asa, and Louis were soon home in Van Winkle and Christine settled in after a long month of travel. Soon after, James Hamilton found reasons to visit Van Winkle and arrange to spend more time in Christine's company.

A Most Unpleasant Journey

SISTERS TOGETHER

WHEN CHRISTINE CAME TO British Columbia in 1874, she wasn't at all certain she would stay, but Caroline and Laura had both encouraged her to come and then decide. Following the death of Joachim, Caroline especially felt the need for her sister's company. Knowing that summer travel in northern British Columbia was comparatively easy, Christine went directly to Van Winkle to visit Laura's home and to see where Caroline and Joachim had lived. The landscape and the small community feel of the place appealed to her. With Theodor living nearby, she felt comfortable in the small extended Lindhard family. The Lindhard-Beedy family was growing quickly. The third child, Josephine Caroline, was born September 6, 1874, a mere month after Christine had arrived. Laura now had three children under the age of three and Christine's help was needed.

Neither Christine nor Laura was surprised when Caroline announced she had married Asahel on September 18, 1874, in Victoria and that they would spend the winter at 150 Mile House. Christine was quickly caught up in the highly active Beedy home and remained in Van Winkle during the brutally cold winter of 1874–75. It was April before she joined Caroline and Asahel for springtime in Victoria. James Hamilton had visited several times during the winter and Christine needed to talk with Caroline about what she should do.

Christine returned to remain with Laura and family during much of the next summer anxiously awaiting word of when Caroline's first baby had arrived. Exira, a daughter, was born August 24, 1875, at 150 Mile House and Christine went to be with Caroline for the next month. Winter was setting in when she returned to Van Winkle to help Laura with her growing family and the Beedy enterprises. The family had recently moved to and opened their new store in Stanley, where Laura and Josiah's fourth child, Winslow, was born January 9, 1876. Now with four small children, Laura was extremely busy and solidly committed to her growing family.

Christine was more prepared for the possible severity of her second winter in Stanley and hoped it might be milder like one she heard the old-timers describe. Some winters in the Cariboo were severely cold and others were warm with little snow, making winter travel much easier. Stanley was located at an altitude of 1,200 metres (3,900 feet) and at latitude 53—that meant winters usually began in October and could linger into May with spring storms and late melting snow. Many miners, business owners, and families left the area in the winter for the warmer locations of Victoria and California, but the Beedy family resided all year. By the 1870s, as mining moved underground on Lightning Creek, year-round operations were possible and companies could employ people the full year. It was essential for stores to remain open to supply miners with their needs throughout the winter and to carry the freight and supplies needed to reach the distant communities.

James Hamilton had been smitten from the day he met Christine Lindhard, so Laura and Caroline did not have to work hard at bringing them together. In 1874, when he first met Christine, James at age thirty-four was one of the most eligible bachelors in the Cariboo. He was a successful and highly regarded businessman, a partner in the highly respected F.J. Barnard and Company, and an extremely competent stage driver. He was ready for a family of his own.

Christine saw both her sisters happily preoccupied with creating their little families. They both approved highly of James as a partner for her.

> **MARRIED** – On the 22d inst., at Stanley, Mr. James Hamilton was united in the bonds of matrimony to Miss Christine Lindhard, the Rev. Mr. C.L. Thompson performing the interesting ceremony. Mr. Hamilton is well known throughout the upper country, for several years past being connected with the enterprising firm of F.J. Barnard & Co. and has a host of friends both here and at Woodstock, New Brunswick, who will be glad to learn that he has formed a life-partnership with so estimable a lady as the bride. He is to be congratulated on all sides.

Christine and James's marriage announcement. DAILY BRITISH COLONIST, APRIL 25, 1876, P. 3

Consequently, it was with their approval that she married James on April 22, 1876. Well known throughout the province and beyond, James's marriage merited special mention in Victoria's daily newspaper.

When the couple married in April, Christine was within days of her twenty-sixth birthday and James had turned thirty-six earlier that month. The small wedding was held at Laura and Josiah Beedy's home with Rev. C.L. Thompson, the Wesleyan Methodist minister at Barkerville, performing the ceremony. Christine declared her religious denomination as Lutheran, and James indicated he was Presbyterian. Their witnesses were Alexander Lindsay and Benjamin Edwards.

James's obligations to F.J. Barnard and Company held him to year-round residency in the northern British Columbia communities. He was currently based in Soda Creek. He was considered manager of the northern section of the stagecoach route and Barnard and Company was a very hands-on organization. The winters usually brought deep snow and treacherous conditions for the stage line and the spring and autumn rains wreaked havoc on the Cariboo Wagon Road. Road maintenance was a constant issue and part of James's responsibility was to see that passengers, freight, express, and mail could safely reach their destinations. While both James and Steve Tingley were partners in the company, they were at times also part of the road clearing and repair crews.

After their wedding, Christine moved with James into their home in Soda Creek. She was 142 kilometres (88 miles) west and south

James Hamilton (1840–83).
IMAGE A-09775 COURTESY OF ROYAL BC MUSEUM AND ARCHIVES

of Stanley, closer to the more temperate climate of coastal Victoria. She would be close to Caroline during the summer months while Asahel captained the *Victoria*. While Laura was some distance away in Stanley, she was closely connected by the stagecoach route.

The summer of 1876 revolved around the babies and young children. Laura and her four children were nearby. Caroline and Asahel's daughter was one years old, and Caroline was expecting their second child. Theodora Levina Bates was born in February of 1877 in Oakland, California.

Christine was soon expecting her first child and Olive Daghmar Hamilton was born July 4, 1877, in Soda Creek. Within days of Olive's birth, Caroline, Asahel, and their two daughters arrived in Soda Creek. Caroline was ecstatic about another daughter in the family and felt an immediate attachment. Christine and Caroline valued their time together throughout the summer in Soda Creek before Caroline and family returned to San Francisco in mid-November for the winter months.

SODA CREEK

Soda Creek is the warmest point along the Fraser River north of Lillooet. It has always been a place favoured by Indigenous people because of the abundance of salmon, venison, wild fruit, and fur-bearing animals in the area. One theory is that it was named for the creek nearby that ran like soda water bubbling through a formation of carbonate of lime.[4] The town grew on a small stretch of flat land on the east side of the Fraser River where steamers could dock and above which the Upper Fraser River was navigable by steamship. The town formed along one long street with Chinatown at the downriver end.

Early entrepreneurs followed the Cariboo Wagon Road as its construction advanced northward, establishing businesses they believed travellers and miners would need in locations that seemed most strategic. Soda Creek soon boasted two hotels, the Colonial built in 1862 by Robert McLeese and Joseph Senay and the Exchange Hotel built beside it the next year by Peter Dunlevy and his partners.

Both McLeese and Dunlevy became long-time residents of the town that became synonymous with their names. They farmed in the area and operated their hotels. They both operated stores, where they sold their farm-fresh produce. The Exchange Hotel had a saloon, served as agent for Barnard's Express, and added a large barn and livery stable behind the hotel.

The Exchange and Colonial hotels competed for business. During the long winter months, they held dances and served as social centres of activity. McLeese, who operated the Colonial Hotel, married Mary Sinclair from Renfrew, Ontario, in 1872. Sadly, she died in 1876 while giving birth to a second child. McLeese later became a member of the provincial legislature and continued to operate the Colonial Hotel until his death in 1898. In the 1860s, Peter Dunlevy, who ran the Exchange Hotel, started a family with an Indigenous woman from Fort Alexandria. In 1873 he married Jennie Huston from Victoria. He and Jennie had five children and he located this family to a house in town beside the Exchange Hotel. The families remained in the town, raised their children, and operated the hotels for decades.[5]

The town and hotels came to life in the summers when the river became active. By the end of 1862, construction of the Cariboo

The Exchange and Colonial Hotels sat side by side on Soda Creek's main street.
COURTESY UBC LIBRARY RARE BOOKS AND SPECIAL COLLECTIONS,
UNO LANGMANN FAMILY COLLECTION OF B.C. PHOTOGRAPHS, I-0053373.0034

Wagon Road had reached Soda Creek, making the town a significant stopping point on the wagon road. In 1863, G.B. Wright built and launched the sternwheeler *Enterprise* to run from Soda Creek to Quesnelmouth, ninety-six kilometres (sixty miles) north on the Upper Fraser River. Steamers on the river competed with stagecoaches on the road to offer passengers speedier travel, and in this upper navigable section of the Fraser River, steamers had an advantage. Even when the wagon road was completed beyond Soda Creek and stagecoaches offered transport on it, travellers preferred the more scenic, entertaining, and comfortable trip on a steamer to the rough and bumpy ride on a stagecoach. The steamers could quickly convey passengers and freight to Quesnelmouth and farther north, to Fort George and beyond. If passengers were continuing east toward Barkerville, they boarded the stage line again in Quesnelmouth for the remainder of the journey.

In the mid-1860s, Soda Creek was a bustling little town. In 1864, 4.5 million dollars' worth of Cariboo gold passed through the town on its way south. However, after 1865, the town declined in importance as the gold rush calmed and the Cariboo Wagon Road was completed. As the Cariboo Wagon Road drew more traffic, the steamers began to operate during summer seasons only. When construction of the Cariboo Wagon Road was completed, Barnard's Express usually travelled the 572 kilometres (356 miles) between Yale and Barkerville twice each week in summer. From May to October each year it was a busy route, but stage and mail services were less frequent during the winter months.

As the enthusiasm for gold slumped, Soda Creek began to build its future on agriculture and was less a centre for provisioning miners and freighters. Wheat was grown on nearby farms and a flour mill opened. There was a blacksmith in town, but the number of permanent residents remained small. The permanent residents were mainly tied to transportation, mining, trapping, farming, blacksmithing, milling flour, and operating the post office and telegraph. Soda Creek didn't have its own school until 1906. The town alternated between bustle and slumber and came to life again in the 1920s when the railroad was extended through the area. Then it slumbered again and faded away. Today, Soda Creek is a rural community from which people commute to work in the nearby cities and is part of the Cariboo Chilcotin–Gold Rush Trail, a historic destination for tourists.

In the days of old, the stopping houses near Soda Creek became well known for their excellent fresh food in the summer months. Soda Creek drew comment in successive British Columbia directories as an excellent agricultural area. Today, it still produces corn and a range of summer vegetables that one would expect to find only in more southerly growing areas.

It's hard to imagine a larger contrast than what Christine must have experienced in the 1870s between the Copenhagen she left and the Soda Creek where she found herself in 1876. Founded in the eleventh century, Copenhagen surrounded her with history and a lively renaissance in science, literature, and art. Workers in Copenhagen enjoyed some of the highest living standards in Europe.[6] The city's population was about 200,000 and enjoyed many cultural pastimes in music, theatre, museums, gardens, exhibitions, and art. Weather in Victoria and San Francisco would be similar to what she had left behind—ocean-moderated temperatures that were neither as cold nor as hot as the interior of British Columbia at Soda Creek and Clinton. Soda Creek was a gold-rush town showing signs of decline in 1876—a temporary settlement in the unsettled and evolving frontier of British Columbia.

The Hamiltons lived quietly in Soda Creek. James was committed to his work and neither he nor Christine sought attention in the societal pages of the newspapers. Their children's births were not announced. Because there were many other Hamilton families in the province, when "Mrs. Hamilton" was listed as a passenger on a stagecoach or steamer, it was impossible to determine whether it was Christine. Their activities were hard to discern.

Soda Creek

In 1878, spring came early. The winter had been unusually warm, and the mining season opened a month earlier than normal, as miners returned to the north in large numbers in mid-May. Caroline and Asahel sailed from San Francisco on May 30 on the *Dakota* that was filled with families returning for the summer months.[7] Two days earlier, they had arranged the burials of their children Theodora Levina and Exira Sumner in the Bates burial plot in Oakland's Mountain View Cemetery. Caroline was tired and devastated over losing both their daughters in a matter of months. On arrival in Victoria, Caroline was shocked to learn of the death of little nine-month-old Anna Beatrice, the infant daughter of her friends Julie and Gustavus B. Wright in New Westminster. Christine and James travelled to Victoria to meet Caroline and Asahel on their arrival and spent a few days in the capital city soaking in the changes around them.

Life in Victoria churned on, with concerns different from the province's interior. Mary Baines complained to municipal council of being attacked on Birdcage Walk by a vicious cow and again that same evening on Menzies Street.[8] Council had further complaints about cattle, mules, and horses running freely in the town, damaging people's property, chasing and terrifying citizens. They debated whether the new streetlights they were planning to install should be gas or electric. F.J. Barnard had imported two thoroughbred horses from Oregon to add to his breeding stock on the BX Ranch. The Hudson Bay Company offered its farm at Langley for sale. The Theatre Royal advertised entertainment by soubrette Miss Carrie Clarke in the comedy *The Rough Diamond*, and an Irish farce *Barney the Baron*. The San Francisco Grand Opera House Combination offered four nights of the melodrama *Octoroon*. The men still played cricket at Beacon Hill Park. Mining engineers John Harper and E.N. Riotte held different opinions on the value of the minerals in the Cariboo quartz, but the miners remained optimistic. Smoked oolichans were popular in Victoria, salmon were plentiful this summer, and fresh strawberries could be ordered from Wm. Clarkson in New Westminster.[9]

PART THREE: CHRISTINE LINDHARD HAMILTON

Christine knew she could count on Caroline to care for Olive whenever she needed someone during the summer. Caroline's despondency caused by the death of their two daughters was only assuaged by being with Olive and delighting in her every move and sound. Having Caroline near enabled Christine to travel to Victoria with James again that summer. They were joined on the return trip from Victoria to Yale by Francis Jones Barnard and Ellen Stillman Barnard. Christine enjoyed the time away and was able to learn more about the Express Company and the challenges it faced. Ellen had lived in Quebec City and then in Toronto early in her marriage before joining her husband in Yale in 1860 with their two youngest children. Now that the children were older, she often accompanied her husband on his frequent trips to the interior and eastern Canada.

Soda Creek

A NORTHERN PARTNERSHIP

JAMES HAMILTON HAD BEEN in British Columbia for over twelve years when he met Christine in 1874. He was born April 18, 1840, in Woodstock, New Brunswick, the fourth son and fifth child of Major and Olivia (Olive) Kerr Hamilton. His father was a farmer who had emigrated in 1823 from Ireland. James's mother died when he was fifteen and he continued to live with his older sister Mary Ann and brothers in Woodstock. Growing up on a farm, he learned at a young age how to work with horses, and it was work that he enjoyed. At age twenty-one he was a stagecoach driver working in New Brunswick. In 1864 as Francis Jones Barnard was pushing north with his express service and putting stagecoaches on the Cariboo Wagon Road, he hired James to drive the Clinton to Lac la Hache section. James was a perfect fit for the company that Barnard imagined—a reliable Canadian with experience in stage line operations. Fellow New Brunswicker Steve Tingley was hired at the same time, primarily for the Yale to Nicomen run. Both fit nicely into Barnard's dream of a highly reputable and reliable stage line that would assure traveller satisfaction and continuation of the Royal Mail contracts Barnard had secured from the colonial government.

James's ties to New Brunswick loosened when his father died in June 1872, and eventually all his siblings moved west. His brothers George and Robert had joined the California gold rush and then made their way to British Columbia where they took pre-emptions in the Nicola Valley and became recognized ranchers and horse breeders, before moving to Alberta to establish ranches there. Brother John, who was eight years younger than James, joined him in British Columbia and drove for the British Columbia Express Company before moving to Alberta and operating a livery stable in Calgary. Sister Mary Ann and brother Samuel also moved to Alberta to join their siblings in the Calgary area.

Unlike many of the entrepreneurs who came to British Columbia in the 1860s, James focused almost exclusively on the express company. There is no indication he invested in mining companies and if he diversified his investments, it was in partnership with his brothers who lived in an area still designated Hamilton Hill—located outside of today's town of Merritt—where they were well-known ranchers and horse breeders.

In May of 1872, Barnard announced a partnership with both Tingley and Hamilton in which they would each hold one-quarter of the company shares.[10] The *Cariboo Sentinel* commented:

> *Both of these gentlemen are long and favourably known not only for the efficient manner in which they have handled the "ribbons," but more especially for the uniform courtesy and kindness which everyone who has patronized the line has experienced at their hands. We are satisfied that Mr. Barnard has added both to the efficiency and popularity of the Express by joining with him in the business two men so thoroughly acquainted with the country and so deservedly popular with the whole community.*[11]

At this point the official name of the company became F.J. Barnard and Company, but it began to advertise its services under the name of the BX (Barnard's Express) and the BC Express Company, which it later officially became. While both Hamilton

A Northern Partnership

and Tingley were company owners, they continued to drive stagecoaches and when needed to get the express or passengers through to their destinations, they arranged the opening of snowy or debris-laden roads, improvised water crossings when bridges washed out, and did whatever it took to ensure the company operated efficiently. James was described as the "attentive manager of the upper end of the route"[12] and these responsibilities took him often into Stanley and Barkerville.

By 1878, James was ready to pull back on his obligations with the F.J. Barnard and Company. In March of that year, the company was formally incorporated by an act of the British Columbia legislature, after which he held one-sixth of the company shares. With incorporation, company creator Francis Jones Barnard and his son, Francis Stillman Barnard, together retained 499 shares out of 1,000. Company directors James Hamilton, Steve Tingley, and Barnard's brother-in-law George Sargison held the remainder of the shares. Shortly after the first meeting of the company directors, Barnard declared insolvency as he was unable to pay his debts on schedule. However, this action enabled him to negotiate a repayment schedule with debtors and avoid bankruptcy.[13]

On January 1, 1879, when Asahel Sumner Bates died in San Francisco, neither Christine nor Laura was able to travel to be with their sister Caroline. It was a very cold winter in the Cariboo. January 1879 was described as "very severe; the thermometer at Stanley recording 30' below zero; 27' at Boyds on the same day; 20' at Quesnelle two days after; 37' at the 150 Mile post and 35' at the 100 Mile post."[14]

News from the interior of the province always reported on weather and the road conditions:

> *Sleighing is good for 280 miles from Barkerville to Cache Creek; thence to Kanaka Bar wheel coaches are running; from the latter place to Yale good sleighing again; from Yale the canoe*

affords communication to New Westminster. At Cheam, on the Fraser, the river is blocked with ice and a portage has to be made.[15]

In addition to the cold and complex transportation, both Laura and Christine were expecting babies. On March 14, Laura gave birth to Josiah Crosby Beedy at Stanley. On May 25, Christine gave birth to George Harold Hamilton at Soda Creek.

Christine felt isolated in Soda Creek with two small babies and missed being physically close and able to support and be supported by Caroline. In summer when Laura's husband, Josiah, began to feel unwell, Christine and James visited. When Josiah died in January of 1880, James, one of the executors of his will, assisted Laura as best he could. Despite the cold and difficulty of travelling in February, Caroline, accompanied by her stepson Otis (a.k.a. John) Bates, who was almost thirteen years old, came to be with Laura and Christine. Caroline convinced Christine, who was expecting her third child to accompany her and Otis back to San Francisco, where the better weather would be good for her and the children. Since James would be in Victoria during much of the spring, it seemed like a good idea for Christine to get away.

Hamilton and Tingley were in Victoria for most of April 1880 representing the BC Express Company at meetings related to Barnard's insolvency. During this time, Barnard's suit against the Dominion government for cancellation of his contract to build the Pacific Telegraph Line from Cache Creek to Edmonton continued, and his ability to pay creditors hinged on a settlement with the Dominion government. The insolvency case was settled by the end of April, when Barnard agreed to pay his creditors in full plus interest over the next thirteen months. "The offer was unanimously accepted. The feeling of the creditors as indicated by proceedings of meeting was that of great confidence in and sympathy with Mr. Barnard."[16] In June, Hamilton was in Victoria as one of the executors of J.C. Beedy's estate, along with Hector McKenzie and Laura Beedy, participating in the probate of the will.

On June 26, 1880, Christine gave birth to Josephine Lindhard (Linda) Hamilton in Oakland. As 1880 turned into 1881 in British Columbia, optimism entered, and the *Daily British Colonist* wrote:

> *We may yet find that 1880 has marked a turning point in the career of the province. During the year just over we have seen the drydock and railway works fairly commenced. We have witnessed an active and steady demand for agricultural products and manufactures spring up; we have seen the almost forgotten gold fields of Cariboo instinct with new life and yielding their hidden treasures to well directed efforts with a generous hand and we enter 1881 full of hope that the great project of a Canadian Pacific Railway is about to be fairly launched upon a basis that will at least insure its completion within the next decade.*[17]

In December of 1880, James joined Christine and the children in Oakland. Little George's health was failing, and he died in February 1881. On February 16, he was buried in the Bates/Beedy family plot in Mountain View Cemetery in Oakland. The recorded cause of death was cerebritis. On April 11, Christine, James, Olive, and baby Linda caught the *Dakota* in San Francisco and returned to Soda Creek—but only briefly.

James was deeply saddened by his son's death, and it was the impetus to move the family that summer to the southern end of his route in Clinton. Christine found it almost impossible to leave her sisters Caroline and Laura, now both widowed and living in Oakland, and return with her small family to British Columbia. She had agreed to come to British Columbia so they could all live close together and now she was alone in the remote interior without them.

The summer of 1881 in Clinton may have seemed quiet. News from Clinton in August suggested things may have been almost boring:

Even Clinton had its own Palace Hotel, which still exists as a tourist attraction today. 1909.
IMAGE A-03069 COURTESY OF ROYAL BC MUSEUM AND ARCHIVES

Clinton—The news from this part is meager. Rains are almost continuous during this month, retarding the ripening of grain and damaging the hay crops. Business is slack and scarcity of money the general complaint.[18]

But events within the large family and business networks kept life on edge. Earlier that year F.J. Barnard had a stroke that left him with some lingering paralysis that he struggled to overcome. There were the usual minor accidents with the stagecoaches, and in August much of the town of Yale burned. The BC Express Company lost their new building that had opened earlier that year, their offices and stables.

Christine and James experienced their first winter in Clinton where the weather in late January was reported as very cold at forty degrees below. But winter was a time for weddings and births that gave fresh hope to communities, offsetting the otherwise bleakest

A Northern Partnership

time of year. The quietness of winter gave people time to party, celebrate, and dance. Clinton is famous for its annual Clinton Ball. In January 1882 the ball coincided with three weddings and Christine and James would surely have been part of the celebrations.[19] The announcement read:

> **GRAND DOINGS AT CLINTON — MARRIAGE BY WHOLESALE — MUSIC AND DANCING.**
> *The annual Clinton Ball ... has filled the town with visitors. Forty-two ladies and seventy-five gentlemen attended the courthouse where the Ball was held ... There were three newly-married couples on the floor who had just been tied up by the Rev. Mr. Chappell. They are: Mr. J.B. Leighton of Cache Creek to Jennie Uren of Savona; Jas. Woods of Woods Creek to Alice Salter of Maiden Creek; and J.S. Chenhall of Clinton to Nellie Walker of Harrison River. Clinton Choral Association aided in the festivities and sang several quartettes and solos. The dance is likely to be continued for two or three nights.*[20]

J.B. Leighton was James Buie Leighton, who at the young age of thirteen came to the Cariboo to work for his uncles, the Buie brothers, who were merchants in Lytton and Barkerville. He worked as a clerk for the Buie brothers in Barkerville and as an agent for Barnard's Express in 1865. He worked for other Cariboo merchants over the years and held the mail contract from 1881 to 1886 from Cache Creek to Okanagan Mission. For sixteen years he held various positions with the BC Express Company in several different locations.[21] Jennie Uren was the daughter of James Uren and Malvina Toy who operated the Clinton Hotel and later a hotel at Savona. J.B. and Jennie Leighton eventually became ranchers in the Savona area.

Francis Stillman Barnard increasingly took leadership of the BC Express Company as his father became involved in Dominion politics and the elder Barnard's health began to fail. While James was in

Victoria supporting the Barnards through the insolvency hearings, Francis Stillman first floated to him the idea of creating the Victoria Transfer Company and suggested that he might be interested in leading the new company that would be based in Victoria, a city more suited to James's growing family.

On March 12, 1883, the bill requesting incorporation of the "Victoria Transfer Company" was read in the British Columbia legislature. The principals of the company were James Hamilton, Edgar Marvin, Frank S. Barnard, and Thomas Earle. The purpose of the company was to construct and operate street railways in Victoria, Esquimalt, and districts surrounding Victoria and to carry on a general transfer, delivery, hack, and livery business.[22] The Act to Incorporate the Victoria Transfer Company Limited was passed on May 12 that year.

The Hamilton's stay in Clinton was short since plans were underway to open the Victoria Transfer Company and James had accepted the position of superintendent. He hoped a move to Victoria, with closer proximity to San Francisco, better educational opportunities,

---

VICTORIA

CARRIAGE & TRANSFER COMPANY.

THE STOCK, PROPERTY & GOODWILL of Mr. J.W. Williams having been acquired by this company, it is their intention to

MATERIALLY INCREASE THE PRESENT LARGE STOCK OF HORSES CARRIAGES, BUGGIES ETC.

And the Public are informed that

CARRIAGES WILL BE SUPPLIED

AT ANY HOUR
OF THE
DAY OR NIGHT
AND A
FIRST-CLASS
LIVERY BUSINESS
conducted at their
STABLES, CORNER OF GOVERNMENT
AND JOHNSON STREETS
ALSO
HORSES, AND VEHICLES OF ALL DESCRIPTIONS WILL BE KEPT CONSTANTLY ON HAND FOR SALE.

TELEPHONE CALL NO. 129

JAMES HAMILTON
Superintendent

DAILY BRITISH COLONIST, FEBRUARY 2, 1883, P. 2

and the warmer climate, would be better for his family. He now had the future of three daughters to consider. Minerva Christine had been born in Clinton on August 2, 1882.

James had seen the BC Express Company through almost two decades of its beginning and early challenging years. From its inception as Barnard's Express, it eventually carried the mail over the Cariboo Road for a period of almost fifty years until the mail contract was lost in 1913. "This unique achievement was due to the energy and capability of the partners, particularly of Tingley and Hamilton. Both men were expert handlers of four or six-horse teams, and Hamilton is never known to have had an accident all the years he drove on the road."[23] By 1882, James was ready for a gentler life and a closer involvement with his growing family.

Within months of Minerva's birth, Christine and James travelled to Victoria on the *Enterprise* from New Westminster. They met with Captain William Raymond Clarke, whose home, Thanet Cottage, at the corner of Quadra and Chatham streets was for sale. They bought it fully furnished for $5,100 and moved in immediately.[24] The house was later described as containing "nine lofty rooms and a bathroom with outhouse, woodsheds, etc., and the garden nicely planted with trees. The house is handsomely furnished, carpets, etc. nearly new."[25]

A few years earlier, Victoria had been described as dull and declining, characterized by vacant lots, dusty streets, and a financial depression. But by 1882 the tone was optimistic. The building of the railway on the mainland and talk of a railway for Vancouver Island along with a new dry dock in Esquimalt brought renewed life to the city. Victoria was coming of age and imagining a new future that included tourism and a diversified economy.

Earlier that year, the popular Driard Hotel had burned, destroying several of the top floors and the adjacent Bowman's livery stable. The *British Daily Colonist* seized the opportunity to point out the need for a grander hotel:

PART THREE: CHRISTINE LINDHARD HAMILTON

Of late years Victoria has grown in favour with tourists, who come from far and wide to enjoy its cool, bracing climate and pure oxygen, its fine drives, grand romantic scenery and sylvan retreats. The Driard House just destroyed by fire, has had a more prosperous season ... What is wanted is a larger and better appointed and more modern hotel. People who can afford to travel nowadays expect luxurious quarters and all the modern conveniences which money can purchase.[26]

The winter of 1882–83 was pleasant for the Hamilton family. Settled in a new house in Victoria, Christine enjoyed the lectures, theatre, concerts, and shopping the small city had to offer. In March, Caroline's new love interest, Captain Charles Henry Harrison (a.k.a. Commodore Harrison), came to Victoria and travelled into the Cariboo to assist both Laura and Caroline with unfinished business around their remaining British Columbia properties. He spent time with the Hamiltons and other friends in Victoria. On September 7, 1883, Harrison and Caroline married in a quiet ceremony in the apartment of friends at the Palace Hotel in San Francisco.

On October 3, 1883, James left the Victoria Transfer Company stables, driving his horse and buggy and heading home. He tied his horse at the front of the house, staggered and collapsed on the front steps. Helped to his bed, he died of an aneurysm of an aorta, an ending that was not totally unexpected. In announcing his death, the *Daily British Colonist* wrote, "Mr. Hamilton was a sterling man and highly esteemed by all."[27] He was forty-three years old. At his funeral held at Christ Church Cathedral, chief mourners were F.J. Barnard and F.S. Barnard. Pallbearers were Edgar Marvin, Joseph Loewen, Robert Burns McMicking, Dixi Ross, Theodore Lubbe, Stephen Tanner, Anton Henderson, and William Dodd.[28] James was buried in Ross Bay Cemetery, Victoria. One report noted, "As evidence of the respect felt for the memory of the deceased, it may be mentioned that twenty-three private carriages followed the procession from Christ Church to the cemetery."[29]

Christine and James Hamilton moved to Thanet Cottage in Victoria when he became superintendent of the new Victoria Transfer Company in 1882.

IMAGE B-04910, COURTESY OF ROYAL BC MUSEUM AND ARCHIVES

In times of tragedy and sadness the Lindhard sisters came together when they could. Christine's daughters were ages six, three, and one. Laura and Caroline came to Victoria with their families to be with Christine. She had their support during the funeral and for several days after they helped her settle property and legal matters before returning to San Francisco. Christine quickly decided on her next steps. With Caroline and Laura both living in the San Francisco area, she would join them as soon as possible.

By the end of November, Christine had advertised the Victoria house and furniture for sale. The law firm of Davie and Pooley in Victoria were appointed to handle the estate and sale of property.[30] In

PART THREE: CHRISTINE LINDHARD HAMILTON

early December, Caroline and Charles returned to Victoria and took time to reconnect with friends. On December 3, the second session of the fourth Legislative Assembly opened and the "Who's Who" of Victoria packed the public galleries to hear the Lieutenant Governor read the opening speech. Caroline and Charles attended, along with many friends that included the Barnards, Finlaysons, Wrights, Onderdonks, Dunsmuirs, Douglases, Shakespeares, and a long list of Victoria's notables.[31]

On December 14, Christine and her three young daughters, accompanied by Caroline and Charles, left Victoria on the steamship *Mexico* for San Francisco.[32] She had been nine years in British Columbia and now she saw a future for herself and her daughters in Oakland, California.

LOSING FAMILY, FINDING FAMILY

CHRISTINE HAD CHANGED DURING her nine years in British Columbia. She had lived in four different places, set up three different homes, borne four children, and experienced the death of her husband and one child. She had experienced the remote small towns and the largest city the province had to offer. They were intense busy years and now she was left on her own after seven years of marriage with her three small children. She had enjoyed Oakland three years earlier when James had joined her there for the winter months. Now with Laura's help, she located a suitable home and settled in.

Christine did not seek the spotlight. She enjoyed a quiet life with books, music, and a few close friends. However, in her large extended family, life moved at a fast pace. The following year, Laura told her she was thinking of returning to Stanley and marrying William Wright Dodd. Laura and her children were missing the north and her boys could benefit from the experience of working in the store. Laura married again and returned to Stanley, British Columbia, with her children in 1885. The same year, Caroline left to travel with Charles on an extended trip of over a year in England and Europe. The tight sisterly bonds began to fray.

Christine was on her own in Oakland. The following year was a turning, a crisis year for Christine, when she found herself alone with three small children. She remembered how alone she had felt when she was in Clinton and Laura and Caroline were both in Oakland. Now she was in Oakland, and they were both far away with their husbands and families. She felt abandoned and realized that the closeness of childhood was no longer there with her sisters. She couldn't understand Laura's return to Stanley, a place she regarded as a cold inhospitable hinterland. She was not attracted to the social elite lifestyle that Caroline so energetically sought. She began to explore social spaces and ideas that drew her interest.

It's impossible to know what attracted Christine to the Bureau of Equitable Commerce, a cooperative living movement that was actively recruiting members in San Francisco and evolved into the Koreshan Unity Commune. In the late 1880s, she began to attend the Camp Golden Gate of the Society Arch-Triumphant that met every Tuesday evening in the parlours of the Koreshan Unity at 218 and 220 Noe Street in San Francisco. In *The Flaming Sword*, a widely read publication of the Koreshan Unity, a regular invitation was published:

> *You are cordially invited to attend these meetings, where every phase of theological, scientific and sociological thought is discussed in an original, striking and convincing manner, through the application of law by logical methods.*
>
> *If you are a thinker, unshackled by prejudice and not committed to the well-beaten lines of investigation, you will find the discussions undertaken in the meetings of this Society, "a feast of reason and a flow of soul."*[33]

She was curious. The Bureau of Equitable Commerce was incorporated in San Francisco in April 1891:

> *The Bureau ... filed articles of incorporation yesterday. The members are associated for the purpose of dealing in real estate, personal property, groceries, provisions, fruit, vegetables, meat,*

coal and wood, hay and grain, cutlery, crockery, agricultural implements, manufactured articles, stationery, printing materials and all kind of goods, wares and merchandise.

The society will construct and operate a printing office if it is found necessary. Its place of business is this city, and its capital stock is $1,000,000 of which $56,730 has been subscribed. There are 100,000 shares valued at $10 each, of which 2000 have been purchased by E. Christine C. Hamilton.

Many of the subscribers are women, most of whom have but one share. The Directors are Cyrus R. Teed, George C. Ludmington, Royal O. Spear, I.R. Marston, Mary E. Knight, Tillie P. Marston of this city and E. Christine C. Hamilton, the principal stockholder, who resides at Sausalito.[34]

The Koreshan Unity Commune was based in Chicago and the second group that formed in San Francisco brought considerable wealth to the organization. Mary E. Knight was from Oakland and may have been Christine's friend. Mary's children were grown. She was apart from her husband and ready for a new life direction, so it's possible that she and Christine decided together to commit to the Bureau of Equitable Commerce. They may have been drawn to the idea of cooperative communal living or the idea of investing in a caring Christian community. Christine and Mary joined at the same time and remained part of the movement for the rest of their lives.

The leader of the Koreshan movement, Cyrus Teed, was described as extremely charismatic, with powerful oratory and powers of persuasion. Teed was a licensed Doctor of Medicine in New York state. He was fascinated by and continued to experiment with alchemy, metaphysics, and electromagnetism. When he was thirty, he had a mystic experience in which an angel came to him and proclaimed him as "chosen to redeem the race."[35] Following this experience, Teed began to organize his beliefs into a set of principles that became part of Koreshanity. He sought to reconcile science and religion.

PART THREE: CHRISTINE LINDHARD HAMILTON

His religio-science was a mix of millennialism, mesmerism, the beliefs of Swedenborg, Theosophy, Spiritualism, mind healing, Buddhism, the primitive Christian church, Egyptian myth, Gnosticism, electromagnetism, and more. He wove them together like an eclectic doctor blended different medical techniques. He called his system Koreshanity, giving no credit to others, and he proclaimed that it contained the answers to every question.

But for all he claimed to know, Teed kept himself unknowable. For his followers, there would always be a mystery around the corner, always more to know about Koreshanity, and it would be translated through him as they became capable of understanding it.[36]

The vision Teed held for the cooperative included economic, spiritual, and social elements. He claimed to advance theories of astronomy and geology. He believed the earth was hollow and that we lived on the inside of a giant sphere. On joining the organization, the followers gave up their private wealth, practised celibacy, regarded Dr. Teed as a second Messiah, and accepted every phase of the doctrine advanced by him, which he claimed evolved from the Bible, astronomy, psychology, and various other things not fully understandable to most ordinary mortals, unless they studied long and attentively.[37] Members had to devote time to the study of social problems and working out Teed's theory of salvation.

America in the nineteenth century was a time of existential searching and saw the birth of many breakaway Christian groups and communes that adhered to alternate lifestyles. The contemporaneous organizations of Mormons, Shakers, Economites, and Oneida communities all had some influence on Teed's evolving doctrines. The Koreshans published a subscriber-based weekly newsletter each Friday called *The Flaming Sword*, in which Teed laid out his shifting beliefs, extended invitations to potential members, and engaged in dialogue with readers. The byline for the newsletter was "The Leader of Scientific and Social Reform. Best thoughts of Modern Times on all Leading Subjects." In another column, the Koreshans were self-described as "devoted to the promulgation of the Social Theocracy and Equitable Commerce, destined to revolutionize commercial methods and to crush the iniquitous money power."[38] A certain openness was displayed in *The Flaming Sword.* One section of the newsletter, titled "Sphere of Women," was headed by Mrs. Ordway and considered topics of "prohibition, enfranchisement of women, and woman's true relation to the essential reforms of the age." Like many newspapers of the time, the newsletter ran segments of news gathered, from a wide variety of newspapers in the United States and listed major world events that had occurred each day of the past week.

Teed offered something for everyone and the movement attracted many women. He produced numerous documents on the role and rights of women. He espoused that women were equal to men and marriage was a form of slavery for women with their rights surrendered to husbands. Within the Koreshan movement women found respect. They had control over their own bodies and a strong sense of mission. They had a safe place in a communal home where they participated equally with men. Celibacy enabled nineteenth-century women to avoid debilitating and repeated childbearing and was viewed as liberatory by some.[39] Communal cooperation in childcare and domestic tasks had considerable appeal for many women. Christine was not as enthusiastic as Caroline and Laura about children and domestic life in nuclear families. The communal arrangements may have made her feel sheltered and protected from bearing alone the trauma and tragedies of birthing, caring for, and losing those one loved. One commune member remembered her as having been assistant matron at Beth Oprah, the Chicago residence. "One of her beliefs was that children and dogs are all right in their place, but their place is not in the house."[40]

One researcher studied the publications of the Guiding Star Publishing House that was a core Koreshan enterprise. In Estero, Florida, the Publishing House occupied a large, impressive building at the centre of the settlement that housed state-of-the-art equipment and facilities that "possibly matched or surpassed any publishing venture in Florida . . . Evelyn Bubbett managed a staff of twenty-five people who ran the printing press." The Publishing House was an enterprise where women held some "equity":

> In 1910... women represented only about 14.7 per cent of all workers involved in publishing and printing in Florida. At the Koreshan Unity, women comprised 40.5 per cent (nine of the twenty workers in the print shop). While not demonstrating true equality between the sexes (men held most of the editorial and supervisory positions), the high percentage of women working in printing did reflect the Koreshans' belief and practice of allowing women "their vision of equity" in facets of community life other than domesticity.[41]

Christine became part of the San Francisco group of Koreshans and moved to the Koreshan residence in Washington Heights,

Dr. Cyrus Teed, founder of the Koreshan Unity Commune, in front of the group's Chicago home in Washington Heights. COURTESY STATE ARCHIVES OF FLORIDA, IMAGE KOR1750, KORESHAN UNITY COLLECTION N2009-3, PAPERS, CA1887-1990, BOX 20

Losing Family, Finding Family

Chicago, in May 1892 with her daughters Minerva and Linda. Newspaper reports noted the two wealthiest donors to the commune at the time were Christine Hamilton and Mary Knight. Some reported their contributions at $50,000 each.[42]

The years in Chicago were spent building the Koreshan movement, and on at least one occasion, Christine was involved in a recruitment meeting. She, Mrs. Boomer, and Mrs. Ella Castle were reported at a meeting "intended to interest their colored sisters in the principles of Koreshanity." They told the women attendees of the planned development in Estero Florida and "invited all to be partners."[43]

Chicago was a temporary stop for the Koreshans, as Teed dreamed of creating a utopia that wasn't possible in the urban setting of Chicago. The Chicago neighbours were not tolerant, and the city newspapermen were harassing. Teed searched for a place where the group could live harmoniously and productively and located land in Florida at Estero Bay south of Fort Myers. He was excited about the place he saw as sunny, fertile, and teeming with fish. It seemed the ideal place where a self-sufficient utopian community could thrive. In 1894 he secured the land from Gustav Damkohler, and work began. Over the next decade, members gradually moved from Chicago to the Estero settlement.

Christine remained in Chicago for nine years and was one of the last to leave in 1903. In 1895, when Christine's daughter Linda was fifteen, Koreshan attendance records show Linda began to attend the regular Tuesday meetings of the commune. Her attendance was not as frequent or faithful as Christine's was, but she did attend meetings during the next three years. Minerva started to attend in 1896, when she was fourteen, and attended intermittently until 1899. In 1900, both Minerva and Linda left the Koreshans to live with their aunt Caroline in Sausalito California. Their move was not unlike that of many other young people who grew up in the commune, attained some education and marketable skills, and chose to live away from the commune. In 1900, Linda was twenty years old and Minerva was eighteen, clearly an age when they could

PART THREE: CHRISTINE LINDHARD HAMILTON

decide their future. Their departure was at the urging of their aunt Caroline and possibly sister Olive, who both wanted them within the big family enclave in Sausalito.

In 1903 when Christine moved to Florida, she was fifty-three and one of the commune elders. As an early member and one who made a significant financial contribution at the crucial beginning, Christine became a member of the first Planetary Court, an administrative group of five women appointed while the group was still based in Chicago. In Florida, the Planetary Court grew to include seven leading women that included Christine. They occupied the most beautiful building on the grounds of the Florida compound; a Victorian-style house with two storeys, a balconied cupola, a wrap-around porch, and large windows. They held leadership roles and were esteemed within the community.

Planetary Court officers. *From left to right:* FIRST ROW: Lou Staton, Evelyn Bubbett, Cyrus Teed (Koresh), Annie Ordway (Victoria), Emma Norton, Andrew Howard. SECOND ROW: Virginia Andrews, Christine Hamilton, Bertha Boomer, Etta Silverfriend, Elizabeth Robinson, Esther Stotler, Addison Graves. THIRD ROW: Rollin Grey, George Hunt, Henry Silverfriend, Samuel Armour, James H. Bubbett, John Sargent. FOURTH ROW: Charles Hunt, George Hussey, Thomas Gay, Ross Wallace, Moses Weaver. COURTESY OF STATE ARCHIVES OF FLORIDA, IMAGE KOR1097, KORESHAN UNITY COLLECTION, N2009-3 PAPERS, CA1887-1990, BOX 3, FOLDER 1

When the Koreshans moved to Florida, the state was still frontier-like. Estero, Florida, in the 1890s has been described as the "wilds of Florida" that represented "the epitome of pioneer living." There were few roads and people relied on ox teams to clear land. There were a few Spanish people who herded cattle brought into Fort Myers from Cuba. Herculean efforts were required to convert the swamp into productive land for food and to turn the settlement into a self-sufficient community. Christine had experienced pioneering in the cold hinterlands of British Columbia, but Florida required pioneering in the hot, insect-infested swamps. Everybody's labour was needed.

Christine preferred to live quietly, privately, and did not seek attention. She didn't write articles for the Koreshan newsletters like many of the other women did. But like other commune members, she participated in a variety of work roles. In the two consecutive censuses of 1900 and 1910, she described herself as a seamstress.[44] She was described by others as an assistant matron. In a letter to Jennie Campbell in 1908, she described the role she fulfilled at that time as "matron" and having "to listen to so many and varied disagreements as well as woes—without being able to relieve, and then I feel it such a waste of time."[45]

Christine's letter to Jennie Campbell was written while Dr. Cyrus Teed lay near death in Estero. In a second letter to Jennie Campbell, Christine expressed the faith she held for Teed at the time: "We have never comprehended the greatness of His mind and work, but only now get the faintest glimps [sic] of what it means. He is the great alchemist—have now entered the crucible and become the sacrifice by which the world is to be transformed."[46] The woes and anxiety she had to deal with were experienced by the commune members as they awaited Teed's death and the test of his immortality following death when they expected him to rise and enter the eternal state.

Teed died December 22, 1908, and was buried on the Koreshan property in Estero. In 1921, a hurricane demolished the mausoleum where he lay, and his body was washed out to sea. After Teed's death, the colony began to diminish, as some members left. Leadership fell to long-time members and the commune became more open, with an emphasis on communal, cooperative living. The commune newsletters continued to publish excerpts from Teed's early and ample writings, in addition to current news and writings from members.

Before his death, Teed witnessed the early success of his imagined utopia. By 1906, the group had acquired nearly 2,800 hectares (7,000 acres) of land and held capital assets of nearly a quarter million dollars. There may have been as many as three hundred members. They became a self-reliant township and had their own source of electricity. They produced everything from concrete to shawls. They operated a school, university, general store, bakery, print shop, tin-shop, machine shop, sawmill, boat works, ferry, and mail service. They engaged in innovative horticulture and grew a variety of crops that included citrus, sugar cane, rubber, and bananas.

The commune proved to be a roaring success in self-sufficiency, and they traded with and entertained their non-commune neighbours.[47] The Koreshan Unity Art Hall hosted concerts and events for commune members and surrounding community organizations. The Koreshan Unity Line operated motorboats and launches between Fort Myers and Estero that carried passengers and cargo up and down the coast.[48] There were lectures on osteopathy, dentistry, history, art, and music. During World War I, the Estero Auxiliary Red Cross was highly active in raising funds. In two months, the Koreshan Unity women knitters produced thirty-two sweaters to send to "the boys at the front" and over a six-month period made ninety-one "refugee garments" for the Red Cross effort.[49]

As one of the early investors and long-term members of the Koreshan Unity, Christine enjoyed a comfortable life, although there were times of hardship when money and food were scarce. The Koreshans have been described as a "gay lot," unlike many communal societies. Their photo collection reveals many "outings," picnics, travel, and celebrations. Teed's intellectual bent placed great emphasis on music, art, and dancing.

The commune had a renowned band and orchestra.[50] The Koreshan Orchestra held regular performances and gave benefit performances for various causes. The Koreshan Band played for dances in Fort Myers and other nearby communities. The Koreshan theatre group mounted regular productions of Shakespeare plays. A report of one orchestra performance in aid of the Children's Home at Jacksonville commented, "These people do things awfully well, and this amount was a generous donation, considering the population of this little village."[51]

The commune attendance records show how its structure evolved over the years. For the first three years, Christine was recorded in the attendance record as Christine Hamilton, listed alphabetically by the family name. Then the family name was dropped, and the attendance records listed "Sister Christine." At times members were listed alphabetically by first names, then in 1898 evidence of a hierarchy emerged in which the first members listed were "Koresh" and "Victoria Gratia" followed by the new "Planetary Court," sisters Berthaldine, Christine, Elizabeth, Evaline, and Virginia. The titles of "sister" and

The Koreshan sisters on the porch of the Planetary Court. From left to right: Christine Hamilton, Evelyn Bubbett, Elizabeth Robinson, Berthaldine Boomer, Virginia Andrews, Emma Fiske (standing), and Etta Silverfriend and Jennie Campbell sit on the steps.
COURTESY OF STATE ARCHIVES OF FLORIDA, IMAGE KOR1102, KORESHAN UNITY COLLECTION, N2009-3 PAPERS, CA1887-1990, BOX 3, FOLDER 1

"brother" began to be used. Christine found a new family and new sisters among the women who had spent almost as many years in the commune as she. Her new sisters were other commune members, names such as Emma Fiske, Jennie Campbell, Virginia Andrews, Evelyn Bubbett, Etta Silverfriend, Elizabeth Robinson, Berthaldine Boomer, and Esther Stotler.[52]

Christine was mentioned for the last time in a newspaper article as part of the Lindhard-Beedy-Harrison family in 1888. When she joined the Koreshans in 1892, she was described as a "widow ... very well connected in this city ... worth between $25,000 and $50,000."[53] Her decision to join the commune broke her connections with, and banished her from, her biological family. Ideologically, she took a path that sharply contrasted with the beliefs that drove Caroline. A central belief of the Koreshans was that the root of evil resided within capitalism, a competitive system that could not be reconciled with brotherly love and Christian values and would lead to the downfall of society.

While Laura might have been more understanding of Christine's commitments than Caroline, the obligations each showed toward their children's future differed considerably. After Cyrus Teed died in 1908, the commune members followed fewer restrictions and the boundaries were more permeable. Members left for periods of time when they were needed by their biological families and later returned. Others came from the outside to live temporarily and work at the commune. There were more visitors. But Christine never left and did not visit her biological family again.

For Christine, the Koreshan Unity Commune became a new family. Once she moved to Chicago and Estero, it appears that she never returned to visit Sausalito or Oakland. Having invested her worldly possessions in the commune, she committed her future to it. The ties to her biological sisters Laura and Caroline were severed. Even the ties with her children, Minerva and Linda, were broken

Losing Family, Finding Family

when they left the commune in 1900. While there was some correspondence about family events, there were no visits.

After extensive recent research on the Koreshan Unity Commune, Millner concluded, "The Koreshans were not a bunch of wackos. The Koreshans were well-educated people with high standards and [they believed] that they were important somehow."[54] And, she concluded with a cautionary note that may partially explain Teed's attraction to dedicated followers, "The man who makes life easy for you always has a chance of making you believe anything."[55]

By 1921 about one hundred members of the commune remained. The newsletter internal to the commune in August 1922 noted, "We regret to record in this issue the passing out of Sister Christine Hamilton." The newsletter quoted from *The American Eagle* of July 27:

Mrs. Christine Hamilton, who has been ill for some weeks past, died here on Monday morning, about one o'clock, aged 72 years. Deceased was a native of Copenhagen, Denmark, and for many years resided in British Columbia, later removed to Pasadena, Cal., where she became interested in the Koreshan Unity, then in San Francisco, later removing to Chicago, and finally to Estero, having been a member of the colony for thirty years preceding her death. She was a woman of high education and culture, highly esteemed by all who knew her, by whom she will be sadly missed. She is survived by two daughters, one living in California and the other in Canada.[56]

In 1961, Florida named 123 hectares (305 acres) of the Koreshan Unity property as the Florida Koreshan State Park. The site's natural heritage includes the tallest pair of monkey puzzle trees in the country, the largest tamarind tree in the state, as well as mangoes, grapefruit, guavas, Surinam cherries, decorative Washington palms, and many more ornamentals.[57]

PART THREE: CHRISTINE LINDHARD HAMILTON

NIECES *of* CAROLINE
and COMMODORE HARRISON

❦

IN 1892 WHEN CHRISTINE left San Francisco with the Koreshan Unity, her daughter Olive Daghmar Hamilton turned fifteen that summer. Olive always had a close bond with her aunt Caroline, and she chose to live with her in Sausalito rather than accompany her mother and sisters to Chicago. This decision severed Olive's relationship with her mother and her sisters Minerva and Linda. Olive would not connect with her sisters again for eight years.

Olive was six years old when her father died and had been old enough to remember her father and the places she had lived in British Columbia. During the 1890s when she lived with aunt Caroline in Sausalito, her Beedy cousins often also lived there. Josiah who was one year younger, became a good friend, as did Josephine, who was three years older. Josephine attended Stanford University from 1894 to 1897, and Olive got to know her well.

Aunt Caroline took great pride in her nieces and nephews and was committed to seeing them do well in life, and for the nieces that meant marrying well. Consequently, Olive became very involved and well known in the Sausalito community. In 1895, had one of the principal parts in a play, "Russian Honeymoon" that a community theatre group offered at "the beautiful residence of Commodore Harrison next Friday night."[58] Her name appeared regularly in the

Society column of the *Sausalito News* when she participated in receptions, teas, weddings, and community social events.

In May of 1897, Olive, in the company of her cousin Josephine, travelled to British Columbia to explore all the old places of meaning for the Hamilton and Beedy families. Aunt Laura and cousins Asa and Winslow were operating the Provision Store in Stanley and Olive and Josephine based themselves there for most of the seven months they were away. This was a significant trip for Olive, as she discovered the places her parents had lived and the people they knew.

The experiences of Olive's sisters Minerva and Linda were considerably different during the eight years that they were apart. Minerva was ten years old and Linda was twelve when they accompanied their mother to Chicago with the Koreshan Unity. They were from their sister, and also from their mother even though she was nearby. The Koreshan living arrangements were communal, which meant that the children lived together, the adults separated into living quarters for women and living quarters for men. Difficult times were reported during the Chicago years, when good nutritious meals were lacking and winters were severely cold.

The Koreshans valued education and training in practical skills and experiences. They operated their own school and the children also learned by participating in the daily life of the community. The girls often worked along with the women in gardening, food preparation, sewing, knitting, and caring for clothes. They participated in the Guiding Star Publishing House activities and learned office practices.

As the children matured, they took part in the regular Tuesday meetings of commune members. One report indicated that Linda didn't always live in the Koreshan commune. She learned to play the violin and was part of the Koreshan Orchestra. During the first year she was in Chicago, her cousin Josephine was also in Chicago attending the Girls' Collegiate School where her aunt Mary Elizabeth Beedy was co-principal. They were probably in touch during this time and Linda may have attended school and lived outside the commune at times. Linda began attending the Koreshan commune meetings each Tuesday, beginning in 1895, and attended often for three years, although not as faithfully as her mother. She was listed in the Koreshan attendance records as "Sister Lindhard" and her name no longer appeared in the attendance records after 1898. "Sister Minerva" was listed in attendance records intermittently from 1896 to 1899.

The turn of the century brought a new beginning for Christine's daughters. Influenced by Aunt Caroline's commitment to family, and as the oldest sister, Olive kept in touch with her younger sisters. In the spring of 1900, Olive travelled to Calgary to visit her Hamilton uncles who lived there. While three of her late father's brothers, Robert, George, and John, had lived in British Columbia and been involved in ranching and horse breeding with James Hamilton, they had moved to the Calgary area by the mid-1880s. By 1900, Uncle George and Aunt Mary Ann had died, but Samuel along with Robert and John were well-known ranchers and horsemen in the area. Olive visited for several months, getting to know her uncles and their families.

It's not known if it was on the instigation of Olive and possibly the participation of an uncle or two, but in the summer of 1900, Minerva and Linda Hamilton left the Koreshan Unity to join Olive in living with their aunt Caroline in Sausalito. Their first outing was attending a Halloween party that fall, accompanied by their aunt Caroline, organized by the Las Amigas Club and held at the San Francisco Yacht Club House. It was a costume party with a Puritan theme, and the report commented that, "The Las Amigas Club again distinguished itself socially."[59]

The Social column in the *Sausalito News* leaves the impression that life for young people in the community was a constant swirl of social events:

Nieces of Caroline and Commodore Harrison

SAUSALITO NEWS, *October 12, 1901*—*"The Progressive Proposal Party" given by Miss Belle Harmes at the family residence on Bulkley Avenue last Saturday evening, was one of the most delightful events of the season. The lawns were brilliant with Japanese lanterns and inside the house flowers and ferns were most effective. Music and dancing were among the features of the evening. The usual delicious refreshments were served. An air of hospitality pervaded, and all departed with high appreciation for the able and gracious manner in which they were entertained by their charming hostess. Following are the names of those that were present: Linda Hamilton, Olive Hamilton, Minerva Hamilton, Louis Beedy, Winslow Beedy, Josiah Beedy and about fifty others too numerous to copy.*

On November 30, 1901, Olive was travelling with her friend Fannie Shoobert and Winslow Beedy on the ferry steamer *San Rafael* that ran between Sausalito and San Francisco. In dense fog it collided with another ferry steamer, the *Sausalito*. Both steamers were owned by San Francisco and Northern Pacific Railway. The *Sausalito* had a few passengers on board, while the *San Rafael* had between 150 and 200 passengers. The *San Rafael* was badly damaged and within a short time it sank in the bay. Winslow was lauded for his skillful and heroic actions:

> *Miss Olive Hamilton, niece of Commodore Harrison of Sausalito, is proud of her cousin, Winslow S. Beedy, and her pride is justified. On the night of the sinking of the* San Rafael *young Beedy showed presence of mind, strength and courage. He saved the lives of his cousin Olive and her friend Fannie Shoobert. . . . "for over ten minutes Mr. Beedy kept both of us afloat. We yelled and finally a boat was lowered from the* Sausalito. *The men in the boat were helpless. Mr. Beedy had to take charge of the boat. We rescued a little boy who had been*

clinging to a stick of wood and saved several other persons. Then we were rowed to the Sausalito."[60]

The drama of the crash continued for Olive and Winslow. The little boy they rescued was separated from his parents and they had to take him home until his parents could be located the following day. As many as twenty lives were lost in the collision and it took days to identify all who were missing.

When Commodore Charles Harrison died on June 18, 1902, all at Hazel Mount were deeply saddened. He had generously provided his beautiful home for his nieces and nephews to enjoy, and he delighted in their company, youthful talents, and energy. His death ended a very happy marriage of almost twenty years with Caroline. Laura, who was living nearby in San Francisco, once again drew close to Caroline. And Caroline soon busied herself more deeply with the young lives of her nieces and nephews and the social swirl of Sausalito.

In early February of 1904, Olive announced her engagement to her cousin Winslow. The San Francisco newspapers ran the headline, "Sausalito Society Belle Will Become the Bride of Winslow L. Beedy." It elaborated:

> *Miss Hamilton is the niece of Mrs. Harrison widow of the late Commodore Harrison, and her home has been for a number of years at the beautiful Harrison residence in Sausalito, where she has been an acknowledged belle in the town's social element and always been one of the handsomest and most attractive girls at the dances and among the gay set seen driving bareheaded about the terraced roads.*[61]

In September, Linda Hamilton announced her engagement to Charles Albert Wright, son of Gustavus Blin and Julie Wright, old friends of Caroline from her days in British Columbia. Both weddings took place the following year. At Olive's wedding on April 25,

Nieces of Caroline and Commodore Harrison

Olive Hamilton (1877–1906) lived most of her life with her aunt Caroline Harrison.

P3958 BARKERVILLE HISTORIC TOWN ARCHIVES

1905, Caroline gave her away and Olive wore a bridal gown she had sewn herself, "made of shimmering white satin embroidered in pearls."[62] When Linda married on June 6, she wore the same dress. The sisters had created the dress together.[63] Minerva was a bridesmaid at both weddings. Hazel Mount was the setting for a reception following Olive's wedding and it was also the setting for Linda's small wedding and reception. The year concluded with the family reunion on Christmas Day at Hazel Mount with Laura, Caroline, all the nieces and nephews, wives, husbands and the first grandchild, Louis Beedy's daughter, Mary Elizabeth. Asa was also present as he had recently left Barkerville and planned to remain in the Sausalito area. But all ties to Canada were not broken.

In the aftermath of the very devastating earthquake that struck San Francisco on April 18, 1906, Linda and Olive began their families. On July 1, 1906, Olive gave birth in San Francisco to a daughter, Caroline Lindhard Beedy. On July 30, Linda gave birth to her first daughter, Anna Beatrice Wright. Joy and hope ran high. But due to complications following birth, Olive died eighteen days later, on July 17.

DEATH OF MRS. BEEDY

The sad death of Mrs. Winslow Beedy, one of last year's brides, has attracted much attention and much sympathy has been expressed for the bereaved young husband. Mrs. Beedy was Miss Olive Hamilton. She leaves also a seven weeks' old infant. The mother's death resulted from a fever following the birth of the child.[64]

The sadness and grief were overwhelming, but the family once again pulled together. Aunt Caroline was especially bereaved. She had adored her niece Olive from the moment she was born and had taken great pride in the young woman she had become. Aunt Caroline spread the big family tent to take in her grandniece Caroline and her father, Winslow Beedy, who made Hazel Mount their home for most of the next decade.

Minerva and Linda had remained close as they found their way outside of commune life and in the care of their aunt Caroline. Minerva had been ten years old in 1892 when she left San Francisco with her mother and Linda for the Koreshan Unity Commune in Chicago. She was eighteen when she left the commune to live with Aunt Caroline in Sausalito. Caroline introduced both Minerva and Linda to social life in Sausalito, and for several years the sisters were frequent guests at many parties and socials in the community and in people's homes. Often, they were accompanied by some of their Beedy cousins. They were described in the social columns as "the attractive Hamilton girls," part of the "smart set" of the Bay Area, and "popular nieces of Mrs. C.H. Harrison."

Nieces of Caroline and Commodore Harrison

When not attending social events, Minerva was active in community charitable causes. She worked in the Coffee Kitchen that was opened to serve the San Francisco Earthquake refugees in April 1906. She and her cousin Josephine frequently helped their aunt Caroline receive guests at teas hosted at Hazel Mount. In the lead-up to the 1911 vote in California on women's suffrage, Minerva participated in Sausalito's campaign to get women registered for the vote. She assisted Mrs. Shoobert in receiving guests at a suffrage card party that the *San Francisco Call* referred to as "the intellectual or polite side of the campaign."[65]

In the summer of 1912, Minerva went to Calgary to visit her uncle John Hamilton, a livery stable operator. He was the only Hamilton uncle still alive and she extended her stay with him into the autumn. In November she was summoned back to Sausalito because Aunt Caroline was seriously ill. On February 7, 1913, Caroline died, and Minerva stayed in Sausalito until August. Aunt Caroline had been generous in dividing her estate among nieces and nephews, but Minerva may have felt the division had not been equitable. Perhaps Minerva hadn't been highly favoured by Caroline; her bequest to Minerva showed constraint. Minerva was bequeathed $500 and one lot in Sausalito.

In 1913, Minerva returned to Calgary and made it her new home. Mrs. Frank Findlay hosted a tea in her honour when she departed Sausalito in August. The following August, she married George Crooks in Calgary and lived there for the next thirty-four years.[66]

Linda perhaps fit more easily into Sausalito life. She was an accomplished violinist who had played in the Koreshan Orchestra for several years, entertained at Sausalito events, and played first violin in the Sausalito Orchestral Society in the 1920s. When Aunt Caroline died, she bequeathed Hazel Mount Cottage to Linda. With her husband and children, Linda became a lifelong resident of Sausalito.

PART THREE: CHRISTINE LINDHARD HAMILTON

Christine Lindhard Hamilton had for over thirty years been estranged from her sisters and biological family. There had been some contact with Minerva and Linda after they left the Koreshan Unity Commune, because she did learn of Olive's death in 1906. But she had clearly adopted the commune "sisters and brothers" as her family. Her existence had not been acknowledged in any wedding or death announcement, social event, or accomplishment of her daughters for over forty years. She had seen the Koreshan commune develop and grow. She remained loyal through the difficult and glory days in Chicago and Estero. It had given her a quiet, secure existence and a meaningful life. She was productive and held power within the Planetary Court in giving guidance to the commune. She was respected and cared for in her later years. She died on July 21, 1922, and was quietly buried on the Koreshan lands in Estero, Florida.

Nieces of Caroline and Commodore Harrison

CONCLUSIONS

THE LIVES OF LAURA, Caroline, and Christine Lindhard can be interpreted through multiple lenses. It makes most sense to me to view them as entrepreneurial women. They seized the opportunity of travelling with and being supported by their cousins who had gone before them to North America. They experienced limited opportunities for themselves in Denmark in work and marriage and yet sensed they were at the forefront of greater freedoms for women and that their lives could be better elsewhere. They accepted the risk of an unknown future in a new country and had the youthful energy and enthusiasm for the adventure.

"Marrying well" was the single most important step for nineteenth-century women. It was one decision they could make that would have the largest consequence for their economic and social future and that of their children. In her first marriage Caroline was too young and too much of a romantic to hold the pragmatic view of marriage that both Laura and Christine had when they married. But all three came to recognize that marriage was the most consequential entrepreneurial decision they would make.

From an entrepreneurial perspective, leaving Denmark for the Cariboo in the 1870s was a perfectly wise decision. The Cariboo offered a surplus supply of men from which to choose a partner. Many of the men were entrepreneurial adventurers who had established themselves in business and mining and had acquired sufficient wealth that they were now seeking life partners.

Historians of businesswomen debate whether women who inherit their businesses from men (usually their husbands) should be considered true businesswomen. But this question is posed at the same time as women in business have often been invisible behind the man in their life. "Even if a man was feckless, drunk or incapable and his wife in reality ran the business, it was still his name above the door."[1] It is unclear who possesses the expertise and power when a life partnership is also a business partnership. Nothing in the lives of the Lindhard sisters suggested that they would have sat back passively in their houses waiting for events to happen to them. Rather, they acted as smart capable women. Consequently, I assumed that they carried their spirit of adventure into their marriage and business partnerships and were alert and astute learners along the way.

After brief first marriages, all three sisters were thrown into the business side of their marriages, whether they had been prepared for that role or not. All three sisters had their husbands die at times when each appeared on the cusp of a brighter economic future with considerable wealth from their ventures. After a decade of digging and draining the Van Winkle claim, Joachim Lindhard died before he experienced the valuable extractions from Lightning Creek in 1874 and 1875. Caroline, however, benefitted from the peak value of $14,000 paid to her by the Van Winkle Company for his shares. There was excitement about the valuable potential of Beedy's quartz ledge on Burns Mountain when Josiah Beedy died in early 1880. It's unclear how much Laura received for the quartz ledge when she sold it the next year to James Reid, but it continued to be mined for many years after she sold. Similarly, Christine and James Hamilton were at a turning point in their lives with a new home in Victoria and a position that put him in charge of the new Victoria Transfer Company when he died.

The legalities of deaths, wills, properties, company shares, probates, and inheritances placed the women in a position of having to

Conclusions

make significant financial decisions. Both Laura and Christine had to consider the impacts of their decisions on their children. Laura was faced with the precise situation Melanie Buddle found had commonly led British Columbia women into self-employment. Left with families to support and an inherited business, women chose self-employment out of economic necessity.[2]

The social fluidity that characterized remote and open frontier societies granted Laura a social setting where her ambitions and self-sufficiency could be achieved. In remote Stanley, she was not limited by being a woman and having to retail items for women only as she might have been in a city. She dealt in a broad range of items, everything from overshoes to hay to fresh milk and meat, and whatever the miners needed. She had autonomy. She financially supported her children by regularly sending money to them and to Caroline for their care. She had learned how to be a retail merchant from her husbands and from her sons who studied business. In Stanley and Barkerville, she and her sons were well known and respected retail merchants. The Beedy family was present in the area for over forty years, and this qualified them as "pioneers" and "settlers" even though they ultimately departed for their final years in California. By Buddle's definition of success, Laura was a successful businesswoman. She ran a business that supported her family, and she managed her family and business in a way that both found success.

When Caroline married her cousin Joachim on the way to the Cariboo in 1870, it was an impulsive rather than strategic act. However, it may not have been for Joachim. Marrying cousins was a way to retain wealth within a family and Joachim may have been aware of his precarious health condition. After three years of marriage, Caroline was left with an estate she claimed was valued at $40,000, a significant amount in 1874 (well over $800,000 in today's dollars). At age twenty-two, she had significant wealth in her possession. Caroline liked the idea of wealth, the status and social connections it brought. However, she made some costly mistakes when she lost control of it to her second husband, Ahasel Bates. Under the tutelage of third husband Charles Harrison, she took control of the properties she held and began strategic decisions in buying, selling, mortgaging, and building a real estate portfolio.

Caroline experienced deep loss and grief in birthing and raising her own children, which drove her determination to build an extended family base in Sausalito. She embraced all her nieces and nephews, and she guided their futures. She supported Laura's children by offering a home base when the children needed to secure higher education. She accommodated Christine's children, presumedly at her own expense, throughout their teen and early adult years. She was particularly attentive to her nieces, guided their marriage decisions, shared her life lessons, and financially cared for them in her will.

Caroline found her home among the social elite of Sausalito and San Francisco. She and Charles built their wealth through real estate, and she committed her energy to charity and community causes. She provided social capital and "generational power" that facilitated her nieces' and nephews' entrances to professional careers and "good" marriages.[3] Caroline maintained long friendships that began in British Columbia and continued in Sausalito, with families such as Gustavus Blin and Julie Sutton Wright and the Schoobert-Dunsmuir families, among others. These family networks were an essential part of fulfilling her social and family goals.

Christine's decisions indicated a clear preference for life in the warmer California climate. Her stays in the northern communities of Stanley, Soda Creek, and Clinton were brief and inhospitable. She departed Victoria with her daughters within months of James Hamilton's death. But Oakland did not hold her either. Her decision to commit her wealth and life to the Koreshan Unity Commune was in stark contrast to and can be considered a rejection of the life Caroline chose. It broke their supportive sisterly relationship. But the economics of everyday life could not be escaped. While the Koreshan commune members turned their worldly wealth over to the commune, they operated internally on a system of tracking and recording labour units contributed by members. All members were expected to contribute through work and Christine did her share. She was a member of a commune that by most accounts was highly successful and entrepreneurial albeit in an alternative economic system that operated internally.

Marie Elliott concludes that women of whatever class and ethnic background had to be strong, mentally and physically, to endure the hardships they faced in the isolated communities of the Cariboo.[4] Laura, Caroline, and Christine would agree with this assessment. Winters were often brutally cold in Stanley. In 1862, when miners rushed into the Upper Fraser River area, most had never experienced searching for gold in such a northern climate before. They had to develop new knowledge about how to work and thrive in the harsh environment. The common pattern was to flee the Cariboo in winter for the more hospitable climates of San Francisco and Victoria, sometimes to seek medical help and often with hope of restoring health.[5]

By the time the Lindhard sisters reached the Cariboo, mining was becoming a year-round activity that tied their husbands to the area. Domestic living conditions usually meant that hard physical labour fell to the women. It was usually the women who gathered summer berries and grew the vegetables that they canned and preserved for winter eating. Times were such that laundry was hand done using washboards and tubs—a backbreaking task. The sisters were capable sewers, knitters, and menders of clothing, so it's difficult to imagine that their hands were idle. They often employed cooks or house helpers, but they also did their own domestic work.

Learning from neighbours and friends who were experiencing similar conditions was crucial to everyday life. The remoteness of the Cariboo was particularly felt in winters when storms made outside contact impossible for weeks at a time. The stagecoaches and sleighs ran infrequently in winter so that mail and supplies did not always arrive. Conditions demanded planning and self-sufficiency. If accidents happened or people were ill, women were called on to be caregivers and knowledgeable nurses. The winter isolation continued until better roads and railways reached the area in the 1900s.

Given the opportunity, Christine and Caroline quickly fled the inhospitable weather of the north for the preferred climate of California. Many women given the opportunity to live elsewhere did so. If husbands and fathers were tied to business in the Cariboo, mothers and children sometimes moved without them to Victoria or California during the harshest months. Schooling beyond elementary levels was not available in the early years and parents sent their children away to Victoria, Ontario, Europe, or California where secondary and post-secondary education was available.

The most extreme example of married couples living apart may be Joshua Spencer Thompson and his wife. They lived together in Hope in 1859, but when he followed the gold rush to the Cariboo, Mrs. Thompson refused to go further and returned to San Francisco. Thompson worked for Buie brothers as a clerk in Williams Creek and was a leading citizen of Barkerville. He participated in the Cariboo Amateur Dramatic Association, helped organize the first school district, and was a three-term member of Parliament. Only when he died suddenly in 1880 and his widow claimed his estate did some people who knew them twenty-one years earlier remember that he had a wife![6]

Another telling story is about Mary Caroline Schram Agassiz who, with her four little children in tow in 1862, planned to accompany husband Lewis Nunn Agassiz to the Cariboo. She reached Yale and looked at the new Cariboo Wagon Road—cut out of solid rock, sheer mountain above, and sheer precipice down to the roiling Fraser below. Beyond this, the old trail looked like a scratch, winding in and out among the mountain. "Is that the road we have to travel to reach the promised land?" she asked. "I would rather go back to Victoria and take in washing."[7] Her refusal to go any further ended the Cariboo dream for that family. They returned to Hope where

Conclusions

Lewis secured a position as chief constable and postmaster and later pre-empted farmland in a nearby valley, where the community of Agassiz now bears his name.

The harsh climate and geographic remoteness made life difficult, but on a variety of fronts British Columbia failed the Lindhard sisters. When they arrived in the 1870s, women could not pre-empt land nor become citizens. The colonial administrators and provincial legislators could not imagine granting women rights and liberties equal to men. The women were welcomed as wives or potential wives but any deviation from a man as head of the household was far too disruptive a notion for the majority to embrace. Thus, despite the Married Women's Property Act of 1873,

> Married men continued to hold the right to their dependants' unpaid labour under the common law, [so] they controlled any income or property acquired through the collective efforts of family members. Married women's unwaged contributions to family were not recognized by the MWPA. They gained no rights in jointly accumulated family property, and they could still be left penniless by their husbands.[8]

Changes occurred in granting rights for women, but they came slowly in British Columbia as they did elsewhere. The suffrage movement began in British Columbia in the 1880s, but it was April of 1917 when British Columbia became the fourth province in Canada to grant women the right to vote in provincial elections and to run for provincial office. A similarly long struggle in California resulted in women gaining suffrage there in state elections in 1911.

The right to citizenship also came slowly. It wasn't until February 11, 1888, that "Mrs. Stovall, a native of Kentucky, United States appeared before Mr. Justice Crease at Nanaimo on Wednesday and applied for admission to the rights of a British subject. His lordship admitted the lady and congratulated her on being the first foreign lady in this province to become a naturalized British subject."⁹ Ultimately, the sisters' aspirations exceeded the opportunities they found.

The ties between Victoria, British Columbia, and San Francisco, California, in the north–south corridor of the Pacific Slope were strong during the latter half of the nineteenth century. The cities were intricately linked through communication, transportation, trade, and family networks that have endured to the present.

The *Daily British Colonist* regularly commented on economic and political progress in British Columbia, and they lamented the slow growth of industry and opportunity in the province:

> *For 23 years, nearly—since the first gold rush of 1858—there has been a steady drain of money from the country. What has become of the $60,000,000 in gold dug from the Cariboo mines? Gone to enrich a foreign state. Sent away to buy goods manufactured from raw material that exists here in abundance. Is there any room for wonderment that the country has not retained either wealth or population and that scores of her young men and women "native and to the manor born" are yearly forced to seek homes elsewhere. Naturally, unable to find employment they have drifted off in the same direction as our gold, and like our gold, are lost forever.*[10]

The *Daily British Colonist* implied but didn't name the United States or California. Victoria and British Columbia were slow to provide opportunities for basic and advanced education. Children had to go away for schooling, as the Beedy children did, and new friendships and job opportunities drew the next generation into new communities. Both A.S. Bates and J.C. Beedy were American citizens and consequently their children could claim citizenship and certain privileges there. There was little that held the Lindhard sisters to British Columbia. By the time Laura left Stanley in 1899, all of her children except Asa had established themselves in the San Francisco area.

Conclusions

Imagine how British Columbia would be different had someone back in 1870 actually welcomed women as citizens, maybe even encouraged them as miners and entrepreneurs on an equal basis with men. The stories of Laura, Caroline, and Christine Lindhard add to the collection of voices that continues to expand about this crucial period of newcomer arrival in British Columbia. Their stories differ from those we have of the ruling class of women who left notes and journals and often wrote as outsiders with a tone of superiority. The Lindhards sought opportunity and a chance for a better life. Within the limited opportunities granted women at the time, they constructed three distinctly different lives and throughout most of their time maintained supportive sisterly bonds. But women's power and influence were curtailed by the dominant patriarchal values and the lack of rights to vote, hold citizenship, and participate as autonomous individuals. Women did build and exercise power and influence within their families and communities that, while unrecognized at the time, had the potential to confound the colonial project that was unfolding at the time.

ACKNOWLEDGEMENTS

I HAVE BEEN FORTUNATE TO have a cast of characters behind the scenes who helped during the writing of this book. My sister Donna Stout, whose profound fascination with families and her genealogical expertise constantly amaze me, was a great collaborator. She generously researched family connections and mapped family trees that linked the main characters of the story. I am grateful for Ken Mather who kindly shared his extensive knowledge of British Columbia history and engaged in many conversations that helped sustain the project. It was during his research for writing *Stagecoach North* that I opened the question, who was the lesser-known partner in Barnard's Express, James Hamilton? What did we know about him? That question introduced me to the Lindhard sisters, and our conversation has not stopped! Other family members are drawn into projects like this, as was Colin Stout. He provided expertise in enhancing old photographs and greatly improved several photos included in this book.

Many people readily responded to emails of inquiry. It was always tremendously exciting to receive a message from a family member who descended from the Lindhard sisters. They very kindly shared photos, letters, memories, and objects that had been passed down through the generations in their families. Every trace and piece of information they so generously shared is deeply treasured, and I am grateful to Jean Beedy Young, Jan Pasnau, Ted Beedy, and Tish Sandos.

A trip to Barkerville Historic Town and time spent in the Barkerville Archives were essential parts of this project. While it wasn't a first trip to Barkerville for me, I fell in love with the place and the landscape. I may have caught a case of what Art Downs called Caribooitis, the result of which one is continually drawn back to the place. A special thank you to Mandy Kilsby, Caroline Zinz, and Christian Keller for their generous archival assistance. The Lindhard story belongs to Barkerville/Stanley and all royalties from the sale of this book will go to the Barkerville Archives.

I am thoroughly grateful to so many others for their help and interest. Poul Erik Rasmussen kindly assisted with translation and interpretation of Danish documents. I thank the Danish Heritage Society and the Scandinavian Cultural Centre for their interest and support. I appreciate the assistance of archivists in all the archives I visited: The Quesnel Archives (Brandee Schutz), Museum of the Cariboo Chilcotin, City of Vancouver Archives, Kamloops Archives, Merritt Archives, Ashcroft Archives, Rare Books and Special Collections at the University of British Columbia library in Vancouver, and Royal British Columbia Museum and Archives.

I worked on this book during a time when many archives across North America were closed. However, many were kindly responsive to my email inquiries. I acknowledge assistance from the Skeetchestn Indian Band, Roman Catholic Diocese of Kamloops, Clinton Museum, Provincial Archives of New Brunswick, Victoria Heritage Foundation, Antioch College Archivist, Crawford County Historical Society, Vancouver City Archives, California State Archives, Oberlin College Archives, Oberlin Heritage Center, Museum of Danish America, Ohio History Connection, Library of Congress, Williams Lake Indian Band Genealogy Project, British Columbia Post Office Research Group, Sausalito Historical Society, and State Archives of Florida.

I am deeply grateful for the interest, support, and editorial assistance from Heritage House, and especially Nandini Thaker and Jesse Marchand for their valuable guidance and suggestions.

NOTES

INTRODUCTION

1. Kathryn Bridge, *By Snowshoe, Buckboard and Steamer, Women of the British Columbia Frontier* (Victoria, BC: Royal British Columbia Museum, 1998, 2019) and Kathryn Bridge, *Henry & Self, an English Gentlewoman at the Edge of Empire* (Victoria, BC: Royal British Columbia Museum, 1996, 2019).
2. Bill Gallaher, *The Promise, Love, Loyalty & The Lure of Gold* (Surrey, BC: TouchWood Editions, 2001) and Jim Nesbitt, "Old Homes and Families" (n.d.), Kamloops Museum and Archives, Stephen Tingley Bio files.
3. Rosemary Neering, *Wild West Women: Travellers, Adventurers and Rebels* (North Vancouver: Whitecap Books, 2000) and Richard Thomas Wright, *Barkerville, Williams Creek, Cariboo* (Wells, BC: Winter Quarters Press, 1998), p. 48–49, document the various establishments of Fanny Bendixen.
4. Marie Elliott, "Women in the Fraser and Cariboo Gold Rushes, 1858–70," in *New Perspectives on the Gold Rush,* ed. Kathryn Bridge (Victoria, BC: Royal British Columbia Museum, 2015), p. 115, and Marie Elliott, "Women of the Fraser River Gold Rush" in *The Trail of 1858,* ed. Mark Forsythe and Greg Dixon (Madeira Park, BC: Harbour Publishing, 2007), p. 75.
5. Peter A. Baskerville, "She Has Already Hinted at 'Board': Enterprising Urban Women in British Columbia 1863–1896," *Histoire sociale – Social History* 26, no. 52 (November 1993), p. 205–227. Baskerville uses the term entrepreneurial to mean activity other than wage work in the capitalist marketplace. He considered three types of activity: women as property holders, women as borrowers, and women in business.
6. For example, see Kathryn Bridge, ed., *New Perspectives on the Gold Rush* (Victoria, BC: Royal British Columbia Museum, 2015), p. 23. In her recent book, *Gold in British Columbia* (Vancouver: Ronsdale

Press, 2020), Marie Elliott tracks the activities of several women entrepreneurs in early British Columbia, but they are add-ons to the main story of colonial administrators, miners, and male entrepreneurs.

7   Eileen Boris and Nupur Chaudhuri, "Introduction: Standpoints on Hard Ground," in *Voices of Women Historians: The Personal, the Political, the Professional*, ed. Eileen Boris and Nupur Chaudhuri (Bloomington: Indiana University Press, 1999), p. xi.

8   Lenore Davidoff, *Thicker Than Water: Siblings and Their Relations, 1780–1920* (Oxford University Press, 2013), p. 69.

9   Melanie Buddle, "Skirting the Boundaries: Businesswomen in Colonial British Columbia, 1858–1914," in *Female Entrepreneurs in the Long Nineteenth Century*, eds. Jennifer Aston and Catherine Bishop ([Cham, SI]: Palgrave Macmillan, 2020), p. 315–336.

10 *Cariboo Sentinel*, September 12, 1874, p. 2.

11 *Cariboo Sentinel*, July 6, 1872, p. 2.

12 *Cariboo Sentinel*, September 28, 1872, p. 3.

13 *Cariboo Sentinel*, June 14, 1873, p. 2.

14 Jean Barman, *Sojourning Sisters: The Lives and Letters of Jessie and Annie McQueen* (Toronto: University of Toronto Press, 2003), p. 3.

Part One—LAURA LINDHARD BEEDY DODD

1   John A. Hall, Ove Korsgaard, and Ove K. Pedersen, eds., *Building the Nation: N.F.S. Grundtvig and Danish National Identity* (Montreal & Kingston: McGill-Queen's University Press, 2015).

2   Hall, Korsgaard, and Pedersen, *Building the Nation*, p. 417.

3   Tine Damsholt, "Hand of King and Voice of People: Grundtvig on Democracy and the Responsibility of Self," in *Building the Nation*, eds. Hall, Korsgaard and Pedersen, p. 156.

4   Kristian Hvidt, *Flight to America, The Social Background of 300,000 Danish Emigrants* (New York: Academic Press, 1975), p. 37.

5   Hvidt, *Flight to America*, p. 124, 200.

6   "Danish-American Culture," Museum of Danish American, online at https://www.danishmuseum.org/explore/danish-american-culture/viewed-through-the-lens/confirmation-coming-of-age-in-denmark-and-the-us

7   Hvidt, *Flight to America*, p. 178.

8   Communication with Vice Consul, Royal Danish Consulate, Vancouver, May 18, 2022. The pepper tradition dates back to the 1500s. If unwed at age

thirty, women and men were sprinkled with pepper as a fun gesture and a reminder by their friends that they should be looking for a life partner. This evolved into an early reminder at age twenty-five by sprinkling the unwed with cinnamon (a gentle reminder that pepper is getting close). Today the more likely gesture is to gift an unwed thirty-year-old with a pepper grinder rather than throwing spice at them.

9   Aime Guilloteau and D.A. Edgar were partners in a small commercial merchant company based in Victoria known as Edgar & Aime. Aime was French, Edgar likely American with strong ties to the commercial merchants of San Francisco. By 1867 the partnership in Victoria had dissolved, and Guilloteau moved on to the Cariboo. See Nancy Oke and Robert Griffin, *Feeding the Family: 100 Years of Food & Drink in Victoria* (Victoria, BC: Royal British Columbia Museum, 2011), p. 122, 127.
10 *Cariboo Sentinel*, October 16, 1869, p. 3.
11 "Adventurers of the Cariboo, Part 1," *The Province*, March 16, 1935, p. 57.
12 "Harry Jones Was Last of Adventurers," *The Province,* February 29, 1936, p. 5.
13 *Cariboo Sentinel*, September 29, 1869, p. 3.
14 Jenny Clayton, *The Lieutenant Governors of British Columbia* (Madeira Park, BC: Harbour Publishing, 2019), p. 26.
15 Louisa May Alcott, May Alcott, and Daniel Shealy, *Little Women Abroad: The Alcott Sisters' Letters From Europe, 1870–1871* (Athens: University of Georgia Press, 2008), p. xvii.
16 Alcott, Alcott, and Shealy, *Little Women Abroad*, page lxxviii.
17 Alcott, Alcott, and Shealy, *Little Women Abroad*, p. 8.
18 Royal British Columbia Archives, Letters to Douglas 1859, F995.
19 William Fraser Rae, *Westward by Rail: The New Route to the East* (London: Longmans, Green and Company, 1870), p. 7.
20 Day in Castle Garden, New York. *Harper's Monthly*, volume 42, June to November 1870. Accessed at: https://www.gjenvick.com/Immigration/CastleGarden/1871-03-ADayInCastleGardenImmigrantStation.html.
21 Rae, *Westward by Rail*, p. 26.
22 Ibid. p. 225.
23 Ibid. p. 228.
24 Ibid. p. 309–310.
25 "USCS Active," Wikipedia, https://en.wikipedia.org/wiki/USCS_Active.
26 *Daily British Colonist*, April 12, 1870, p. 3.

27 Alice Trueman, "Playing the Game: The Education of Girls in Private Schools on Vancouver Island," master's thesis (University of Victoria, 2009).
28 Barnard's Express would later be known as F.J. Barnard & Company, and still later as the BC Express Company.
29 Willis J. West, *Stagecoach and Sternwheel Days in the Cariboo and Central B.C.* (Surrey: Heritage House, 1985), p. 10.
30 Ken Mather, *Stagecoach North* (Victoria, BC: Heritage House, 2020), p. 114.
31 Branwen Patenaude, *Trails to Gold, Roadhouses of the Cariboo* (Surrey, BC: Heritage House, 1996), p. 133.
32 West, *Stagecoach and Sternwheel*, p. 10.
33 Fred Ludditt, *Barkerville Days* (Langley, BC: Mr. Paperback, 1980), p. 59.
34 For the range of stories about Lightning Creek, see Forsythe and Dickson, *The Trail of 1858*, p. 96; Milton and Cheadle's 1863 journal *Cariboo Gold Rush* (Victoria, BC: Heritage House, 2013) p. 80; Agnes Laut, *The Cariboo Trail* (Victoria, BC: Touchwood, 2013), p. 34; Richard Thomas Wright, *Barkerville and the Cariboo Goldfields* (Victoria, BC: Heritage House, 2013), p. 95; Donald E. Waite, *The Cariboo Gold Rush Story* (Surrey, BC: Hancock House, 1988), p. 33.
35 Gordon R. Elliott, *Barkerville, Quesnel & the Cariboo Gold Rush* (North Vancouver: Douglas & McIntyre, 1958, 1978), p. 25.
36 Wright, *Barkerville, Williams Creek, Cariboo*, p. 137.
37 A fine wet silt that is heavy and gummy to handle.
38 *City Directory*, Manchester New Hampshire, 1852, p. 78, accessed through ancestry.ca.
39 *The Engineering and Mining Journal*, 53 (April 23, 1892): 446. J.C. Beedy may have followed his older brother Jonathan Winslow Beedy's path to Spanish Flats, where he had succumbed to smallpox at age twenty-three in 1853.
40 Nathan Crosby, *A Crosby Family* (Lowell, MA: Stone, Huse & Company, 1877), p. 72.
41 Mather, *Stagecoach North*, p. 32.
42 *The Victoria Daily Times*, December 31, 1887, p. 5.
43 *Daily British Colonist*, November 30, 1860, p. 3.
44 Mather, *Stagecoach North*, p. 29.
45 *Daily British Colonist*, April 18, 1861, p. 3.
46 *Montreal Gazette*, January 3, 1878, p. 1, 2.
47 Elliott, *Gold in British Columbia*, p. 70.
48 *Weekly Butte Record*, December 14, 1861, p. 1. Also carried in *Sacramento Daily Union*, December 12, 1861, p. 4.

49 Fred Ludditt, *Barkerville Days* (Vancouver: Mitchell Press, 1969), p. 23.
50 Elliott, *Gold in British Columbia*, p. 402.
51 *New Westminster British Columbian*, June 18, 1862, p. 3. Eves was born January 6, 1831, in Barbourville, Kentucky. In 1860 he resided in Sierra County California and had been in the Cariboo for less than two years when he died. He was buried in the Yale Pioneer Cemetery.
52 *Victoria Daily Times*, November 9, 1886, p. 3. Magirl was also from Crawford County, Pennsylvania—the same hometown as J.C. Beedy.
53 Ernest S. Cowper, "Miners of '63 Ate Bacon—at $1.75 a Pound," *The Province*, December 18, 1934, p. 23.
54 Elliott, *Gold in British Columbia*, p. 405.
55 *Cariboo Sentinel*, July 19, 1868, p. 3 and August 25, 1869, p. 3.
56 Letter, J.C. Beedy to father, July 3, 1869, courtesy of Jean Beedy Young.
57 *Cariboo Sentinel*, June 8, 1868, p. 2 and June 16, 1869, p. 4. Merchants' Line operated a regular schedule of packet ships that carried mail and freight between Victoria and San Francisco. A packet ship was originally a boat that carried post office mail packets to and from British embassies, colonies and outposts. During the 1800s, the service catered to retailers who required scheduled and reliable transport and was a new service at the time.
58 *Victoria Gazette,* July 21, 1858.
59 *Victoria Gazette,* September 11, 1858.
60 *Victoria Gazette,* November 13, 1858.
61 Royal BC Archives, Colonial Correspondence, file 995, GR1372_141-1.
62 William Mark, *Cariboo, A True and Correct Narrative* (Stockton: W.M. Mark, 1863), p. 22. http://collections.barkerville.ca/tales/cariboo.
63 Belle Rendall, *History of Harrison Hot Springs and Port Douglas Area* (Harrison Lake Historical Society, 1981).
64 Milton and Cheadle's 1863 journal in *Cariboo Gold Rush* (Surrey, BC: Heritage House, 1987, 1999), p. 73. Patenaude, *Trails to Gold*, p. 273, identifies Beedy and Lindhard as operators of this roadhouse in 1863.
65 *Cariboo Sentinel*, October 4, 1866, p. 4.
66 Royal BC Archives, Colonial Correspondence, file 995, GR1372_141-1.
67 *Cariboo Sentinel*, May 6, 1867, p. 1.
68 *Cariboo Sentinel*, August 18, 1869, p.4.
69 Melanie Ihmels, "The Mischiefmakers, Woman's Movement Developments in Victoria, British Columbia, 1850–1910," master's thesis (University of Victoria, 2013).

70 J. David Hacker, "Decennial Life Tables for the White Population of the United States 1790–1900." https://www.ncbi.nlm.nih.gov/pmc/articles/PMC2885717/#S2title.

71 Jacqueline Gerson, Austin Wadle, and Jasmine Parham, "Gold Rush, Mercury Legacy: Small Scale Mining for Gold Has Produced Llonglasting Toxic Pollution, from 1860s California to Modern Peru," *The Conversation*, May 28, 2020. https://theconversation.com/gold-rush-mercury-legacy-small-scale-mining-for-gold-has-produced-long-lasting-toxic-pollution-from-1860s-california-to-modern-peru-133324.

72 *Cariboo Sentinel*, August 4, 1870, p. 3.

73 *Cariboo Sentinel*, February 4, 1871, p. 2.

74 *Cariboo Sentinel* March 18, 1871, p. 3, and April 8, 1871, p. 3.

75 *Cariboo Sentinel*, March 25, 1871, p.3.

76 Patenaude, *Trails to Gold*, p. 226.

77 Ibid., p. 224.

78 Louise Shaw, "Ryder Lake—Up on the Hill," in *The Chilliwack Story*, ed. Ron Denman (Chilliwack Museum and Archives, 2007), p. 287–301.

79 Barkerville Archives, RG 085, RG 398, RG 004, RG 086.

80 Patenaude, *Trails to Gold*, p. 224–227.

81 Royal British Columbia Archives, GR-0216, 104 Volume 74.

82 *Daily British Colonist*, January 31, 1871, p. 2.

83 *Cariboo Sentinel*, February 11, 1871, p. 3.

84 *Cariboo Sentinel*, April 29, 1871, p. 1.

85 Mather, *Stagecoach North*, p. 146–150.

86 Ken Mather, "Barkerville Hosts Canada's First Dominion Day (Before Being Part of Canada!)," *Barkerville, 150 Years of Pure Gold, Prince George Citizen*, June 7, 2012, p. 16–19. https://issuu.com/pgcitizen/docs/barkerville.

87 *Cariboo Sentinel*, July 8, 1871, p. 3.

88 *Cariboo Sentinel*, July 8, 1871, p. 3.

89 *Cariboo Sentinel*, October 7, 1871, p. 3.

90 Dixi and Lucy's infant son Josiah Beedy Ross died at Cottonwood in 1872. The Ross family moved to Victoria in 1873 and Dixi partnered with J. Cameron and later F. Neufelder before opening his own grocery store on Government Street. Dixi H. Ross became a much-loved grocery store located at 117 Government and later at 111 Government Street, after Dixi's son Harry took over. The store remained in business in Victoria for about fifty years and had a reputation for innovative

advertising, an abundant stock of food and liquor, and hospitable treatment of customers. See Oke and Griffin, *Feeding the Family*, p. 28–29. https://hcmc.uvic.ca/~taprhist/content/documents/article.php?article=ross.

91 Certificate of Death 106, North Carolina State Board of Health, September 5, 1941. Lora stated she was born October 13, 1865, in Quesnelle.

92 *Cariboo Sentinel*, May 16, 1874, p. 2.

93 Patenaude, *Trails to Gold*, p. 260.

94 *Cariboo Sentinel*, May 13, 1874, p. 1 and p. 3. Also, *Daily British Colonist*, May 26, 1874.

95 I have been unable to find any information about Lora DeLora. It's believed she was of Indigenous heritage. Her and Josiah's child Lora lived as part of the Harriet Beedy Ross family and attended higher education in Chicago. She pursued a career in medicine and was one of the first group of women who graduated as a doctor from the College of Physicians and Surgeons, University of Illinois, in 1899. She lived and worked at times in Oregon and Michigan, and settled in Asheville, North Carolina. She never married and died in Asheville in 1941.

96 *Cariboo Sentinel*, November 28, 1874, p. 3.

97 *Daily British Colonist*, September 5, 1880, p. 3.

98 *Cariboo Sentinel*, May 9, p. 3 and June 6, 1874, p. 3.

99 *Daily British Colonist*, June 16, 1874, p. 3.

100 *Cariboo Sentinel*, September 12, 1874, p. 3.

101 *Cariboo Sentinel*, June 20, p. 3 and October 31, 1874, p. 3.

102 Elliott, *Gold in British Columbia*, p. 344.

103 *Cariboo Sentinel*, August 7, 1875, p. 3. It appears that the store built in 1875 was also the Beedy family's new residence. Stanley gradually became the dominant town, although the names Van Winkle and Stanley are used sometimes separately and sometimes together to designate the separate settlements that for a period of time were indistinguishable. To add to the confusion, the Van Winkle post office continued to be called Van Winkle even after it was physically moved to Stanley.

104 British Columbia Public Schools Report 1879–1885, Supplementary Report. http://saltspringarchives.com/reports/docs/1879.pdf.

105 *Guide to the Province of British Columbia for 1877–78* (Victoria: T.N. Hibben and Company, 1877), p. 368. https://open.library.ubc.ca/collections/bcbooks/items/1.0222279.

106 *Daily British Colonist*, July 4, 1878, p. 3.

107 *Daily British Colonist,* July 14, 1878, p. 3.
108 See the mining file summary at https://minfile.gov.bc.ca/Summary.aspx?minfilno=093H%20%20037.
109 *Daily British Colonist,* March 29, 1879, p. 3.
110 *Daily British Colonist,* November 30, 1879, p. 3.
111 *Daily British Colonist,* March 9, 1881, p. 1. Richfield was the location of the courthouse that served the Barkerville area. Barkerville consisted of four small mining towns within four miles on Williams Creek. Richfield was farthest upstream on the creek, Camerontown farthest downstream. Barkerville grew up in the middle, and Marysville was the fourth site scattered on the flats below Camerontown.
112 Royal British Columbia Archives, GR-1304, reel # B08878, Victoria Supreme Court—probate/wills.
113 *Daily British Colonist,* September 5, 1880, p. 3.
114 *Daily British Colonist,* November 20, 1880, p. 3.
115 *Daily British Colonist,* March 19, 1881, p. 3.
116 *Daily British Colonist,* May 2, 1880, p. 3, and Royal BC Archives, GR-0216.103 Volume 73, Lightning Creek Bills of Sale and Transfers, 1880–1908.
117 *Daily British Colonist,* March 31, 1881, p. 2.
118 *Daily British Colonist,* May 3, 1881, p. 2.
119 *Daily British Colonist,* March 30, 1884, p. 2.
120 *Daily British Colonist,* May 1, 1884, p. 4.
121 *Daily British Colonist,* April 12, 1885, p.3.
122 *Daily British Colonist,* May 11, 1885, p. 4.
123 *Daily British Colonist,* May 12, 1885, p. 3.
124 *Daily British Colonist,* August 2, 1885, p. 3.
125 *Cariboo Sentinel,* May 23, 1870, p. 3 and October 5, 1872, p. 3.
126 *Cariboo Sentinel,* July 1, 1870, p. 3.
127 *Cariboo Sentinel,* April 29, 1871, p. 3.
128 *Cariboo Sentinel,* January 7, 1871, p. 3.
129 Joe Hough was an artist with a satirical newspaper *The Comet* published in Victoria in 1873. See Royal BC Archives photo A-02136.
130 *Cariboo Sentinel,* October 19, 1872, p. 3.
131 *Cariboo Sentinel,* July 5, 1873, p. 3.
132 *Cariboo Sentinel,* April 19, 1871, p. 3 and May 9, 1874, p. 3.
133 *Cariboo Sentinel,* April 3, 1875, p. 3.

134 William M. Hong, *. . . And So . . . That's How It Happened: Recollections of Stanley-Barkerville 1900–1975* (Barkerville: Friends of Barkerville, 1978) p. 217.
135 Downs, Arthur." https://abcbookworld.com/writer/downs-art/.
136 Edward Mallandaine, *The British Columbia Directory 1887* (Victoria: E. Mallandaine and R.T. Williams, 1887), p. 274.
137 *Daily British Colonist*, May 18, 1880, p. 3.
138 *Daily British Colonist*, October 20, 1886.
139 *Daily British Colonist*, November 11, 1886, p. 3.
140 *Oakland Tribune*, March 12, 1888, p. 1.
141 Dodd block in downtown Spokane. https://www.spokesman.com/stories/2014/jan/13/then-and-now-federal-building-in-dodds-wake/.
142 *Morning Oregonian*, October 27, 1888, p. 8.
143 *Daily British Colonist*, July 20, 1888, p.1.
144 *Daily British Colonist,* November 8, 1887, p. 3.
145 *Daily British Colonist,* February 19, 1988, p.2.
146 W.M. Halliday, *Williams' British Columbia Directory Part 2* (Victoria: R.T. William, 1891). p. 270. https://bccd.vpl.ca/index.php/browse/title/1891/Williams%27_British_Columbia_Directory_Part_2.
147 *Sausalito News,* May 29, 1897.
148 See *Henderson's British Columbia Gazateer and Directory* of 1890, and the 1891 Canada Census.
149 See 1891 Canada Census and *Williams Official British Columbia Directory,* 1893.
150 *The Evening Republican,* Meadville, Pennsylvania, September 13, 1893, and *Titusville Herald,* December 14, 1901.
151 Barkerville Archives, RG085.
152 Patenaude, *Trails to Gold*, p. 241.
153 E-mail correspondence with Ted Beedy, October 6, 2020.
154 Letter A.H. Beedy to Fred Tregillus, April 20, 1900, Barkerville Archives.
155 *The Province,* September 29, 1941, p. 15
156 Hong, *That's How It Happened.*
157 Ludditt, *Barkerville Days*, p. 61.
158 L.G. Henderson, *Henderson's Gazetteer and Directory (*Victoria: L.G. Henderson, 1901), p. 255.
159 The Chinook expression, klahowya (kla'-how-ya), is the ordinary salutation at meeting or parting, meaning, "How do you do?" and "Good-bye."

160 Excerpt from "Good-bye to Cariboo" by W.L.F., from MS-0044-0001 Lottie Bowron fonds, Royal BC Archives.
161 *Sausalito News*, March 15, 1902, p. 12.
162 Barkerville Archives, 1999.0009.0944, Tregillus collection, 1901.
163 United States Census, 1910, accessed through ancestry.ca.

Part Two—CAROLINE LINDHARD BATES HARRISON

1 Alcott, Alcott, and Shealy, *Little Women Abroad*, p. xx.
2 David Oppenheimer's interests moved from Yale to Victoria and Vancouver as he seized new opportunities in the developing cities in merchandising, real estate, lumbering, railroad construction, and a variety of other interests. He served as mayor of Vancouver from 1888 to 1891.
3 Chad Reimer, *Before We Lost the Lake* (Halfmoon Bay, BC: Caitlin Press, 2018), p. 101–103.
4 This ad appeared frequently in the *Cariboo Sentinel*.
5 *Cariboo Sentinel*, November 12, 1870, p. 3.
6 *Cariboo Sentinel*, December 3, 1870, p. 3.
7 *Cariboo Sentinel*, June 4, 1870, p. 3.
8 *Cariboo Sentinel,* September 3, 1870, p. 2, 3.
9 *Cariboo Sentinel*, November 12, 1870, p. 3.
10 *Cariboo Sentinel*, January 6, 1871, p. 2.
11 *Cariboo Sentinel*, November 26, 1870, p. 2.
12 *Cariboo Sentinel*, December 31, 1870, p. 3.
13 *Cariboo Sentinel*, January 14, 1871, p. 3.
14 *Cariboo Sentinel*, February 4, 1871, p. 3.
15 Theodor held shares in Rockdale Company on Chisholm Creek, along with J.W. Lindhard and J.C. Beedy (*Cariboo Sentinel*, August 10, 1872, p. 3). He also held shares in Halliday Company on Peters Creek (*Cariboo Sentinel*, August 24, 1872, p. 3).
16 *Cariboo Sentinel*, August 10, p. 3 and August 24, 1872, p. 3.
17 *Cariboo Sentinel*, June 8, 1872, p. 3.
18 *Cariboo Sentinel,* February 10, 1872, p. 2.
19 *Cariboo Sentinel*, July 6, 1872, p. 3.
20 *Cariboo Sentinel*, August 24, 1872, p. 2.
21 *Cariboo Sentinel*, April 26, 1873, p. 3.
22 Bright's disease was a condition of the kidneys that today is referred to as chronic or acute nephritis. The condition could have been caused by

exposure to toxins, infection, or autoimmune factors. The result was inflammation of the structure of the kidneys and a frequent cause of death at the time.
23 *Cariboo Sentinel*, June 14, 1873, p. 2.
24 *Cariboo Sentinel*, June 14, 1873, p. 2.
25 *The Victoria Daily Times,* December 31, 1890, p. 11.
26 Harry Jones as told to Louis Lebourdais, "Early Days in the Cariboo," *The Province*, March 23, 1935, p. 43.
27 Royal British Columbia Archives, GR-0216.102, Volume 72, Lightning Creek Bills of Sale and Transfers, 1860–79.
28 Lizzie Munro (1853–1952) was the daughter of Alexander Munro, who was with the Hudson's Bay Company and chief factor from 1874 to 1890. In 1875 she married Robert Paterson Rithet, one of Victoria's well-known merchants and a businessman-entrepreneur who was mayor of Victoria in 1885 and a member of the provincial legislature in the 1890s.
29 The Protestant Orphan's Home opened in 1873. One of the founding members was Margaret Barnard Sargison, who, along with Ellen Stillman Barnard, was a regular donor to the Home for many years.
30 *Cariboo Sentinel*, June 6, p. 3 and June 20, 1874, p. 4.
31 Caroline's brother-in-law J.C. Beedy appears to have been an investor in the *Victoria* since his cash book shows receipts and disbursements each autumn from the steamer *Victoria*. Royal British Columbia Archives PR-1173 Beedy and Townsend fonds, 1875–1879.
32 In 1879, Captain John Irving and Robert McLeese of Soda Creek bought the *Victoria*. It continued to work the Upper Fraser River until at least 1886 when it was hauled ashore and left to decay near Fort Alexandria. Its registry was closed in 1897. See *Daily British Colonist*, June 20, 1879, p. 3; Art Downs, *Paddlewheels on the Frontier Volume One* (Surrey: Foremost Publishing, 1967–71), p. 48; and Norman R. Hacking, "Steamboating on the Fraser in the 'Sixties," *British Columbia Historical Quarterly* 10, no. 1 (January 1946): p. 1–42.
33 Nichols Academy was founded in 1815 by wealthy industrialist Amasa Nichols. It has closed at various times, and today operates as the private Nichols College. https://en.wikipedia.org/wiki/Nichols_College.
34 *Hartford Courant*, October 11, p. 2 and October 17, 1849, p. 2.
35 *Daily National Democrat*, March 28, 1860, p. 2.
36 *New Westminster Mainland Guardian*, January 20, 1872.

Notes

37 A.J. Splawn, *Ka-mi-akin—The Last Hero of the Yakimas* (Portland: Kilham Stationery and Printing, 1917), p. 170.
38 Ibid., p. 211.
39 Uncle Dan Drumheller, *Uncle Dan Drumheller Tells Thrills of Western Trails in 1854* (Spokane, WA: Inland-American Printing, 1925).
40 Thomas Menefee and Francis Woodward were both Missourians who were packers; they later partnered in buying the Mission Ranch. Menefee died in Barkerville while attending horse races in 1873 and was buried in the Soda Creek cemetery. Elliott, *Gold in British Columbia*, p. 253–255.
41 Correspondence with Anna Gilbert, Williams Lake Indian Band Genealogy Project, February 4, 2020.
42 Baptismal Record of Williams Lake, St. Joseph's Mission 1866–1882.
43 Andie Diane Palmer, *Maps of Experience: The Anchoring of Land to Story in Secewepemc* (Toronto: University of Toronto Press, 2005).
44 Royal British Columbia Archives, PR-1956 St. Joseph's Mission fonds.
45 *Cariboo Sentinel*, May 28, 1870, p. 3.
46 *Cariboo Sentinel*, July 30, p. 3 and October 1, 1870, p. 3. The company consisted of W.G. Asbury, George Newton, Thomas Jones, Isaac Howell, R.H. Young, Isaac Lipsett, James Moore, George W. Cook, and Ira Crow.
47 *Cariboo Sentinel*, September 19, 1867, p. 3.
48 *Cariboo Sentinel*, October 2, 1869, p. 2.
49 *Cariboo Sentinel*, September 14, 1872, p. 3.
50 *Cariboo Sentinel*, July 27, 1872, p. 2.
51 Robin Skelton, *They Call It the Cariboo* (Victoria: Sono Nis Press, 1980).
52 Art Downs, *Wagon Road North* (Surrey, BC: Heritage House, 1960–93), p. 32.
53 *New Westminster Mainland Guardian*, January 20, 1872.
54 *The Times Picayune New Orleans*, Louisiana, February 28, 1872, p. 8, and *Weekly Oregon Statesman*, Salem Oregon, April 10, 1872, p. 3.
55 *Cariboo Sentinel*, May 8, 1872, p. 3.
56 *Cariboo Sentinel*, October 12, 1872, p. 3.
57 "My Egotism," diary of Jas. N. Thain, *Daily British Colonist*, 1874, October 10, 11, 13, 15, 16, and 17.
58 Hacking, "Steamboating," p. 5.
59 *Daily British Colonist*, August 9, 1874, p. 3.
60 British Columbia Women's Institutes Centennial Cook Book, *Adventures in Cooking* (Victoria: Author, 1958), p. 65.

61 Lara Campbell, *A Great Revolutionary Wave* (Vancouver, BC: University of British Columbia Press, 2020), p. 14.
62 Paulette Falcon, "If The Evil Ever Occurs: The 1873 Married Women's Property Act: Law, Property and Gender Relations in 19th Century British Columbia," master's thesis (University of British Columbia, 1991).
63 *Cariboo Sentinel*, September 20, 1866, p. 3.
64 On Elizabeth Ord, see *Cariboo Sentinel*, July 1, 1867, p. 2; Elizabeth Thurber, see *Cariboo Sentinel*, June 3, 1867, p. 2 and July 30, 1866, p. 4; Fanny Bendixen, see *Cariboo Sentinel*, June 25, 1866, p. 3; Mrs. Gannon, see *Cariboo Sentinel*, July 12, 1866, p. 2.
65 *Cariboo Sentinel*, January 23, 1875, p. 3.
66 *Cariboo Sentinel*, May 1, 1875, p. 3.
67 *Daily British Colonist*, October 22, 1875, p. 1.
68 *Daily British Colonist*, June 8, 1875, p. 3.
69 *Daily British Colonist*, October 22, 1875, p. 1.
70 Peter R. Decker, *Fortunes and Failures: White Collar Mobility in Nineteenth-Century San Francisco* (Cambridge, MA: Harvard University Press, 1978).
71 Patenaude, *Trails to Gold*, 89.
72 *Oakland Tribune*, January 28, 1882, p. 3.
73 Aaron O'Neil, "Child Mortality Rate in Canada, 1830–2020." Statista, June 21, 2022. https://www.statista.com/statistics/1041751/canada-all-time-child-mortality-rate/.
74 *Daily British Colonist*, October 13, 1878, p. 3.
75 *Daily British Colonist*, July 3, 1878, p. 3.
76 Royal British Columbia Archives, PR-1709 E/C/M21.1 Archibald McKinlay letters; Irene Stangoe; *Cariboo-Chilcotin, Pioneer People and Places* (Surrey, BC: Heritage House, 1994), p. 123.
77 *Daily British Colonist*, November 12, 1878, p. 3.
78 *Daily British Colonist*, January 3, 1879, p. 3.
79 *The Daily Citizen*, Ottawa, January 15, 1879, p. 2.
80 David R. Williams, *The Man for a New Country: Sir Matthew Baillie Begbie* (Sidney, BC: Gray's Publishing, 1977), p. 107. The enacting of this law was not as straightforward as it first appeared. "Country wives" and "illegitimate children" were not permitted to file their own claims on an estate. Instead, they had to have an agent do so on their behalf. This required a certain determination to engage the process that some may have chosen to avoid. See Chris Clarkson, *Domestic Reforms,*

Political Visions and Family Regulation in British Columbia, 1862–1940 (Vancouver, BC: UBC Press, 2007), 60.
81 The letter originally appeared in the *Daily British Colonist*, November 7, 1879, p. 3. https://williamslakeband.ca/about/history/.
82 *Daily British Colonist*, December 6, 1879, p. 3.
83 McKinlay was a Hudson's Bay Company employee who moved in 1862 with his family to Lac La Hache, pre-empted land, and started a ranch and roadhouse at 115 Mile. From 1876 to 1878, he was one of three commissioners (with G.M. Sproat and A.C. Anderson) to the Joint Indian Reserve Commission that was tasked with settling land disputes between settlers and Indigenous people.
84 *Daily British Colonist*, December 13, 1879, p. 3.
85 Archibald McKinlay 1876–77 Diary, PR-1709 Royal British Columbia Archives.
86 *Daily British Colonist*, January 11, 1880, p. 2.
87 The position of Indian superintendent was a federal appointment and a position Powell held for seventeen years, beginning in 1872. During this time, Powell, a medical doctor, worked for better education and medicine for Indigenous people. Prior to this appointment by Prime Minister Sir John A. MacDonald, Powell had been a member of the British Columbia Legislative Council and a supporter of British Columbia joining the Dominion of Canada. Sarah Cheevers, Christina Rocha, and Miranda Griffith, eds., *First Nations Water Rights in British Columbia: A Historical Summary of the Rights of the Williams Lake First Nation* (Victoria, BC: Ministry of Environment, Lands & Parks, Water Management Branch, 2001), p. 13.
88 Robert Edgar Cail, "Disposal of Crown Lands in British Columbia, 1871–1913," master's thesis (University of British Columbia, 1956).
89 Elliott, *Gold in British Columbia*, p. 388.
90 *Arizona Daily Star*, March 25, 1880, p. 2.
91 *Daily British Colonist*, June 15, 1879, p. 2.
92 *Daily British Colonist*, June 21, 1879, p. 2.
93 *Oakland Tribune*, September 6, 1880, p. 3 and *Oakland Tribune*, September 12, 1881, p. 3.
94 Hixon led a group of five prospectors in May 1866 into an area known as Canyon Creek, from which there had been reports of a gold-bearing creek discovered by "some Chinese." The area was about fifty miles north of Quesnelmouth, which Hixon described

as a "continuation of the Cariboo mountains" and "very valuable." *Cariboo Sentinel,* July 9, 1866, p. 2. The town of Hixon and Hixon Creek are now named for Hixon as "discoverer" of the area. In 1872 Hixon was bankrupt. See *The British Columbia Gazette,* August 17, 1872 https://open.library.ubc.ca/collections/bcbooks/items/1.0357399#p174z-3r0f:Hixson. In 1879, J.F. Hixon served as an agent for the estate of A.S. Bates and plaintiff versus W.W. Houseman in a case of the estate being owed $150 for cattle (GR 570, volume 2, Royal BC Archives, County Court records Quesnelmouth and Soda Creek). Hixon may also have served as Otis Bates' agent in making a claim on the Bates estate, as required in the *Destitute Orphans' Act.* See Clarkson, *Domestic Reforms.*

95 *San Francisco Examiner,* November 18, 1881, p. 4.
96 *San Francisco Examiner,* May 14, 1882, p. 3 and August 17, 1883, p. 4; *Oakland Tribune,* May 29, 1882, p. 4.
97 *Oakland Tribune,* May 11, 1882, p. 2.
98 *Oakland Tribune,* May 24, 1883, p. 3.
99 "Bates v. Bates," *The Pacific Reporter* 12 (January 1887), p. 223–224.
100 *Oakland Tribune,* July 12, 1883, p. 3.
101 In the 1880s, Alban Nelson Towne was general manager of the Southern Pacific Railway Company.
102 *San Francisco Examiner,* November 24, 1888, p. 2.
103 *The Elite Directory for San Francisco and Oakland* (San Francisco: Argonaut Publishing, 1879), p. 21.
104 Dorothy Harriet Huggins, "San Francisco Society: From the 'Elite Directory' of 1879," *California Historical Society Quarterly* 19, no. 3 (1940), p. 225–239.
105 Huggins, "San Francisco Society," p. 235.
106 *San Francisco Examiner,* July 14, 1889, p. 3.
107 *San Francisco Examiner,* March 2, 1884, p. 3.
108 *San Francisco Examiner,* June 22, 1891, p. 5.
109 *San Francisco Chronicle,* June 22, 1891, p. 5.
110 *San Francisco Examiner,* November 24, 1888, p. 2.
111 *Oakland Tribune,* August 4, 1883, p. 8 and July 30, 1885, p. 2.
112 *San Francisco Examiner,* November 24, 1888, p. 2.
113 *San Francisco Examiner,* December 8, 1888, p. 4 and *Oakland Tribune,* December 7, 1888, p. 8. Some reports indicate the Claremont estate was where Caroline, A.S. Bates, and family, including Otis, lived for

several years. Claremont is now a neighbourhood straddling the city limits of Oakland and Berkeley.
114 U.S. Spanish American War Volunteers Index to Compiled Military Service Records, 1898, accessed through www.ancestry.ca.
115 *Oakland Tribune*, March 14, 1904.
116 *Sausalito News*, November 19, 1904, p. 2.
117 *San Francisco Call*, April 30, 1899, p. 15.
118 *Marin County Tocsin*, February 24, 1900, p. 3.
119 *Sausalito News*, June 21, 1902, p. 2.
120 *Berkeley Daily Gazette*, September 27, 1904, p. 3.
121 *San Francisco Call*, July 28, 1907, p. 36.
122 *San Francisco Call*, April 5, 1903, p. 42, July 19, 1903, p. 42. and May 11, 1904, p. 40; *San Francisco Chronicle*, May 2, 1903, p. 4.
123 *San Francisco Call*, November 18, 1895, p. 8.
124 *The San Francisco Examiner*, March 23, 1905, p. 7.
125 *Sausalito News*, April 28, 1906, p. 1.
126 *Sausalito News*, April 28, 1906, p. 4.
127 *San Francisco Call*, December 28, 1906, p. 15, *The San Francisco Examiner*, February 8, 1907, p. 5; *The Recorder* (San Francisco), September 23, 1908, p. 3.
128 *Marin County Tocsin*, February 3, 1912, p. 1.
129 *Sausalito News*, February 8, p. 1 and February 15, p. 1.

Part Three—CHRISTINE LINDHARD HAMILTON

1 *Daily British Colonist*, July 28, 1874, p. 3.
2 *Daily British Colonist*, July 28, 1874, p. 3. Lydia Pinkham was beginning to build her reputation as an herbalist, promoting her vegetable compound and other "medicinal" concoctions that appealed to women and others in a family-operated business that lasted into the 1930s.
3 Barnard's Express company name officially changed in 1872 to F.J. Barnard and Company, when Stephen Tingley and James Hamilton each became one-quarter owner-partners in the company. The common name in usage remained Barnard's Express and over the decade came to be referred to as the BX Express and then the BC Express Company.
4 Garnet Basque, "Soda Creek," *Canadian West* 17 (Fall, 1989), p. 83–91. There are usually several stories about why places are named as they are. For Soda Creek, another is that it was named for "the white alkali

powder that dries on the rocks" along the Fraser River at this place. Forsythe and Dickson, *Trail of 1858*, p. 200.
5   Patenaude, *Trails to Gold*, p. 129–138.
6   Ekaterina Khaustova and Paul Sharp, "A Note on Danish Living Standards through Historical Wage Series, 1731–1913," *EHES Working Papers in Economic History* 81 (July 2015), p. 1. http://www.ehes.org/EHES_81.pdf.
7   *Daily British Colonist*, June 1, 1878, p. 3.
8   Because of their architectural style, the first government administration buildings built in 1859 were dubbed the "bird cages." They occupied the same location as the current Legislative Building, facing James Bay. The section of Government Street with address numbers in the 500s was known as Birdcage Walk from 1859 to 1905. Today it is part of Government Street south of the Legislative Building, a BC Heritage site, still identified as Birdcage Walk.
9   *Daily British Colonist*, May 30 to June 6, 1878.
10 *Cariboo Sentinel*, May 4, 1872, p. 2.
11 *Cariboo Sentinel*, May 4, 1872, p. 3.
12 *Inland Sentinel*, June 10, 1880.
13 Mather, *Stagecoach North*, p. 176–77, 180–81.
14 *Daily British Colonist*, January 23, 1879, p. 3.
15 *Daily British Colonist*, January 23, 1879, p. 3.
16 *Daily British Colonist*, April 25, 1880, p. 3.
17 *Daily British Colonist*, January 1, 1881, p. 2.
18 *Daily British Colonist*, August 21, 1881, p. 3.
19 The Clinton Annual Ball, now in its 155th year, prides itself on being the longest running event of this kind. See https://www.clintonannualball.com.
20 *Daily British Colonist*, January 21, 1882, p. 3.
21 Mark S. Wade, *The Cariboo Road* (Victoria: Haunted Bookshop, 1979), p. 196–99.
22 *Daily British Colonist*, March 15, 1883, p. 2.
23 Wade, *The Cariboo Road*.
24 *Daily British Colonist*, October 29, 1882, p. 3. Captain Clarke was harbour master in Victoria, a city councillor and an auctioneer. His wife, Mary, age 37, had died on September 28. The cottage was likely named for Thanet, a coastal district on the northeastern tip of Kent, England.
25 *Daily British Colonist*, November 21, 1883, p. 1 and December 12, 1883, p. 3.

26 *Daily British Colonist,* October 4, 1882, p. 2.
27 *Daily British Colonist,* October 4, 1883, p. 3.
28 Edgar Marvin was vice-consul of the United States in Victoria, an entrepreneur-partner in the hardware company Marvin & Tilton, and a founding director of the Victoria Transfer Company. Joseph Loewen was a part owner of Victoria Brewery and a distributor of beer throughout the province. Robert Burns McMicking set up the first company to bring electric lighting to Victoria and established Victoria's first telephone exchange. Dixi Ross was a nephew of J.C. Beedy and operated a grocery store in Victoria. Theodore Lubbe was a fur merchant and miner associated with developing electrical power by damming Goldstream River to power Victoria's streetlights and street cars. Stephen Tanner was manager for Victoria Truck & Dray Company. Anton Henderson was born Antoni Hendriksen in Denmark. In 1880, he became an agent for the BC Express Company in Cache Creek. He succeeded James Hamilton as superintendent of the Victoria Transfer Company. William Dodd was agent for the BC Express Company and government agent in Yale during the 1870s and 1880s.
29 *Daily British Colonist,* October 6, 1883, p. 3.
30 *Daily British Colonist,* November 21, 1883, p. 1.
31 *Daily British Colonist,* December 4, 1883, p. 3.
32 *Daily British Colonist,* December 14, 1883, p. 3.
33 *The Flaming Sword,* January 9, 1892, p. 8.
34 *The San Francisco Call,* April 21, 1891, p. 3. Royal Spear was a charismatic recruiter who toured the Midwest and California promoting Teed's ideas.
35 Lyn Millner, *The Allure of Immortality* (Gainsville FL: University Press of Florida, 2015) p. 21.
36 Millner, *The Allure of Immortality* p. 22.
37 *San Francisco Examiner,* July 8, 1891, p. 4.
38 *The Flaming Sword,* February 11, 1898, p. 2.
39 Wendy E. Chmielewski, Louis J. Kern, and Marlyn Klee-Hartzell, eds., *Women in Spiritual and Communitarian Societies in the United States* (Syracuse, NY: Syracuse University Press, 1993).
40 Koreshan Memories of Marie McCready, accessed at www.ancestry.com.
41 Irvin D. S. Winsboro, "The Koreshan Communitarians' Papers and Publications in Estero, 1894–1963," *The Florida Historical Quarterly* 83, no. 2 (2004), p. 184.

42 *St. Louis Globe-Democrat*, May 4, 1892, p. 1, and *San Francisco Chronicle*, April 28, 1892, p. 7.
43 *The Inter Ocean*, March 2, 1894, p. 4.
44 United States Census, 1910.
45 Christine Hamilton letter to Jennie Campbell, December 1, 1908. State Archives of Florida, Koreshan Collection, N2009-3_B234_FF19.
46 Christine Hamilton letter to Jennie Campbell, December 8, 1908. See the interpretation by Katherine Adams, "Life Inside the Earth: The Koreshan Unity and Its Urban Pioneers, 1880–1908," master's thesis (The Florida State University, 1910), p. 43–44. Jennie Campbell was a schoolteacher within the commune.
47 James E. Landing, "Cyrus Reed Teed and the Koreshan Unity," *America's Communal Utopias*, ed. Donald E. Pitzer (Chapel Hill & London: University of North Carolina Press, 1997), p. 375–95.
48 *News-Press*, Fort Myers, August 15, 1913, p. 3; July 4, 1914, p. 3; and November 14, 1914, p. 3.
49 *News-Press*, Fort Myers, January 24, 1919, p. 3.
50 Irvin D.S. Winsboro, "The Koreshan Communitarians' Papers and Publications in Estero, 1894–1963," *The Florida Historical Quarterly* 83, no. 2 (2004), p. 173–90.
51 *News-Press*, Fort Myers, December 31, 1918, p. 8.
52 Emma Norton (1857–1950) was Teed's sister and a faithful follower from the beginning. Virginia Andrews (1846–1921) was the wife of Abie Andrews, longtime friend and supporter. Initially a reluctant supporter, after her husband died, she became a committed follower and moved to Estero with her children. She was secretary until she died in 1921. Evelyn Bubbett (1854–1935) joined the Koreshans in Chicago in 1888. She moved to Estero in 1894 with her husband and children and was the owner of the Koreshan's publishing house. Etta Silverfriend (1866–1944) was a member of the Chicago group in 1888. She and her brother were board members and Etta was the treasurer. Esther Stotler (1852–1932).
53 *San Francisco Chronicle*, April 28, 1892, p. 7.
54 Millner, *Allure of Immortality*, p. 255
55 Ibid., p. 280.
56 D.J. Richards, "Current Events in Our Community Life," August 1922, p. 92, accessed at https://www.yumpu.com/en/document/read/3699339/current-events-in-our-community-life-by-d-j-the-koreshans.

Notes

57 See https://www.floridastateparks.org/parks-and-trails/koreshan-state-park.
58 *San Francisco Call*, August 25, 1895, p. 19.
59 *Sausalito News*, November 3, 1900, p. 1.
60 *San Francisco Examiner*, December 2, 1901, p. 11.
61 *San Francisco Examiner*, February 8, 1904, p. 7.
62 *Sausalito News*, May 6, 1905, p. 3.
63 Information provided by family. The dress was donated to a museum in Tennessee by Minerva Wright Matthews.
64 *Oakland Tribune*, August 25, 1906, p. 8.
65 *San Francisco Call*, May 28, 1911, p. 34.
66 *San Francisco Examiner*, August 2, 1914, p. 44.

CONCLUSIONS

1 Helen Doe, "Gender and Business," *Female Entrepreneurs in the Long Nineteenth Century*, eds. Jennifer Aston and Catherine Bishop ([Cham, SI]: Palgrave Macmillan, 2020), p. 347–57.
2 Melanie Buddle, "Skirting the Boundaries: Businesswomen in Colonial British Columbia, 1858–1914," *Female Entrepreneurs in the Long Nineteenth Century*, eds. Jennifer Aston and Catherine Bishop ([Cham, SI]: Palgrave Macmillan, 2020), p. 315–36.
3 On ideas of generational power and settler futurity, see Laura Ishiguro, "'Growing Up and Grown Up . . . in Our Future City': Discourses of Childhood and Settler Futurity in Colonial British Columbia," *B.C. Studies* 190 (Summer, 2016), p. 18.
4 Elliott, *Gold in British Columbia*, 216.
5 Prins, "Seasons of Gold."
6 *Daily British Colonist*, April 13, 1881, p. 3.
7 Bridge, *By Snowshoe, Buckboard and Steamer*, p. 20.
8 Chris Clarkson, *Domestic Reforms*, p. 52.
9 *Daily British Colonist*, March 11, 1888, p. 4. While citizenship could offer a sense of identity and some privilege, it didn't assure continued residency. Theodor Lindhard became a naturalized citizen on July 4, 1875, but he left Stanley in the early 1880s and returned to Denmark.
10 *Daily British Colonist*, April 20, 1881, p. 2.

BIBLIOGRAPHY

Alcott, Louisa May, May Alcott, and Daniel Shealy. *Little Women Abroad: The Alcott Sisters' Letters from Europe, 1870–1871*. Athens, GA: University of Georgia Press, 2008.

Aston, Jennifer, and Catherine Bishop, eds. *Female Entrepreneurs in the Long Nineteenth Century : A Global Perspective*. Cham, SI: Palgrave Macmillan, 2020.

Barman, Jean. *Sojourning Sisters: The Lives and Letters of Jessie and Annie McQueen*. Toronto: University of Toronto Press, 2003.

———. *The West Beyond the West*. Toronto: University of Toronto Press, 2004.

———. "Sophie Morigeau, Free Trader, Free Woman." In *Recollecting: Lives of Aboriginal Women of the Canadian Northwest and Borderlands*. edited by Sarah Carter and Patricia McCormack, 175–195. Edmonton: University of Alberta Press, 2011.

Barman, Roderick J. "Biography as History." *Journal of the Canadian Historical Association/ Revue de la Societe historique du Canada* 21, no. 2 (2010): 61–75.

Baskerville, Peter A. "She Has Already Hinted at 'Board': Enterprising Urban Women in British Columbia 1863–1896." *Histoire sociale – Social History* 26, no. 52 (November 1993): 205–227.

———. "Women and Investment in Late-Nineteenth Century Urban Canada: Victoria and Hamilton, 1880–1901." *The Canadian Historical Review* 80, no. 2 (June 1999): 191–218.

Basque, Garnet. "Soda Creek." *Canadian West* no. 17 (Fall 1989): 83–91.

Beedy, Mary E. "The Joint Education of Young Men and Women in American Schools and Colleges (1873)." In *The Education Papers:*

Women's Quest for Equality in Britain, 1850–1912, edited by Dale Spender, 248–267. New York: Routledge, 1987.

Beeton, Isabella. *The Book of Household Management*. New York: Penguin Books, 1861.

Boris, Eileen, and Nupur Chaudhuri, eds. *Voices of Women Historians: The Personal, the Political, the Professional*. Bloomington: Indiana University Press, 1999.

Bridge, Kathryn. *By Snowshoe, Buckboard and Steamer: Women of the British Columbia Frontier*. Victoria, BC: Royal British Columbia Museum, 1998, 2019.

———. *Henry & Self, an English Gentlewoman at the Edge of Empire*. Victoria, BC: Royal British Columbia Museum, 1996, 2019.

———. ed. *New Perspectives on the Gold Rush*. Victoria, BC: Royal British Columbia Museum, 2015.

British Columbia Women's Institutes Centennial Cook Book. *Adventures in Cooking*. Victoria, BC: Author, 1958.

Buddle, Melanie. "Skirting the Boundaries: Businesswomen in Colonial British Columbia, 1858–1914." In *Female Entrepreneurs in the Long Nineteenth Century*, edited by Jennifer Aston and Catherine Bishop, 315–336. [Cham, SI]: Palgrave Macmillan, 2020.

Campbell, Lara. *A Great Revolutionary Wave: Women and the Vote in British Columbia*. Vancouver and Toronto: UBC Press, 2020.

The Canadian Home Cook Book, Containing 739 Valuable Recipes. 1919.

Cheevers, Sarah, Christina Rocha, and Miranda Griffith eds. *First Nations Water Rights in British Columbia: A Historical Summary of the Rights of the Williams Lake First Nation*. Victoria: Ministry of Environment, Lands & Parks, Water Management Branch, 2001.

Chmielewski, Wendy E., Louis J. Kern, and Marlyn Klee-Hartzell, eds. *Women in Spiritual and Communitarian Societies in the United States*. Syracuse, NY: Syracuse University Press, 1993.

Clarkson, Chris. *Domestic Reforms, Political Visions and Family Regulation in British Columbia, 1862–1940*. Vancouver, BC: UBC Press, 2007.

Clayton, Jenny. *The Lieutenant Governors of British Columbia*. Madeira Park, BC: Harbour Publishing, 2019.

Crosby, Nathan. *A Crosby Family*. Lowell, MA: Stone, Huse & Company, 1877.

Dalley, Lana L., and Rappoport, Jill, eds. *Economic Women: Essays on Desire and Dispossession in Nineteenth-Century British Culture*. Columbus, OH: University of Ohio Press, 2013.

Damsholt, Tine. "Hand of King and Voice of People: Grundtvig on Democracy and the Responsibility of Self." In *Building the Nation*, edited by John A. Hall, Ove Korsgaard, and Ove K. Pedersen, 151–168. Montreal & Kingston: McGill-Queen's University Press, 2015.

Davidoff, Lenore. *Thicker Than Water: Siblings and Their Relations 1780–1920*. Oxford: Oxford University Press, 2013.

Decker, Peter R. *Fortunes and Failures: White Collar Mobility in Nineteenth-Century San Francisco*. Cambridge, MA: Harvard University Press, 1978.

Denman, Ron, ed. *The Chilliwack Story*. Chilliwack, BC: Chilliwack Museum and Archives, 2007.

Downs, Art. *Wagon Road North*. Surrey, BC: Heritage House, 1960–93.

Downs, Art, ed. *Cariboo Gold Rush*. Surrey, BC: Heritage House, 1987, 1999.

———. *Paddlewheels on the Frontier, BC Volume One*. Surrey, BC: Foremost Publishing, 1967–71.

Drumheller, Uncle Dan. *Uncle Dan Drumheller Tells Thrills of Western Trails in 1854*. Spokane, WA: Inland-American Printing, 1925.

Elliott, Gordon R. *Barkerville, Quesnel & The Cariboo Gold Rush*. North Vancouver, BC: Douglas & McIntyre, 1958, 1978.

Elliott, Marie. *Gold and Grand Dreams: Cariboo East in the Early Years*. Victoria: Horsdal & Schubart, 2000.

———. "Women of the Fraser River Gold Rush." In *The Trail of 1858*, edited by Mark Forsythe & Greg Dixon, 74–75. Madeira Park, BC: Harbour Publishing, 2007.

———. "Women in the Fraser and Cariboo Gold Rushes, 1858–70." In *New Perspectives on the Gold Rush*, edited by Kathryn Bridge, 109–124. Victoria, BC: Royal British Columbia Museum, 2015.

———. *Gold in British Columbia: Discovery to Confederation*. Vancouver: Ronsdale Press, 2020.

Epp, Marlene, Franca Iacovetta, and Frances Swyripa, eds. *Sisters or Strangers? Immigrant, Ethnic and Racialized Women in Canadian History*. Toronto: University of Toronto Press, 2004.

Eyford, Ryan C. "Close Together, Though Miles and Miles Apart: Family, Distance and Emotion in the Letters of the Taylor Sisters, 1881–1921." *Histoire sociale/Social History* 48, no. 96 (May 2015): 67–86.

Forsythe, Mark, and Greg Dixon, eds. *The Trail of 1858*. Madeira Park, BC: Harbour Publishing, 2007.

Gallaher, Bill. *The Promise, Love, Loyalty & the Lure of Gold*. Surrey, BC: TouchWood Editions, 2001.

Guide to the Province of British Columbia for 1877–78. Victoria, BC: T.N. Hibben and Company, 1877.

Hacking, Norman R. "Steamboating on the Fraser in the 'Sixties." *British Columbia Historical Quarterly* 10, no. 1 (January 1946): 1–42.

Hale, Frederick, ed. *Danes in North America*. Seattle and London: University of Washington Press, 1984.

Hall, John A., Ove Korsgaard, and Ove K., eds. *Building the Nation: N.F.S. Grundtvig and Danish National Identity*. Montreal: McGill-Queen's University Press, 2015.

Halliday, W.M. *Williams' British Columbia Directory, Part 2*. Victoria, BC: R.T. William, 1891.

Hawk, Angela. "Going 'Mad' in Gold Country: Migrant Populations and the Problem of Containment in Pacific Mining Boom Regions." *Pacific Historical Review* 80, no. 1 (February 2011): 64–96.

Haworth, Paul L. "On the Headwaters of Peace River." In *Peace River Chronicles*, edited by Gordon E. Bowes, 327–345. Vancouver, BC: Prescott, 1963.

Henderson, L.G. *Henderson's Gazetteer and Directory*. Victoria, BC: L.G. Henderson, 1890.

———. *Henderson's Gazetteer and Directory*. Victoria, BC: L.G. Henderson, 1901.

Herbert, Christopher. *Gold Rush Manliness: Race and Gender on the Pacific Slope*. Seattle, WA: University of Washington Press, 2018.

Hong, William M. *. . . And So . . . That's How It Happened: Recollections of Stanley-Barkerville 1900–1975*. Barkerville: Friends of Barkerville, 1978.

Huggins, Dorothy Harriet. "San Francisco Society: From the 'Elite Directory' of 1879." *California Historical Society Quarterly* 19, no. 3 (1940): 225–39.

Hume, Stephen. *Lilies & Fireweed, Frontier Women of British Columbia*, Madeira Park, BC: Harbour Publishing, 2004.

Hvidt, Kristian. *Flight to America: The Social Background of 300,000 Danish Emigrants*. New York: Academic Press, 1975.

Irwin, Mary Ann. "Going About and Doing Good: The Politics of Benevolence, Welfare, and Gender in San Francisco 1850–1880." *Pacific Historical Review* 68, no. 3 (1999): 365–96.

Ishiguro, Laura. "Growing Up and Grown Up . . . In Our Future City: Discourses of Childhood and Settler Futurity in Colonial British Columbia." *BC Studies* 190 (2016): 15–37.

Khaustova, Ekaterina, and Paul Sharp. "A Note on Danish Living Standards through Historical Wage Series, 1731–1913." *EHES Working Papers in Economic History* no. 81 (July 2015): 1–25.

Kidd, Benjamin. *Social Evolution*. Cambridge: Cambridge University Press, 1894.

Laut, Agnes. *The Cariboo Trail*. Victoria, BC: Touchwood, 2013.

Landing, James E. "Cyrus Reed Teed and the Koreshan Unity." In *America's Communal Utopias*, edited by Donald E. Pitzer. Chapel Hill & London: University of North Carolina Press, 1997.

Ludditt, Fred. *Barkerville Days*. Vancouver: Mitchell Press, 1969.

———. *Barkerville Days*. Langley, BC: Mr. Paperback, 1980.

Mallandaine, Edward. *First Victoria Directory, Fifth Issue*. Victoria, BC: Author, 1874.

———. *The British Columbia Directory 1887*. Victoria, BC: E. Mallandaine and R.T. Williams, 1887.

Mather, Ken. *Stagecoach North*. Victoria, BC: Heritage House, 2020.

Millner, Lyn. *The Allure of Immortality*. Gainsville, FL: University Press of Florida, 2015.

Neering, Rosemary. *Wild West Women: Travellers, Adventurers and Rebels*. North Vancouver: Whitecap Books, 2000.

———. *The Canadian Housewife*. North Vancouver, BC: Whitecap Books, 2005.

Oke, Nancy, and Robert Griffin. *Feeding the Family: 100 Years of Food & Drink in Victoria*. Victoria: Royal British Columbia Museum, 2011.

Palmer, Andie Diane. *Maps of Experience: The Anchoring of Land to Story in Secewepemc*. Toronto, ON: University of Toronto Press, 2005.

Patenaude, Branwen. *Trails to Gold: Roadhouses of the Cariboo*. Surrey, BC: Heritage House, 1996.

Perry, Adele. "Hardy Backwoodsmen, Wholesome Women, and Steady Families: Immigration and the Construction of a White Society in Colonial British Columbia, 1849–1871." *Histoire sociale/Social History* 33, no. 66 (November 2000): 343–60.

Rae, William Fraser. *Westward by Rail: The New Route to the East*. London, UK: Longmans, Green and Company, 1870.

Reimer, Chad. *Before We Lost the Lake*. Halfmoon Bay, BC: Caitlin Press, 2018.

Rendall, Belle. *History of Harrison Hot Springs and Port Douglas Area*. Harrison Lake Historical Society, 1981.

Shaw, Louise. "Ryder Lake—Up on the Hill." In *The Chilliwack Story*, edited by Ron Denman. Chilliwack, BC: Chilliwack Museum and Archives, 2007.

Skelton, Robin. *They Call It The Cariboo*. Victoria, BC: Sono Nis Press, 1980.

Spender, Dale, ed. *The Education Papers: Women's Quest for Equality in Britain 1850–1912*. New York: Routledge, 1987.

Splawn, Andrew Jackson. *Ka-mi-akin: The Last Hero of the Yakimas*. Portland, OR: Kilham Stationery and Printing, 1917.

Stangoe, Irene. *Cariboo-Chilcotin: Pioneer People and Places*. Surrey, BC: Heritage House, 1994.

Wade, Mark S. *The Cariboo Road*. Victoria, BC: Haunted Bookshop, 1979.

Waite, Donald E. *The Cariboo Gold Rush Story*. Surrey, BC: Hancock House, 1988.

West, Willis J. *Stagecoach and Sternwheel Days in the Cariboo and Central BC*. Surrey, BC: Heritage House, 1985.

Williams, David R. *"The Man for a New Country": Sir Matthew Baillie Begbie*. Sidney, BC: Gray's Publishing, 1977.

Winsboro, Irvin D.S. "The Koreshan Communitarians' Papers and Publications in Estero, 1894–1963." *The Florida Historical Quarterly* 83, no. 2 (2004): 173–90.

Wright, Richard Thomas. *Barkerville, Williams Creek, Cariboo*. Wells, BC: Winter Quarters Press, 1998.

———. *Barkerville and the Cariboo Goldfields*. Surrey BC: Heritage House, 2013.

ARCHIVAL SOURCES

Barkerville Historic Town Archives
- RG 004 J.C. Beedy, 2 boxes, 11 books
- RG 085 W.W. Dodd, 2 boxes, 1 book
- RG 086 Van Winkle and Stanley store ledgers
- RG 398 Account book Hudson's Bay Company Store 1876 to 1880
- Fred Tregillus Collection

Florida State Archives
- Koreshan Unity Papers, N2009-3
- Box 234, FF19.
- Box 30, FF 16, 28, 29, 30
- Member files, series 4, box 170, FF 11

Kamloops Archives, Stephen Tingley Bio files, newspaper clippings

Royal British Columbia Archives
- GR-0216.102 Volume 72, Lightning Creek Bills of Sale and Transfers, 1860–1879
- GR-0216.103 Volume 73, Lightning Creek Bills of Sale and Transfers, 1880–1908
- GR-0216.104 Volume 74
- GR-1372_141-1, file 995 Colonial Correspondence
- GR-1304 reel # B08878, Victoria Supreme Court – probate/wills
- MS-0044-0001 Lottie Bowron fonds
- PR-1173 Beedy and Townsend fonds, 1875–1879
- PR-1709 Archibald McKinlay 1876-77 Diary
- PR-1709 E/C/M21.1 Archibald McKinlay letters
- PR-1956 St. Joseph's Mission fonds

ONLINE SOURCES

Ancestry. www.ancestry.com.

City Directory, Manchester New Hampshire, 1852.

Koreshan Memories of Marie McCready

U.S. Spanish American War Volunteers Index to Compiled Military Service Records, 1898.

"Downs, Art." ABC Bookworld. https://abcbookworld.com/writer/downs-art/.

British Columbia Census, 1881. http://data2.collectionscanada.gc.ca/e/e329/e008211654.jpg.

Williams' British Columbia Directory Part 1. 1891. British Columbia City Directories 1860–1955. Vancouver Public Library. https://bccd.vpl.ca/index.php/browse/title/1891/Williams%27_British_Columbia_Directory_Part_2.

The British Columbia Gazette, vol. 11, 1872. https://open.library.ubc.ca/collections/bcbooks/items/1.0357399.

Minfile Record Summary, No. 093H 037. British Columbia Ministry of Energy, Mines and Petroleum Resources. https://minfile.gov.bc.ca/Summary.aspx?minfilno=093H%20%20037.

British Columbia Public Schools Report 1879–1885, Supplementary Report. Saltspring Archives. http://saltspringarchives.com/reports/docs/1879.pdf

Chief William Statement, 1879. Williams Lake Band. https://williamslake-band.ca/about/history/.

Richards, D.J. "Current Events in Our Community Life." August 1922, p. 92. https://www.yumpu.com/en/document/read/3699339/current-events-in-our-community-life-by-d-j-the-koreshans.

Day in Castle Garden, New York. *Harper's Monthly*, volume 42, June to November 1870. https://www.gjenvick.com/Immigration/CastleGarden/1871-03-ADayInCastleGardenImmigrantStation.html.

Khaustova, Ekaterina, and Paul Sharp, "A Note on Danish Living Standards through Historical Wage Series, 1731- 1913." *EHES Working Papers in Economic History* 81 (July 2015): 1. http://www.ehes.org/EHES_81.pdf.

The Engineering and Mining Journal, volume 53, April 23, 1892, p. 446 https://books.google.ca/books?redir_esc=y&id=ZdI2AQAAMAAJ&q=Beedy#v=onepage&q=Beedy&f=false.

The Flaming Sword http://iapsop.com/archive/materials/flaming_sword/.

Gerson, Jacqueline, Austin Wadle and Jasmine Parham, "Gold Rush, Mercury Legacy: Small scale mining for gold has produced long-lasting toxic pollution, from 1860s California to modern Peru." *The Conversation*, May 28, 2020. https://theconversation.com/gold-rush-mercury-legacy-small-scale-mining-for-gold-has-produced-long-lasting-toxic-pollution-from-1860s-california-to-modern-peru-133324.

Guide to the Province of British Columbia for 1877–78 (Victoria: T.N. Hibben and Company, 1877), 368. https://open.library.ubc.ca/collections/bcbooks/items/1.0222279.

Hacker, J. David. "Decennial Life Tables for the White Population of the United States 1790-1900." https://www.ncbi.nlm.nih.gov/pmc/articles/PMC2885717/#S2title.

Henderson's Gazetteer and Directory https://bccd.vpl.ca/index.php/browse/title/1901/Henderson%27s_BC_Gazetteer_and_Directory.

Koreshan State Park. https://www.floridastateparks.org/parks-and-trails/koreshan-state-park.

Mather, Ken. "Barkerville hosts Canada's First Dominion Day (before being part of Canada!)," *Barkerville, 150 Years of Pure Gold, Prince George Citizen*, June 7, 2012, 16–19. https://issuu.com/pgcitizen/docs/barkerville.

Museum of Danish America. https://www.danishmuseum.org/explore/danish-american-culture/viewed-through-the-lens/confirmation-coming-of-age-in-denmark-and-the-us.

O'Neil, Aaron. "Child Mortality Rate in Canada, 1830–2020." Statista, June 21, 2022. https://www.statista.com/statistics/1041751/canada-all-time-child-mortality-rate/.

Pacific Coast Business Directory, 1867. https://open.library.ubc.ca/collections/bcbooks/items/1.0308093#p812z-3r0f.

"Bates v. Bates," *The Pacific Reporter* (Volume 12, January 1887), West Publishing Company, 223–224. https://play.google.com/books/reader?id=Jk3DTL9RsikC&hl=en&pg=GBS.PA69.

Ross, Harry G. https://hcmc.uvic.ca/~taprhist/content/documents/article.php?article=ross.

United States Coast Survey. https://en.wikipedia.org/wiki/USCS_Active.

NEWSPAPERS

The following newspapers were accessed through several online sources and some were a part of more than one collection. Sources were: archive.org, https://newspaperarchive.com, ancestry.com, California Digital Newspaper Collection (https://cdnc.ucr.edu), and BC Historical Newspapers (https://open.library.ubc.ca/collections/bcnewspapers).

Barkerville, *Cariboo Sentinel*
Berkeley, California, *Berkeley Daily Gazette*
Chicago, *The Inter Ocean*
Estero, Florida, *The Flaming Sword*
Fort Myers, Florida, *News-Press*
Hartford, Connecticut, *Hartford Courant*
Marysville, California, *Daily National Democrat*
Meadville, Pennsylvania, *The Evening Republican*
Montreal, *Montreal Gazette*
New Orleans, *The Times Picayune*
New Westminster, *British Columbian*
New Westminster, *Mainland Guardian*
Oakland, California, *Oakland Tribune*
Oroville, California, *Weekly Butte Record*
Ottawa, *Daily Citizen*
Portland, Oregon, *Morning Oregonian*
Prince George, BC, *Prince George Citizen*
Sacramento Daily Union
Salem, Oregon, *Weekly Oregon Statesman*
San Francisco Call
San Francisco Chronicle

San Francisco *Examiner*
San Francisco, *The Recorder*
San Rafael, California, *Marin County Tocsin*
Sausalito, California, *Sausalito Marin Scope*
Sausalito, California, *Sausalito News*
St. Louis, Missouri, *Globe-Democrat*
Titusville, Pennsylvania, *Titusville Herald*
Tucson, Arizona, *Arizona Daily Star*
Vancouver, *The Province*
Vancouver, *Daily Standard*
Victoria, *Daily British Colonist*
Victoria, *Daily Times*
Victoria, *Victoria Gazette*

THESES

Adams, Katherine. "Life Inside the Earth: The Koreshan Unity and Its Urban Pioneers, 1880–1908," master's thesis (Florida State University, 1910).

Cail, Robert Edgar. "Disposal of Crown Lands in British Columbia, 1871–1913," master's thesis (University of British Columbia, 1956).

Falcon, Paulette. "If The Evil Ever Occurs: The 1873 Married Women's Property Act: Law, Property and Gender Relations in 19th Century British Columbia, master's thesis (University of British Columbia, 1991).

Ihmels, Melanie. "The Mischiefmakers: Woman's Movement Development in Victoria, British Columbia, 1850–1910," master's thesis (University of Victoria, 2013).

Mikkelsen, Phyllis. "Land Settlement Policy on the Mainland of British Columbia 1858–1874," master's thesis, (University of British Columbia, 1950).

Prins, Megan Katherine. "Seasons of Gold: An Environmental History of the Cariboo Gold Rush," master's thesis (Simon Fraser University, 2007).

Raun, James Jensen. "The Danish Lutherans in America to 1900," doctoral dissertation (University of Chicago, 1930).

Sherwood, Jay Allen. "Political and Economic History of British Columbia 1871–1903," master's thesis (University of Montana, 1976).

Trueman, Alice. "Playing the Game: The Education of Girls in Private Schools on Vancouver Island," master's thesis (University of Victoria, 2009).

INDEX

70 Mile House, 173
74 Mile House, 35
83 Mile House, 35
100 Mile House, 173, 186
115 Mile House, 35,
141 Mile House, 35
150 Mile House, 112, 120–23, 127, 130, 133, 140, 170, 173, 174–75, 186
1879 Constitutional Convention, 155
1891 Canadian Census, 81

Adelphi Saloon, 32
Agassiz, Lewis Nunn, 223–24
Agassiz, Mary Caroline Schram, 223
Ainsworth, Lawrence Sutton, 158
Alcott, Louisa May, 22–23, 96
Alcott, May, 22
American Independence Day, 6, 14, 51, 54, 57
Andrews, Virginia, 203, 206, 207
Angela College, 30
Anthony, Susan B., 155

Antler Creek, 41, 42
Arbor Society, 162
Armour, Samuel, 203
Ashcroft, BC, 72, 76, 80, 81, 117, 228

Baines, Mary, 182
Baker, Seymour, 86
Ball, H.W., 118
Ball, Henry Maynard, 46, 64
Ballarat Company, 74
Bancroft, Frederick, 159
Bank of British Columbia, 83, 119
Bank of British North America, 67
Bank of California, 130
Bank of Victoria, 83
Bardo, L.M., 85
Barkerville, 2, 4, 6–7, 19, 21, 31–32, 34–36, 38–39, 42–43, 46, 51, 54, 56–58, 60, 64, 66, 69, 73–74, 76–77, 80–82, 83, 84, 87–88, 89–91, 95–96, 98, 102–4, 107, 112, 116–17, 126, 160, 171, 173, 176, 180, 186, 190, 214, 220, 223, 228

Barman, Jean, 8
Barnard, Ellen Stillman, 183
Barnard, Francis Jones, 41–44, 51, 56–57, 59, 182–87, 189, 193
Barnard, Francis Stillman, 186, 191, 193
Barnard's Express, 31–33, 35, 41, 64, 102–3, 108, 112, 178, 180, 182–83, 185, 189, 190, 192. *See also* BC Express Company
Bartlett, Alice, 22
Bates, Alanson, 115
Bates, Asahel Sumner, 35, 66, 111–13, 115–16, 120, 122, 138, 140–41, 144, 151, 169, 173, 186, 225
Bates, Caroline. *See* Lindhard, Caroline
Bates, Ellie, 117–18, 135
Bates, Exira (Ex) Sumner, 127, 132, 175, 182
Bates, John "Otis", 68, 112, 117–18, 130, 134–35, 140–42, 150–53, 187
Bates, Levina Brown, 115
Bates, Theodora Levina, 131, 132, 177, 182
BC Express Company, 81, 89, 185, 187, 189–90, 185, 192. *See also* Barnard's Express
Beacon Hill Park, 182
Beaver Pass Ranch and Roadhouse, 61
Beedy and Company, 42
Beedy, Asa Harold, 7, 59, 64, 67, 72, 76, 80–82, 86–87, 89, 91–92, 106, 110, 153, 160, 162–63, 171, 173, 210, 214, 225

Beedy, Caroline, 161, 163, 215
Beedy, Josephine Caroline, 64, 66–67, 81, 92, 153–54, 162–63, 174
Beedy, Josiah Crosby, 6, 19–21, 37–38, 40–44, 46–47, 49–51, 54–56, 58–59, 60–62, 64–69, 71–72, 81, 85–86, 91–92, 106, 108, 110–12, 140, 153, 155–56, 160, 163, 175–76, 187, 209, 212, 219, 225
Beedy, Laura. *See* Lindhard, Laura
Beedy, Lora, 60–61, 63
Beedy, Ludwig "Louis" Samuel, 59, 64, 67, 76, 80, 82–83, 86, 91–92, 110, 153, 158–59, 163, 171, 173, 212, 214
Beedy, Mabel Hosmer, 158–59
Beedy, Mary Elizabeth (grandchild), 159, 214
Beedy, Mary Elizabeth, 49, 59, 81, 91, 210
Beedy, Olive Hamilton. *See* Hamilton, Olive Daghmar
Beedy, Samuel, 40, 65, 185, 211
Beedy, Winslow Lindhard, 65–67, 82–83, 86–88, 91, 92, 153, 159, 161–63, 175, 210, 212–13, 215
Begbie, Matthew, 90, 99, 117, 135
Belfast, Ireland, 54
Bendixen, Fanny, 2, 126
Birdcage Walk, 182
Black Bear Creek, 119
Board of Trade of Portland, 79
Bonaparte Band, 117
Boomer, Berthaldine, 202–3, 206, 207
Borrowe, Constance, 155

Index

Bowman, W.G., 127, 192
Bowron, Emily Edwards, 126
Bowron, John, 68
Bowron, Lottie, 86, 88, 90
Bowron, Willie, 87
Boyd, Janet, 54–55, 58, 76, 84, 186
Boyd, John, 7, 54, 76, 83–84, 186
Bradley, E.A., 85
Brew, Chartres, 103
Bridge River, 44
Briggs, Thomas, 133
British Columbia Directory, 76, 80
British Columbia Legislative Assembly, 126, 186, 191
British Columbia Supreme Court, 79
Bubbett, Evelyn, 200, 203, 206–7
Bubbett, James H., 203
Budd, Walter, 69,
Buddle, Melanie, 220
Buffalo, New York, 25
Burdett-Coutts, Angela, 30
Bureau of Equitable Commerce. *See* Koreshan Unity Commune
Burns Mountain Quartz Company's mine, 70
Burns Mountain, 66–67, 70–71, 219
BX. *See* Barnard's Express

California Digital Newspaper Collection, 6
California gold rush, 40, 143, 184
California Hotel, 44
California Superior Court, 140
California Title Insurance and Trust Company, 159
Callender, Elizabeth, 160
Cambridge Springs, Pennsylvania, 40, 43, 50, 58, 61, 65, 71, 82

Cameron, Sophia Groves, 2
Camp Golden Gate of the Society Arch-Triumphant, 197
Campbell, Jennie, 204, 206–7
Campbell, Louis, 116
Campbell, Ned, 37
Canadian Pacific Railroad, 107
Cape Horn, 4
Captain Bumsby, 119
Carey, Pat, 86
Cariboo Amateur Dramatic Association, 58, 73, 104, 223
Cariboo Amateur Theatre, 126
Cariboo Chilcotin–Gold Rush Trail, 181
Cariboo Road, 32–3, 45, 51, 54, 95, 98, 192,
Cariboo Sentinel, 7, 46, 48–49, 51, 56, 102, 104, 108, 113, 119, Z123, 185
Cariboo Wagon Road, 4, 32, 34–36, 52–53, 56, 122–23, 171, 176, 178, 180, 184, 223
Carpenter Ranch, 138
Carson, Alfred, 84
Carson, Mary Ann, 84
Cascade Mountains, 104
Castle Garden Immigration Depot, 24, 97
Central Pacific Railroad, 27–28
Chadsey, Chester, 98
Chadsey, George, 98
Chadsey, James, 98
Chadsey, William, 99
Charles H. Dodd and Company, 79
Chenery, Leonard, 159
Cheyenne, Wyoming, 27

Chicago and Northwestern Railroad, 27
Chicago, 25–27, 81, 153, 198, 200–3, 207–10, 215, 217
Chief William, 135–38
Chinatown, 178
Chisholm Creek, 66, 106
Christ Church Cathedral, 193
Christmas ship, 18
Civic League of San Francisco, 163
Claremont Estate, 130, 151
Clarke, Carrie, 182
Clarke, William Raymond, 192
Cleveland Oil and Paint Manufacturing Company, 79
Clinton Hotel, 190
Clinton, BC, 32–33, 35, 64, 68, 77, 125, 171, 181, 184, 188–89, 190–92, 197, 221, 228
Clunes, Mary, 126
Cluxton, John, 116
Cochran, Hugh, 87
Cold Spring House, 7, 54–55, 58, 84
Colonial Hotel, 179
Commodore Harrison. *See* Harrison, Charles Henry.
Common School Ordinance Act of 1869, 104
Company G Infantry, 151
Conklin Gulch, 74
Conly, John, 40
Copenhagen, 13, 63, 110, 167, 181, 208
Cosmopolitan Hotel, 60, 62
Cottonwood House, 51–53, 55–6, 59, 84, 106
Cottonwood Ranch, 106
Cottonwood River, 37, 52

Council Bluffs, Iowa, 27
County Court of Richfield, 60
Crease, Emily, 30
Crease, Henry, 30
Crease, Justice, 224
Crooks, George, 216
Cunningham, William, 37

Daily British Colonist, 6, 31–32, 41, 49, 56, 67–68, 70–71, 76, 80, 128, 134, 137, 139, 150, 176, 188, 191, 193, 225
Dakota, 68, 140, 182, 188
Dale Creek trestle bridge, 27
Dally, Frederick, 32, 39
Damkohler, Gustav, 202
Danish Constitution, 17
Davidoff, Lenore, 5
Davie and Pooley, law firm of, 194
Deacon, Jas, 86
Deep Creek Farm, 35, 138
Deep Creek House, 119, 120
DeLora, Lora, 60
Derrick, Thomas, 51,104
Detroit, Michigan, 25–26
Dodd, Budd and Company, 69, 70
Dodd, Charles Henry, 79
Dodd, Jane Wright, 73
Dodd, Laura. *See* Lindhard, Laura
Dodd, Thomas Steward, 73
Dodd, William Henry Harrison, 70
Dodd, William Wright, 69–71, 73, 77, 85, 196
Dominion Day, 6, 51, 54, 58, 73, 107
Douglas, James, 44, 99–100, 118, 195

Index

Downs, Art, 76, 228
Driard Hotel, 192
Drumheller, Dan, 117
Dudley, Massachusetts, 115
Dunbar Flats, 46, 51
Dunlevy, Peter Curran, 120, 178–79
Dunsmuir, Robin, 143, 159, 195
Duxbury Reef, 64

Earle, Thomas, 191
Eastman Business College, 82
Edwards, Benjamin, 75, 176
Edwardsville, 75
El Monte Hotel, 142
Eldorado Club Rooms. *See* New Eldorado Billiard & Dancing Saloon
Eldorado Saloon. *See* New Eldorado Billiard & Dancing Saloon
Elite Directory for San Francisco and Oakland, 143
Elliott, Andrew Charles, 41
Elliott, Marie, 117, 222
Elwyn, Thomas, 41
England, 4, 14, 61, 64, 73, 90, 99, 100, 145–46, 163, 196
Esquimalt Harbour, 30
Esquimalt, 191–92
Estero, Florida, 200–8, 217
Evans, John, 110
Eves, George, 42
Exchange Hotel, 35, 112, 120, 178–79,
Express Company. *See* Barnard's Express

F.J. Barnard and Company, 1, 175–76, 185–86. *See also* Barnard's Express
First and Second Schleswig Wars, 14
Fiske, Emma, 206–7
Flaming Sword, The, 197, 199, 200
Fleming, Janet, 54, 84
Fleming, John, 84
Florida Koreshan State Park, 208
Florida, 200–4, 206, 208, 217
Fort George, 180
Fort Myers, 202, 204–6
Fort Yale, 41, 60
Foster Gold Mining Company, 74
France, 22–23, 90
Fraser Canyon, 33, 41, 44–45
Fraser River gold rush, 41, 99
Fraser River, 1, 4, 37, 41, 44–45, 113, 127, 131, 170, 173, 178, 180, 222,
Frolic, 145, 148, 156
Fung, Ah, 19, 86, 102

Gay, Thomas, 203
Germany, 15, 22, 90, 98, 168
Girls' Collegiate School in Chicago, 81
Grand Hotel Club, 148
Grant, John, 118
Graves, Addison, 148, 203
Great Western Railway, 25
Grey, Rollin, 203
Griffin, James, 130
Grouse Creek, 86
Grundtvig, Nikolai Frederik Severin, 14–15
Guam, 152

Guiding Star Publishing House, 200, 210
Guillod, Harry, 38
Guilloteau, Aime, 19
Gunn, Mrs. C.M., 162

Halliday Company, 106
Hamburg America Line, 22
Hamburg, Germany, 22, 25, 30, 96, 168
Hamilton, Christine. *See* Lindhard, Christine
Hamilton, Gavin, 133
Hamilton, George Harold, 186
Hamilton, James, 1, 35, 65, 68, 127, 131, 142, 171, 173–75, 177, 184–87, 191–94, 211, 219, 221
Hamilton, John, 35, 216
Hamilton, Josephine Lindhard (Linda), 188, 211–13
Hamilton, Linda, 158–59, 163
Hamilton, Major, 184
Hamilton, Mary Ann,
Hamilton, Minerva Christine, 162, 212
Hamilton, Olive Daghmar, 91, 154, 161, 177, 209, 212, 214–15
Hamilton, Olivia (Olive) Kerr, 184
Hamilton, Ontario, 184
Hanson, Andrew, 41
Harper brothers, 107
Harper, Elizabeth, 2, 32
Harper, John, 182
Harper's Monthly, 24
Harrison Hot Springs, 78
Harrison Lake, 44–45, 78
Harrison, Caroline. *See* Lindhard, Caroline

Harrison, Charles Henry, 82, 141, 142, 146, 150, 158, 193, 209, 212–13
Hartford, Connecticut, 115
Hazel Mount, 145–47, 153, 155–56, 158, 160–62, 213–16
Henderson, Anton, 193
Henley, Charlotte, 158
Hixon, Joseph Foster, 140, 151
Hong, William, 89
Hope, BC, 45, 137, 223
Hosmer, Mabel Elizabeth, 158–59
Hotel de Fife, 103
Hough, Joseph Z., 74
Howard, Andrew, 203
Hudson Bay Company, 182
Hunt, Charles, 203
Hunt, George, 203
Huntingdon Company, 74
Hussey, George, 203
Huston, Jennie, 179

Intestate Estates Act, 135
Irving, John, 133

Jack of Clubs Creek, 74–75
Jones, Harry, 83, 110
Jones, Llewellyn, 74

Kattrup Sogn, 18
Kee, Yee, 103
King Christian VI, 17
King Frederik VII, 14
Kingston, Ontario, 52
Knight, Mary E., 198, 202
Koreshan Unity Commune, 197–98, 201, 207–8, 215, 217, 221
Kurtz, John, 41

Index

Lac la Hache, 184
Lafayette, 22–23
LaFontaine Mines, 89
Laird, Kathleen, 84
Land Ordinance Act, 104
Laramie valley, 27
Legislative Council of British Columbia, 51
Leighton, James Buie, 190
Lenihan, James, 138
Lightning Creek Register of Mortgages (1865–1906), 56
Lightning Creek, 18–20, 37–38, 42–43, 45, 51, 56, 61, 64–67, 70, 80, 83, 89, 96, 102–3, 109, 110, 175, 219
Lightning Hotel, 91
Lillooet Lake, 44, 45, 113
Lincoln Elementary School, 68
Lindhard & Co., 44
Lindhard, Belle Malarkey, 79
Lindhard, Bolette Nielsen, 13
Lindhard, Caroline, 1, 3–4, 7, 54, 58, 63–64, 68, 82–83, 88, 91–96, 102, 105–7, 111, 125, 126, 128, 130–31, 132–33, 135, 139–41, 144–55, 159–62, 167, 169–71, 174–5, 177, 182–83, 186–87, 194–97, 200, 2023, 207, 209, 211, 214–15, 218–26
  birth, 95
  death, 163, 216
  marriage, 29, 66, 77, 97–98, 101, 112–15, 118, 124, 127, 141–42, 145, 193
  immigration, 13, 21–23, 25, 30–32, 35–36, 97–100
  widowed, 60–61, 108–10, 134, 139, 156–58, 188, 213
Lindhard, Christine, 1, 4, 8, 68, 77, 131, 133, 140, 146–47, 153–54, 160, 170, 177, 181–84, 186–90, 192–98, 200–7, 209, 217–23, 226
  birth, 167
  death, 208
  marriage, 65, 127, 131, 175–76
  immigration, 63–5, 110–1, 125, 165–77
  widowed, 142, 193–4
Lindhard, Helen, 91, 154
Lindhard, Joachim "Henry," 4, 13, 16, 18–21, 23, 25, 27, 29–32, 34, 36–38, 43–46, 49–51, 56, 59–61, 66, 95–104, 106–12, 124, 130, 167, 169, 174, 219–20
Lindhard, Jorgen Hansen, 13, 95, 167
Lindhard, Josephine Margrethe Rasmussen, 13, 95, 167
Lindhard, Laura, 1, 7, 10–13, 14–16, 18–21, 35, 49–50, 52, 54–56. 58, 63–67, 69–77, 79–85, 88–92, 96–97, 100, 102, 105, 108, 110, 127, 140, 142, 147, 153–54, 158–59, 160, 167–68, 171, 173–77, 186, 193–96, 197, 200, 207, 210, 213–14, 218–21, 225–26
  birth, 13, 17
  death, 92, 162–63
  marriage, 18, 51, 71, 106, 196
  immigration, 3–4, 23–32, 36, 38, 125
  widowed, 59–61, 68, 78, 187–88
Lindhard, Peter "Harold," 13

Lindhard, Theodor, 13, 18, 21, 23, 25, 27, 29, 59, 61, 95, 98, 106, 110, 169, 174
Lindhard, William Laurist, 17, 79, 139
Lindsay, Alexander, 176
Loewen, Joseph, 193
Lord & Taylor, 125
Los Angeles, 155
Lubbe, Theodore, 193
Lucas, Hattie, 2
Lytton, BC, 30, 33, 38, 190
Lytton, Edward Bulwer, 99

Macy's, 125
Magirl, Robert, 42
Malarkey and Company, 82
Mann, Horace, 81
Married Women's Property Act, 60, 224
Marvin, Edgar, 113, 191, 193
Marysville, California, 54
McArthur, James, 59
McArthur, William, 59
McKenzie, Hector, 68, 187
McKinlay, Archibald, 138
McLaughlin Company, 107
McLeese, Robert, 178–79
McMicking, Robert Burns, 193
Meason Ranch, 138
Menefee, Thomas, 117
Michigan Central Railroad, 26
Millard, C.T., 43
Miller, David, 98
Miller, Laura Chadsey, 98
Mission Ranch, 117
Missouri River, 27
Mountain View Cemetery, 78, 132, 152, 158, 182, 188

Mssrs. Schorling & Company, 19
Munro, Lizzie, 111, 126–27
Musgrave, Anthony, 19–20, 100

Nam, Thomas, 85
Nelson, Hugh, 41
Nevada, 28,
New Brunswick, 32, 184, 228
New Dominion Dining Rooms, 104
New Eldorado Billiard & Dancing Saloon, 74–75
New Orleans, 98, 123
New Westminster Brass Band, 133
New Westminster Mainland Guardian, 122
New Westminster, BC, 4, 31, 104, 133, 136, 140, 171, 182, 187, 192
New York, 4, 22–25, 42, 61, 64, 82, 96–97, 110, 125, 148, 159–60, 168–69, 198
Niagara Falls, 25, 97
Nichol, Thomas, 76
Nichols Academy, 115
Nicola Valley, 185
Nimpmuc reservation, 115
North Pacific Coast Railroad Company, 145
North Pacific Transportation Company, 30
Norton, Emma, 203
Norway, 14, 90

Oakland Long Wharf, 28
Oakland, California, 68, 71, 76–79, 111, 114, 130–32, 134, 139–44, 151–53, 158, 177, 188, 195–98, 207, 221
Oberlin Business College, 81

Index

Old Van Winkle Store, 61
Omaha, Nebraska, 27
Omineca region, 102
Onward, 31, 170–71
Open Library University of British Columbia, 6
Oppenheimer, Charles, 51, 61, 98
Oppenheimer, David, 98
Ord, Elizabeth, 126
Ordway, Annie, 200, 203
Oroville, California, 40, 42
Ottawa Daily Citizen, 134

Palace Hotel, 128–30, 133–34, 142, 144, 147, 151, 189, 193
Panama, 4
Peebles, Ellen Dickie, 89
Peebles, John, 51, 66, 89
Perkin's Ledge, 66
Perkins Gulch, 20
Peters Creek, 106
Philippines, 152
Pima County, Arizona Territory, 138
Pinkney Place, 140, 159
Pioneer Line of Stages, 107
Planetary Court, 203, 206, 217. *See also* Koreshan Unity Commune
Port Douglas, 44–45
Portland, Oregon, 32, 79, 82, 83
Poughkeepsie, New York, 82
Powell, Israel, 137–38
Power, William, 41
Price, Watkin, 83
Prince Alfred, 63
Promontory, Utah, 27
Prussia, 14–15
Puerto Rico, 152

Pullman's Palace Cars, 25
Putnam's Magazine, 22

Queen Victoria, 22, 126
Quesnel Forks, 116
Quesnel Lake, 43
Quesnel, 37, 43, 77, 84, 113, 131, 173, 228
Quesnelmouth, 35, 42, 46, 51, 60, 113, 118, 180

Ralston, William, 130
Read and Cora companies, 74
Red Gulch, 89
Reid, James, 68, 219
Reno, 28
Rice, Rebecca, 81
Richfield, 37, 42, 52, 60, 64, 68, 103, 107, 126
Riotte, E.N., 66, 182
Rip Van Winkle Bar, 38
Roberts, Harmon, 56
Robinson, Elizabeth, 203, 206, 207
Rock Dale Company, 66, 106
Roeder, Henry, 61
Rogers, S.A., 87, 160
Rosborough, A.M., 142
Rose, Alithea, 145
Rose, Frederick, 66
Ross Bay Cemetery, 193
Ross Company, 66
Ross, Dixi H., 50, 58, 193
Ross, Harriet Beedy, 60–61
Ross, Lucy Birchard, 50, 58–59
Royal British Columbia Archives, 90
Ryder Lake, 52
Ryder, John Ferris, 52

Sacramento, 28
Salt Lake City, 27
San Francisco Yacht Club, 142, 145, 146, 155, 211
San Francisco, 4, 5, 7, 9, 28–30, 43, 59, 61, 63–64, 66, 68, 70, 72, 82–83, 91, 97–98, 107–8, 111–14, 125, 127–31, 133, 139–40, 142–48, 150, 155–56, 158, 160–61, 163, 169–71, 177, 181–82, 186–88, 191, 193–95, 197–98, 201, 208–9, 211–16, 221–23, 225
Sargent, John, 203
Sargison, George, 186
Sausalito Land and Ferry Company, 141, 145
Sausalito News, 154, 161, 210–12
Sausalito Women's Club, 155
Sausalito, 82, 88, 91–92, 111, 142, 145–50, 153–56, 158–63, 198, 202–3, 207, 209, 211–16, 221, 228
Savona, BC, 116–17, 190
Saxonia, 22–24, 96
Schleswig-Holstein region, 14
Scotch Jeanie, 103
Selborne Academy (now Tamalpais Boys' School), 82
Senay, Joseph, 178
Seymour, Frederick, 86, 100, 118
Sheldon, Mary, 2
Sherman, Wyoming, 27
Ships
  Active, 29–30, 98
  Enterprise, 31, 122, 133, 140, 171, 180, 192
  Fort Yale, 41, 60

Frolic, 145, 148, 156
Lafayette, 22–23
Mexico, 195
Onward, 31, 170–71
Prince Alfred, 63
Prince of Wales, 113
Princess, 142
San Rafael, 212
Saxonia, 22–24, 96
Silesia, 168
William Tabor, 64, 125, 169
Shoobert, Fannie, 159, 162, 212, 216
Sierra Nevada mountains, 28, 40
Sierra, 28, 40, 42
Silverfriend, Etta, 203, 206
Silverfriend, Henry, 203
Sinclair, Mary, 179
Slough Creek, 89
Smith, Allen, 52
Soda Creek, 35, 57, 65, 112–13, 120, 127, 131–32, 138, 171, 173, 176–81, 187–88, 221
Spanish American War, 151
Splawn, Jack, 116–17
Spuzzum, BC, 41, 44
St. Alice Hotel, 78
St. Joseph's Mission, 118
Stanford University, 81–82, 153, 209
Stanley, BC, 7, 36, 55, 62, 64–66, 68–70, 72–73, 75–77, 79–82, 84, 86, 89–91, 105, 109, 140, 153, 167, 171, 175, 177, 186–87, 196–97, 210, 220–22, 225, 228
Stanley, Edward Henry, 64
Stanton, Elizabeth Cady, 49
Staton, Lou, 203
Stege, Denmark, 13, 16, 20, 44, 95, 98, 167

Index

Stotler, Esther, 203, 207
Sugar Cane Ranch, 138

Tanner, Stephen, 193
Teed, Cyrus (Koresh), 198–205, 207–8
Temescal estate, 130
Thanet Cottage, 192, 194
Thompson River, 116
Thompson, C.L., 176
Thompson, Joshua Spencer, 223
Thorne, Eliza Jane, 98
Thurber, Elizabeth, 126
Tingley, Clarence Harper, 32
Tingley, Elizabeth Harper, 2
Tingley, Steve, 32, 171, 176, 186
Titusville High School, 82
Tlopelkey, 117, 118, 135,
Tolstoy, Leo, 162
Towne, Alban Nelson, 142
Townsend, Alfred, 60–62, 64, 110–11
Trahey, James, 113
Tregillus, Fred, 83, 86–88
Trutch, Joseph William, 118–19
Tupper-Galpin, Kate, 155
Two Sisters Claim, 74

Union Jack Company, 20
Union Pacific Railroad, 27–28
United States Coast Survey, 30
University of British Columbia, 6, 228
University of Victoria, 6
Uren, James, 190
Uren, Jennie, 190
Uren, Malvina Toy, 190
Valley Mountain, 74

Van Valkenburg, Ellen, 154
Van Winkle Company, 20, 51, 61, 66, 102, 106, 110, 219
Van Winkle store, 19, 46–47, 56, 61–62, 101–2, 111
Van Winkle, BC, 4, 6–7, 18–20, 31–32, 35–39, 43, 45–46, 49, 51–52, 56–66, 68, 73, 76, 95–96, 99–104, 106–8, 110-12, 162, 170, 173–75, 219
Vaughan and Sweeney Company, 73
Vernon Park, 140
Victoria Transfer Company, 191, 193–94, 219
Victoria, BC, 192–95, 203, 206, 219, 221–23
Victoria's Protestant Orphan's Home, 111
Virginia City, 28
Vulcan Saloon, 69, 76

W.L.F., 90
Wadham, E.A., 41
Wallace, Ross, 203
Warren Hill, 40
Way, Frank, 41, 44
Weaver, Moses, 203
Webster, Massachusetts, 115
Wells, Fargo & Company, 44
Welsh Mining Company, 66
Wendelbo, Dorethe Katrine Frikke, 18
Wendelbo, Jorgen Andersen, 18
Wheeler, Helen, 159
William Tabor, 64, 125, 169
Williams Creek, 41, 46, 76, 104, 223

Williams Lake, 112, 117–19,
 122–23, 135, 137–38, 228
Willow River mine, 89
Wilson G. Hunt, 133
Wilson, Florence, 126, 133
Women's Auxiliary to the
 California Pioneers, 163
Woodstock, New Brunswick, 184
Woodward, Francis Marion, 117
Wright, Anna Beatrice, 215
Wright, Charles Albert, 158, 159, 213
Wright, Gustavus Blin, 113, 140,
 180, 182

Wright, Julie Sutton, 159, 213, 221
Wright, Linda Hamilton. *See*
 Hamilton, Linda

Xat'sull Band, 138

Yale Steam Navigation Company,
 41
Yale, BC, 4, 7, 20, 31–34, 36,
 41–45, 57, 60, 64, 72, 82,
 98–99, 108, 120, 125, 170–71,
 180, 183–84, 186, 189, 223

ABOUT *the* AUTHOR

LINDA PETERAT IS an author, educator, and researcher. She holds a PhD from the University of Alberta and is professor emerita of curriculum studies at the University of British Columbia. For many years, she directed the home economics teacher education and graduate programs at UBC. She is a founding member of and contributor to the Silver Star Mountain Museum and the BC Food History Network. She resides part time on Silver Star Mountain and part time in Chilliwack.

Discover Heritage House's complete list of
Canadian history books at heritagehouse.ca.

STAGECOACH NORTH
A History of Barnard's Express

KEN MATHER

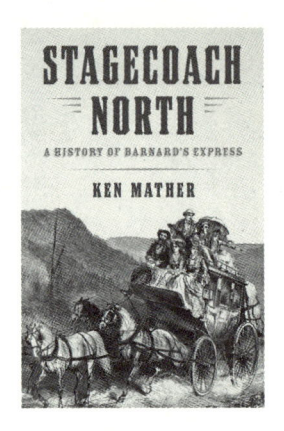

"An essential addition to any bookshelf on BC history." —*British Columbia History*

"In *Stagecoach North*, which includes maps, illustrations, and rare photos, Mather mixes scholarly research with interesting facts. His book is peppered with anecdotes and conveys the risks Barnard and others undertook over the rugged trails of south-central British Columbia." —*Canada's History*

ISBN 978-1-77203-309-0 (paperback)
ISBN 978-1-77203-310-6 (ebook)

WAGON ROAD NORTH
*The Saga of the Cariboo Gold Rush,
Revised and Expanded Edition*

ART DOWNS; KEN MATHER (ED.)

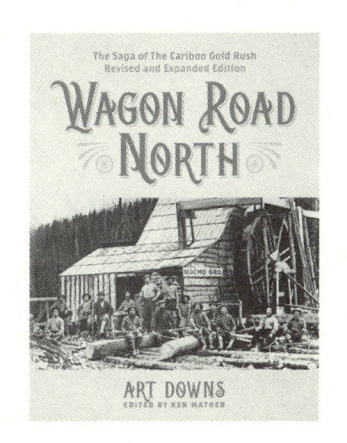

"This book is as informative today as it was six decades ago—especially with [Ken] Mather's additions."—*British Columbia Magazine*

"Updating a classic work is a tricky and dangerous business, but Mather has succeeded admirably here ... Mather's updates will help ensure that Wagon Road North remains a mainstay for years to come."—*BC Studies*

ISBN 978-1-77203-360-1 (paperback)

ISBN 978-1-77203-361-8 (ebook)

BRITISH COLUMBIA AND
YUKON GOLD HUNTERS
A History in Photographs

DONALD E. WAITE

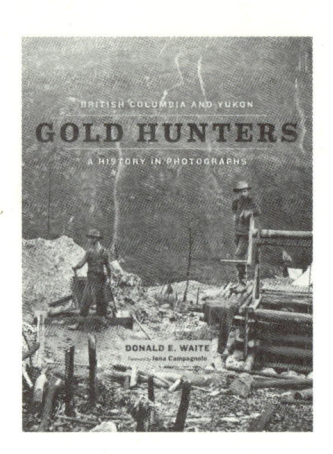

"In the goldfields, Don Waite is to photography what Pierre Berton is to words... Masterful."—Rick Antonson, former president and CEO of Tourism Vancouver and co-author of *Slumach's Gold: In Search of a Legend*

"This book is a gold mine all its own, giving us new insight into the reasons why British Columbia developed the way it did. It is a gem, a vital resource for anyone with an interest in the history of our province."—Dave Obee, Victoria *Times Colonist*

ISBN 978-1-77203-077-8 (paperback)